Person, Soul, and Identity

Philosophy and the Real Self

The Order of the Ages
The Logic of Spiritual Values
Keys of Gnosis
Self and Spirit
The One and the Many
Foundations of Free Will

ROBERT BOLTON

Person, Soul, and Identity

Philosophy and the Real Self

ANGELICO PRESS
SOPHIA PERENNIS

First published in the USA
by Angelico Press/Sophia Perennis 2016
© Robert Bolton 2016

Series editor: James R. Wetmore

For information, address:
Angelico Press
4709 Briar Knoll Dr.
Kettering, OH 45429
angelicopress.com

ISBN 978 1 62138 234 8 pb
ISBN 978 1 62138 235 5 cloth
ISBN 978 1 62138 236 2 ebook

Cover image: Ernst Ludwig Kirchner, *Drei Gesichter*, 1929
Cover design: Michael Schrauzer

CONTENTS

Introduction

The Crisis of the Self

The subject of personal identity (and the question of its essence) has an increasing urgency today because it is less understood than ever before, and because of the resulting conflicts which now surround it. No other issue more clearly reveals the utter chaos of modern consciousness than this one, or more clearly shows the need to rediscover the principles from which the idea of the person arises. The reason why this subject is now a battleground is because on the one hand there is the advance of an aggressive scientific reductionism which is arguing for an outright denial of the very existence of self or soul, and even of mind, assuming that nothing can be real unless it is an object of sense perception; and on the other, there is an invasion of the whole culture by a political agenda which is centered on the rights and freedoms of individual selves or persons. I think it is no exaggeration to say that one side or the other must be talking complete nonsense.

The cult of scientism has banished every idea of God from its domain, and now it does not shrink from denying the reality of soul or self, and therewith the subjective source of its own anti-spiritual assertions. It should be noted in passing that this reductionist denial is also coming to provide the basis for a denial of the reality of suffering, since suffering can no more be measured, weighed or counted than the soul can; but this development is still latent. And this is what is happening in a social context dominated by a flood of legislation to protect the selves of individuals and justify their sense of self-esteem, and this as an absolute right, not a privilege. The reality of mental suffering and the need to prevent it is thus unchallenged in the social and political spheres, and this goes on as though the existence of the self was a mathematical certainty. But although the reality of the inner, subjective self is taken for granted in society, those who so regard it usually do so in spite of having no conception of knowledge apart from the empirical one of the scientists, so that they accept the premises of scientism and deny their consequences.

Inconsistent as it is, this position is society's opposition to the empiricist reductionists who are similarly irrational in their own way. The reality of sense-perception they depend on does not admit of proof, because such proof could only be empirical, and that would *presuppose* sense-perception. These confusions and paradoxes point to the need for a form of knowledge which is subtle enough and comprehensive enough to penetrate the darkness created by modern pretenders to knowledge. It must work below the surface of phenomena and engage with the formative ideas and principles on which the phenomena depend. Such was always the role of metaphysical thought, ever since Plato, with its idea of proof based on the internal logic of ideas. In view of the doctrine that man is made in the Divine image, there should be nothing surprising in the idea that human minds should be able to know at least some kinds of things in the way that God knows all things. Knowledge of that kind will be the main objective in what follows.

The heart of the problem is the nature of personal identity, and a study of it is necessary firstly for its own sake, and secondly in order to dispel the chaos with which it is surrounded today. The difficulty of this problem appears in the deep divide we always find between the ease with which one can identify oneself for relative purposes in fragmentary ways, and the extreme difficulty with which one can conceive one's identity in a way which is true to one's whole being. This difference belongs with that between knowing facts in the outside world and knowing something about the person who knows them *qua* knower. We learn first about things outside us, and about the reality closest to us last of all, insofar as the knowledge is fully conscious and not just intuitive. To compound the problem, knowledge of self is more beset by emotional barriers than any other kind, which implies that even where our reasoning powers may be adequate in themselves, they can still miss the mark because of irrational and social pressures.[1]

To begin with, there are two questions: firstly, whether we are physical beings which possess consciousness, or conscious spiritual beings which possess physical forms? Secondly, should we decide for the latter alternative, would our conscious being be only an accidentally separate part of a universal conscious substance, or an intrinsically unique counterpart to the universal?

Whatever the answers to these questions, the manifest facts may all seem much the same, and yet the answers to them are of immense importance for the meaning of life and for the destiny of the individual. Consequently, most of what follows will be centered around various ways of answering them in a manner which will affirm their reality as issues, and which will seek to rectify the confusions of common-sense assumptions, which are nearly always in conflict because empirical consciousness sees the individual as a collection of phenomena, selected by the observer.

Because of the deep obscurities of this subject, therefore, the main trend of modern thought is against the idea of an objectively real unitary self as the source of the observable manifestations of the person. If in fact there were no such thing, the confusion surrounding identity would be perfectly natural and would not need any explanation outside the realm of the psychology of the irrational. For philosophers this would bring with it the advantage that they could no longer be accused of having failed to understand personal identity and give an account of it. What is not really there cannot really be a challenge.

From this point of view it is quite appropriate that twentieth-century philosophy has consisted largely in an onslaught against dualism and the latter's conception of mind or soul in relation to the body and the material world. Analytical and linguistic philosophy have been united in rejecting the idea of the "thinking substance" associated with Descartes, which had been taken as necessary to posit as the thinker of thoughts. Reductionist criteria are always pursued with a conviction that suggests a belief that the universe is under an obligation to be simple. Body alone is much simpler than body and soul, of course, and its explanation would then be no challenge to scientific minds.

It is typical of modern scientists and philosophers of science to assume that the most true explanation must always be the simplest, by the criterion of Ockham's Razor. But however valid that may be for handling scientific data, it has no place among universal realities. Simplicity was ended by the first thing to be created, and all the subsequent acts of creation, proceeding by division, increased the level of complexity until it was great enough to constitute a world. This is why the commitment to simplicity among modern minds reveals an unconscious or unadmitted urge to reverse creation and bring the world to an end, or, in a word, nihilism.

If, therefore, the real self should add to the complexity of our world, that need not be an objection to it. In reality, a world of thoughts-without-thinkers, even if simpler, is also less intelligible, and that is another kind of complication. William Barrett has argued that without a self or thinking substance no one would be able to manage even something as simple as counting up to five.[2] When "five" has been reached one must know this to be effected by the same reasoning agent who counted "one" a few moments ago, and failing that, the operation must lose all meaning.

Barrett also points out that it is simply the obscurity of our idea of the self, which always seems to comprise too much and too little at the same time, and not a lack of functions for it, which gives skeptical philosophy a seeming justification for trying to disprove its existence. But there is a possible confusion here between the reality of a thing and the extent of our knowledge of it: "the reality of personal identity is so bedrock a fixture of our world that we hardly ever single it out for special comment,"[3] and the deficiencies in our knowledge of it do not alter this. Similarly, we may know next to nothing about our neighbor and still be certain of his existence, and this certainty cannot be increased by getting to know more about him.

In this connection we could appeal to the theory, well-known to modern philosophy, that existence is not a predicate, which I would modify to mean that it is a predicate in a unique category. Thus no amount of ignorance or confusion as to the other predicates of the self need give us grounds for doubting its existence. Failing this, "most of the furniture of our daily world would have to be declared of questionable reality,"[4] and to focus this criticism on the self more than on anything else is merely a sign of prejudice.

Likewise, modern philosophy has made much of the fact that we are frequently not directly conscious of having a self, and that we can do many or most things without the help of such an awareness.

This, according to Barrett, need no more cast doubt on the continuing existence of the self than the inability to see the inside of a room need cause us to doubt the continuing existence of its contents.[5] This kind of criticism of the self could therefore only be compelling for subjective idealists and for those for whom denial of the self is a necessary dogma.

Metaphysics and Science

Besides the above arguments, there have also been behavioristic attempts to reduce the mind's thinking and understanding to patterns of overt action and reaction. Many true statements would denote modes of action in regard to the outside world, but they cannot all be forced into this category. That philosophy abounds in statements to which there could be no conceivable behavioral response is only too well known, but the same is also true of science. What behavioral response can we make to the statements that the universe has been expanding ever since it began, or that life on earth began five hundred million years ago? As with the Verification Principle, this is an anti-metaphysical position which turns out to be anti-scientific as well. Moreover, as Zeno Vendler points out, there are many situations where understanding should imply action, and where one can fail to act while still understanding, and where training can produce the appropriate reaction without understanding.[6]

Nevertheless, this does not mean that I shall be arguing for an uncritical return to Descartes' idea of the thinking substance, because although Descartes expresses ideas of great importance from the present point of view, he often expressed them in ways that were inconsistent and insufficient to account for personality. One could say that he held a Platonic conception of the soul while ignoring the Platonic account of the body and the material world. Such an attempt to combine a spiritual conception of soul with a materialist's' conception of the material world not unnaturally gave rise to an aggravated kind of dualism which defies understanding.

Vendler shows in his treatment of Descartes how he deviates from the essential idea in a passage which could serve to announce the theme of this study:

The soul is a complete substance, the *subjectum inhaesionis* of all its accidents, thus of all its acts, including the specific operations of thought.... This substance, however, remains really distinct from all these operations, which are nothing but actualizations of the soul's faculties (intellect and will), which themselves are really distinct from the substance.[7]

He then adds: "Needless to say, this is not what Descartes means."

Although Descartes can sometimes appear to endorse the above, Vendler shows that in some texts he expresses an idea of the soul which would make it consist wholly in thinking,[8] so as to be "a temporarily extended configuration of thoughts." From this, as we are told, it is but a short step to Hume's idea of the self as a mere aggregate of perceptions. For this reason, the treatment given here to this subject will concentrate not on Descartes but on his sources, notably St. Augustine and those who were sources for him.

Besides the above anti-metaphysical arguments, there is at least one more which should be considered. This one takes language and logic in their role as artifacts, products of the social and historical accidents of their construction. Thus concepts are expressed in words which are to connect ideas with precision, and exhibit intelligibility and certainty because their makers designed them to do so, and not because of objective reality. According to this way of thinking, therefore, the fact that certain truths may be reached by philosophy would be no more remarkable than the fact that our clothes should fit us after we have had ourselves measured for them.

This kind of reasoning ignores the distinction between what is an artifact purely and simply, like a brick or a nail, and an artifact like a photograph, which serves to manifest some other reality. It may not have been impossible for primitive man to have plucked language and logic out of the air, but unless we know this to have been the case, we are free to assume that these things were in fact constructed as representations of reality.

Those who deny this conclusion would be in a stronger position if they were to emulate their idea of primitive man and fabricate new languages and logics which owed nothing to the ones we actually use. However, no such new artifacts are actually produced, and it seems that what this would entail is only a little less improbable than creating a new primary color or a new musical note. We should also remember that the relativization of language and logic still has to be argued for by means of this same language and logic.

Existentialism and the Self

While it is perfectly natural in terms of its reductionist principles that analytical philosophy should have no time for the substantive self or soul, the same cannot be said of another modern school of philosophy, existentialism. This tradition originates in Kierkegaard's reaction on behalf of the concrete individual person against Hegel's attempt to make all reality reside in the universal, where the individual has no meaning. For Kierkegaard, the real self and the immediate certainty of his existence and his quest for salvation, not theoretical knowledge, was the essential route to reality.

But, as Barrett says, "notoriety does not mean that appropriate notice was taken of the message of the founder."[9] He observes that existentialism has been carried along with a general historical movement toward the disintegration of the individual: "But what should surprise us is that philosophers and intellectuals construct theories which, in their intricate and sometimes fanciful ways, serve really to abet this depersonalizing process."[10]

Thus analytical and existential philosophies share a negative attitude to metaphysics, that is, to the idea that man can make nonempirical reality intelligible to himself. This belongs with the scientific background of the former, for which the empirical is its standard of reality, and with the latter as well, for many religious minds such as Kierkegaard's distrust metaphysics because it implies that man, by virtue of the intellect, can in some real sense converse with God independently of ascetic values and faith.

Two of the leading existentialists take an equally negative attitude to the individual *qua* soul. In *Being and Time*, Heidegger writes at great length about the self as it appears as *Dasein*, and all its modalities, but for all the endless detail in which Heidegger describes it, it never seems to be more than an aspect of the real person. Sartre is also unsatisfactory in this respect because he writes about freedom without showing exactly who or what it is that enjoys it. It appears that he thinks that to be specific about the nature of this self would be to put limitations on its freedom. Any definite self-nature would be something which we are not free to change at will. Absolute freedom would then for him mean no self at all, even though the absence of a real self to be changed should deprive its unlimited changes of any meaning.

In a less academic realm, popularized mysticism, mostly of Orientalizing kinds, reveals essentially the same tendency in regard to the self. Its message is usually that acquaintance with the highest reality reveals the truth of a monistic and pantheistic conception of man and God, such that the latter two would not really be different at all. The point of view of such writings, whether they come from Buddhist, Vedantist, or Theosophical sources, is poles apart from that of modern philosophy, but for all that, these reveal once again an agreement as to the de-substantialization of the soul or self, though not about anything else.

When there is agreement about something among extremely disparate types of minds, it is doubtful whether this can be the result of rational persuasion, as there is little likelihood of their all following the same reasonings in the same direction very far. Alternatively, it may mean one of two things: either the point they are agreed upon is dazzlingly self-evident, or their agreement is only a semblance of one, caused by non-rational factors such as unadmitted emotional and cultural pressures.

Since this is a subject where self-evident truths are harder to find than usual, we may rule out the former alternative. But if the likeliest explanation is emotional pressure, of what kind could it be? A premonition of some general doom to which one must surrender in anticipation? This would most probably result from a world-weary longing for escape from the idea of a real self which would commit its possessor to effort. The substantiality of the individual soul implies ultimate responsibility, and an open-ended capacity for action, and even the possibility that one may have to take sides in a morally significant conflict.

Introduction

Failure of Identity in Practice

It is my view that this flight from selfhood satisfies only a relative part of our nature, in disregard for the good of the whole. The great majority are never consulted about the matter, which means that they experience the negative effects of this view of reality while having no ideological commitment to it. Modern society has for a long time been functioning in ways which inflict "self-denial" on those who know nothing of its theoretical content.

This is partly brought about by political and economic means which are collectivistic and anti-libertarian in tendency, but also by many things which are supposed to mean progress. These include highly-prized freedoms in regard to social mobility, the melting of social classes, choice of employment and education, and choice of where to live. In addition to this, there is a universal interpenetration of cultures and religions by means of which individuals are able to respond to many more kinds of influences and modify their identities with them. All these forms of mobility and variety are so much desired that no one considers the penalty that goes with them: the loss of the stable conditions under which true identity can realize itself.

At the same time, there is the constant advance of technology, which makes many skills and occupations unnecessary. This inevitably casts doubt on our convictions as to what we are and what our purpose is. Though the identity in this thesis signifies something much more essential than a mere identification with cultural forms, places, and social groups, it appears that these more superficial forms of it serve as a mirror to the self and so support the discovery of the self which expresses itself through these things, if it is able to continue long enough with them. But this is what is hindered by the endless mobility and cultural variety in the modern world. The products of civilization lose their spiritual function in this way, and so are reduced to amusements, hobbies, exotica and merchandise. This goes hand-in-hand with a corresponding disrelation to nature, where everything gets reduced to its physical and economic functions:

We have on the one hand the self, the abstract ego emptied of all substance except its attempt to transform everything in heaven and on earth into means for its preservation, and on the other, mere stuff to be dominated, without any other purpose than that of this very domination.[11]

This also indicates the paradox that efforts toward the preservation of human life become more and more intense in proportion as one loses belief in a real self to be preserved. The real self thus makes itself felt while being consciously absent, mocking all attempts to deny its reality. Man thus puts himself under the power of the unknown, in the name of enlightenment.

Because the denial of real personhood is unnatural and has no support in popular conviction, it has given rise to universal hunger for a substitute in the form of self-identity. The supply of artificial means of satisfying this need explains many things: for instance, the cult of stars of the entertainment industry comes from a desire for ready-made identities on which one can model one's own. Symbols and gestures of identity are used to conceal the lack of real self at a deeper level.

If the denial of personality from theoretical sources is accepted, however, the result in practice is not no self, but rather the equation of the self with the irreducible minimum required for it to interact with the outside world, commonly referred to as the empirical ego, or just the ego. Since there is most probably something immovable here, it is quite natural that an imposed denial of self should in practice result in the cultivation of the lowest kind of self, whether its promoters intend this or not. There is a possible analogy here between the position I am ascribing to the true self and that of philosophy as such, in that the rejection of philosophy means in practice the adoption of very bad philosophy.

According to Horkheimer,[12] this reduction in the development of personality deprives man of the ability to be either moral or immoral. According to the example he instances, persons without effectual identity are thereby trapped in the present moment, where they may show apparent traits such as laziness and dishonesty, or what would be these things in persons who were effectively self-aware.

On this basis a failure of identity will be manifested in an increase in non-moral and criminal behavior by people who lack the consciousness requisite to be immoral or criminal by choice. Unlike true wickedness, this kind is yet further beyond the reach of either correction or deterrence, since there is no way in which consciousness can interact with unconsciousness. Evils are enacted, not so much by human agents as by dissociated emotional reactions which begin and end in isolated moments which are not grasped as a connected whole. It may sound strange to say that prospects are more hopeful where there is more deliberate moral evil, but such is the case, since only this kind is genuinely human.

The unrealized self is vulnerable to outside pressures, as it fails to differentiate itself from the impressions to which it is subject. This makes one imitative, so as to find security in being like as many other persons as possible, regardless of their suitability to be taken as models. As Horkheimer interprets it,

> The impact of existing conditions upon the average man's life is such that the submissive type mentioned earlier has become overwhelmingly predominant. From the day of his birth, the individual is made to feel that there is only one way of getting along in this world—that of giving up his hope of ultimate self-realization. This he can achieve solely by imitation. He continuously responds to what he perceives about him, not only consciously but with his whole being, emulating the traits and attitudes represented by all the collectivities that enmesh him—his play group, his classmates, his athletic team, and all the other groups that, as has been pointed out, enforce a more strict conformity, a more radical surrender through complete assimilation, than any father or teacher in the Nineteenth Century could impose. By echoing, repeating, imitating his surroundings, by adapting himself to all the powerful groups to which he eventually belongs, by transforming himself from a human being into a member of organizations, by sacrificing his potentialities for the sake of readiness and ability to conform to and gain influence in such organizations, he manages to survive. It is survival by the oldest biological means of survival, namely, mimicry.[13]

In proportion as anyone accepts such conditions, they will be made intolerant of those who are not willing to do so, such that the situation has a potential for self-perpetuation and self-worsening. The pressures go beyond mere conformity, and penetrate to one's inmost scale of priorities.

This reduction of the self, and the consequent proliferation of Jung's "depotentiated individual" has advanced so far as to have penetrated even traditional religion. Though orthodoxy is theoretically at the opposite extreme from this position, a takeover of religious thought from beneath by the secular mentality has now come to seem almost like another orthodoxy in some quarters. It is manifest in a number of things which seem unrelated at first sight:

(1) that the religious message has become increasingly reliant on Biblical literalism;
(2) that social collectivism is preached as a panacea for moral and spiritual ills;
(3) a practical if not theoretical abandonment of sexual morality;
(4) an almost automatic sympathy for secular pressure groups and their demands for more "rights";
(5) a general politicization and de-personalization of religion.

The common factor in all these things can be shown to be the belief that man is merely his empirical ego, that he is nothing more than that part of his personality by which he interacts with external realities. On this basis there would indeed be no point in seeking anything in Scripture deeper than relations of bare facts. Likewise, solitude could have no meaning if what we are is a function of external relatedness. We could hardly even be said to exist except in communal activities.

In this case, no soul could be individually saved or lost, and if the idea of salvation were retained, it could then be only as a collective salvation, as though by means of some psycho-cosmic evolution. Inhuman as this may appear, it is widely accepted today because it is a basis on which one can deny one's own individual guilt and responsibility. Such thought is in any case deeply anti-religious by the standards of most religions, with its practical denial of spirituality.

In regard to sexual morality, there cannot be much point in trying to curb or convert sexually anarchic behavior if external relatedness is all that persons essentially are. To do so would be almost the same as denying their right to exist. Similarly, in the case of secular rights movements one can hardly do otherwise than demand that conditions be made to match the peculiarities of individuals if those things are all they really are. Again, where the politicization of the message is concerned, it is only natural that the "salvation" of the society at large should be a more congenial subject than that of the individual soul when personal identity is seen as something as insignificant as the ego.

This deviation of religion in practice means that the world around us no longer offers anyone any alternative to the materialistic idea of personhood. At the same time, care is still advocated for the infirm and the handicapped without its being noticed that the essential reason for this is the principle that the real self or soul transcends what is manifest at ego-level.

The prevailing atmosphere exists at a level too unconscious for the extreme inconsistency of this to be perceived, but it is not too difficult to see what would result if the idea of man as an empirical ego were applied with full consistency. No doubt the incurably sick or subnormal would be "terminated" forthwith, and those who were less subnormal would presumably be made slaves. Above all, no one would have any right to exist for reasons of his own; the equation of the self with its phenomena would reduce it to an object fit for rape or exploitation. That is implicit in every materialist position.

Dualism and the Soul

What I wish to oppose to the view of self as ego is the conception of identity based on the spiritual soul, the unitary and substantive center of the being, the one to which orthodox religion remains committed, despite certain indications to the contrary. Rather than serving as an assumption, the soul's very existence is what most of our contemporaries think is in need of proof. Indirect means of proof for the soul are not hard to find, however; confirmation of its central presence appears in the facts of error and illusion. Such things show that the world is not something *given*, but is *reconsti-*

tuted in the mind of each person, just as psycho-physical dualism would imply.

Besides error and illusion, one may note the discontinuous existence of most things as experienced by the senses, which belies the continuous existence we believe they have; and the ways in which they appear to change numerous properties, such as shape and size, which we believe to be constant, also give grounds for thinking that the world of experience is a representation and not the world itself. At the same time, the world which physicists and chemists talk about is obviously not the world as we experience it, and this too is an argument for the distinction between appearance and reality. The world which we believe to exist differs in very important ways from the world we actually experience.

This representational aspect of our world strongly suggests the center of activity which we call the soul, that which forms our representations; and the conception of the soul employed in what follows will be Platonic, not Cartesian. In this way, the hard dualism of the body and a soul identified with thought alone is avoided, in favor of a "relaxed" dualism in which the soul performs a range of functions which include those necessary for physical life, along with the rational and intellectual. In this way, the soul is a member of the same world as that of the body, but in a radically different way.

The Meaning of Representation

This approach could still give rise to a misunderstanding as to the meaning of "representation," however, owing to an ambiguity in the word. Is not the image in a camera a "representation" of the objects outside it? This obviously has nothing to do with the activity of a soul. In this case, the optical image is a direct extension of the same physical phenomenon in nature, and is subject to the same laws.

Secondly, the optical representation is available for any number of observers, owing to its being a part of the world it "represents." This contrasts with the subjective representation which is not part of the world from whence it is produced, being a transposition into a different mode of being. The distinction here is like that between calling the précis of a text a "representation" of the text and the writing of it a "representation" of the thought which was expressed in it.

Thirdly, and most radically, a physical representation of other objects consists solely of other sense-objects in a similar category, whereas our conscious representations convey those objects in a mental form, and as parts of *a world*. Unless they did so, our perceptions would be of little use. Thus the perception of the inside of a room is indirectly experienced as one of the whole house, and that of the surrounding area, of a town, of a country, and so on. This shows how misunderstandings of representation can give rise to spurious arguments against dualism.

Psycho-physical dualism, which accepts a common objective cause of our impressions, is the middle way between the extremes of idealism and common-sense realism, which are as it were the ditches on either side of it. Idealism rightly grasps the large subjective element in objective experience, only to end up in a dead-end by making the subjective alone real, and thereby denying that representations represent anything. Realism, on the other hand, insists so much on an objective reality that it is forced to base itself on the premise that the world we perceive is *pure given*, so that our perceptions would be caused by things which were no different from themselves. In this case, the world of experience would absurdly be self-caused, like God.

In spite of this, it is fashionable to believe that there is something especially unbelievable about dualism, even though it does not strain credulity as idealism and realism do, as indicated above. Even where it is part of a philosophy which takes material things as less real than intelligible ones, it remains literally "realistic."

Why Platonism?

Platonism is a suitable approach to this subject because it is concerned so largely with archetypal realities. Personal identity, where it involves a transcendental element, is by nature close to the Platonic Forms, as I propose to show in Chapter 2. According to J.N. Findlay, the full realization of individual identity comes through its assimilation of a certain unique combination of the Forms. Persons may thereby become "glorious elaborations of standard eidetic possibilities." Thus the self "becomes part of what eternally is."[14]

However, it may appear that Platonism depends too much on a subtle and paradoxical treatment of both the ideal and the actual, which is too far from the realities of life for it to be relevant for more than a tiny minority. In reality, it is quite the opposite. The dependence of the actual on the ideal is a universal conviction which even pre-dates Plato. To settle doubts on this score, we have the word of Mircea Eliade that a Platonic metaphysic informs even the most primitive cultures, in which daily activities are conditioned by attempts to make them into re-creations of archetypal realities: "among primitives, not only do rituals have their metaphysical models, but any human act whatever acquires effectiveness to the extent to which it exactly *repeats an act* performed at the beginning of time by a god, a hero, or an ancestor";[15] and, furthermore, "an object or an act becomes real only insofar as it imitates or repeats an archetype."[16]

The implication of this is that "Plato could be regarded as the outstanding philosopher of 'primitive mentality,'"[17] by which Eliade means the thought of archaic man generally. If universality is any recommendation, therefore, we may choose this way with greater confidence. To universality one can add antiquity, because some of the earliest inscriptions speak of archetypal realities: "In Egypt, places and nomes were named after the celestial 'fields': first the celestial fields were known, then they were identified in terrestrial geography";[18] and "All the Babylonian cities had their archetypes in the constellations: Sippara in Cancer, Nineveh in Ursa Major. . . ."[19]

Besides this, the concepts of *menok* and *getic* in ancient Iranian cosmology express a particularly developed form of the conception of invisible originals and earthly instances. There are also Egyptian sources referring to the soul as a separable entity which show that this conception goes back to around 3400 BC[20] Since it has continued with little alteration in Christian belief, it has thus an effective recorded history of over five thousand years, which is something for the historical imagination to conjure with; while we recall by way of contrast that systematic denials of it in our culture are extremely localized both in time and in influence.

Introduction

But beyond its historical background, this form of philosophy calls for some more detailed introduction, as its point of view runs counter to the tendency of most modern thought. As a metaphysic, it seeks the key to non-intellectual realities in terms of those which are specifically intelligible, and this is where it most conflicts with common sense.

The option of interpreting both the intellectual and the physical from the side of the intellectual, taken as a criterion of the real, belongs with an intuition of the metaphysical reality in ordinary experience. The empiricism which would resist this attitude gains strength from certain impressions received by us in the earliest part of life. In the earliest state of our consciousness our world effectively did consist of a collection of objects. The process of development which followed that stage has consisted largely in an increasing realization that invisibles have as much title to reality as have visibles. The law of cause and effect, moral laws, and numerical relations become known in an ever-increasing number of realms and instances.

Nevertheless, the earliest impression of reality gives a material or empiricist bent to our instinctive judgments, however much we have outgrown it with the reasoning mind. Material concretes have therefore in their favor a comfortable familiarity which preexists all attempts to reach the objective truth; common-sense materialism is abetted by an intellectual laxity or skepticism.

Modern Accounts of Platonism

However, the main problem with justifying Platonic metaphysics lies in the question of freeing it from objections according to which it results from the confusion of self-predication. Were this justified, the explanations given by it would be as useless as the satirical explanation of the power of opium: "*facit dormire quia habet virtus dormitiva.*" If white things are white because they participate in the Form of Whiteness Fw, all white things will be in a sense unified by this Form. But if the White itself is also white, its relation to all its instances should perhaps be subject to yet another Form Fw1 embracing it and its instances, and give rise to an infinite regress. So it also would be if, say, the Beautiful itself is beautiful—and we cannot conceive it to be ugly, even if it is not what we normally call beautiful. So how can it and all the others be worthy of its name without being an instance of itself?

R.E. Allen states the problem as follows: "the Form is a universal which has itself as an attribute and is thus a member of its own class, and by implication, that it is the one perfect member of that class. The language suggests that the Form has what it is: it is self-referential, self-predicable."[21] However, Plato does not really mean it in this way, because he argues that the Three itself does not contain three members, but rather is the reality which can only be manifest in the grouping of things which we designate as "three." Likewise, the Equal itself cannot really be equal to anything, and Being itself is not an existent. Thus the Forms cannot really be treated as specimens of the things they cause without an absurdity which Plato could not have failed to see, one which would have meant that "the man who first explicitly distinguished between universals and particulars confused them; and finally, that a central thesis of his ontology, the doctrine of degrees of being and reality, rests on this elementary mistake."[22] Even the question of mistakes arising from the unfamiliarity of the subject is not likely to be a factor for a philosopher of Plato's stature.

However, it is not true that self-predication must result simply from saying that the Just itself is just, or that the Beautiful itself is beautiful. For that to be the case, the attributes of, say, justice would have to be univocally true of both the Form and its instances. Plato nowhere gives grounds for such a supposition. In reality, when we say that the Just is just, we are not saying the same kind of thing as when we say this of a particular action which is just.

At *Phaedo* 78e, Plato says that Forms are called by the same names as their instances, but this should not cause difficulties, because the way in which the same attribution can have different meanings can easily be clarified. For example, the writings of both Aristotle and Alexander of Aphrodisias can be called "Aristotelian," though the same designation conceals a basic difference between them.

Aristotle would seem to acknowledge this dual function of designation in his account of the Forms: "Sensible things, Plato said, were all named after the ideas, *and in virtue of a relation to them*; for the many existed by participation in the Ideas that have the same form as they."[23]

Here, as in the above example, the implication is that the name in question designates the Form as such, and the instantiated things in only a derivative manner. The same verbal attribution is thus either a statement of identity (e.g., "Shakespearian verse" applied to Othello) or a statement of relation (e.g., "Shakespearian verse" applied to verse written so as to resemble Shakespeare). There is a class of things which have a given property on account of producing or originating it, alongside with the class of those which have this property as a result of having received it. When we say that something is good, for example, we mean that it is ontologically dependent on the Good itself, besides manifesting its quality. This is why, as R.E. Allen expresses it, "Forms themselves are proper nameables; what appear to be self-predicative statements are identity statements; and what appear to be attributive statements are relational statements."[24]

Another interesting example of this distinction is to be found in regard to standards of measure, such as the Imperial Standard Yard. Clearly we can equally well declare "measures one yard" both of an object of our choice and of the I.S.Y. itself, and equally clearly the same major difference in meaning arises here also, the systematic ambivalence which is comprehended in Plato's conception of instantiation.

However, modern treatments of this doctrine emphasize this difference in degrees of reality to so large an extent that one could not speak of relationships between Forms and instances at all. Here they apparently diverge from Plato, who says that the instances copy the Forms, just as though they were comparable things, so giving an opening for the Third Man Argument, though this is probably only a difficulty of language. Two equal lengths can resemble two equal weights in being equal, but this does not mean that they resemble the Equal itself, since that has no need of being equal to anything.

If instances are to their Forms as pictures to their subjects, the point is made even clearer; as a picture of a house, for example, is in no way a house at all, no matter what qualities it has in common with it. This idea of resemblance or imitation therefore relates categorically different things to one another. This community of quality resides on different levels, just as "visibility" can be attributable both to the sun and to the things that can be seen by its light.

At this stage, however, the objection could still be made that the instances resemble the Forms, even though they are not things in the same category. There would still seem to be some restricted scope for self-predication on this basis, so we must look more closely at what is involved in this qualitative resemblance. If one looks at the reflection of one's face in a mirror, it could be said that the reflection resembles one's face, though this could still be misleading. The face-reflection is not a face at all, and to say that it resembles the face is to make too much of it as an entity. Rather, it should be called a *resemblance* of a face, in view of its being wholly a relational entity. Similarly, the property of having eyes cannot be ascribed in the same sense to both face and reflection because the reflection-eyes are not really eyes.

The difference in degree of reality here between the face and its reflection fittingly expresses that between the Form and its instances. In all such examples, the same attributive form of words masks a deep difference in degrees of reality. According to Allen, modern criticisms of Plato's theory are wrong because they represent the difference between Form and instance as being purely one of quality. The Form is thought to possess the quality to perfection, while the instances possess it only imperfectly; but this is too superficial a distinction. The difference between them is really one of category. In reality, it subsists between categorically different things, and this is at least consistent with what Plato says, and must needs be the case if he did not make the mistake of positing self-predication. As reflections depend on their objects for both their character and their existence, so instances depend in both these ways on their Forms.

Allen sums this up in a way which practically negates the reality of the physical and instantial world, in his attempts to put the theory beyond criticism: "Particulars have no independent ontological status; they are purely relational entities. . . . Because their being is relational, adjectival, and dependent, relations to bind them to the Forms are neither possible nor required."[25]

Consequently there would seem to be no simple yes-or-no answer to the question as to whether the instances of the Forms constitute an addition to them. They both do and do not do so, depending on how the question is treated. This is not a compromise, as both answers are equally true, as is the case with metaphysical realities which are so much more complex than the individual concretes for which human language seems to have been devised.

However, though modern forms of Platonism are well defended against critical attack, this is at the price of ignoring one side of the above distinction, which in turn downgrades the whole distinction between the ideal and the physical. The thinking behind this is not very consistent, because on the one hand there is said to be no interval between the Forms and their instances, such that we do not need to conceive relations between them; and on the other there is said to be so profound a difference between them that the instances have only a quasi-existence, in relative terms, at least.

Can the instances really be so insubstantial if they are so directly affiliated with the Forms? Or if they are insubstantial, must not the Forms be so as well? Neither Allen nor Findlay appears to address this problem. Moreover, the existence of the material or instantial world is the one thing upon which all are agreed, whether they are Platonists or not, and in view of this it seems a strange tactic to treat it as being almost an illusion for the purpose of accommodating Platonism to its opponents' arguments. This is not putting it too strongly, since this treatment of the physical world would unavoidably make it consist only of "entities in which resemblance and dependence so combine as to destroy the very possibility of substantiality."[26]

But the peculiar dependence of the instantial world on the Forms does not entitle us to dispense with the reality of this world at its own level. Its existence is never fully separate, because it contains many things of the eidetic order, including souls, inhering in it *per se*, whence it cannot be illusory. Besides this, it reveals a distinct reality in all its limitations and imperfections, which are clearly substantial enough to prevent our seeing through them to the eidetic realities they are traducing.

If there really were "nothing substantial to be laid hold of apart from them (the Forms),"[27] one would expect to find all the perfections of the Forms here in this world, and not what we actually find. In short, the "two-world" conception cannot be simply a mistake, however misleading it can be if taken without qualification. To make the material world unreal *qua material* or instantial can be shown to undermine the reality of the Forms themselves. The supposed nullity of the instantial world must entail that of the Forms themselves, whose causal power is wholly responsible for it. If they could not cause anything substantial, what substantiality could they themselves have? There is an absurdity in investing the Forms with a plenary reality and causal power while denying that anything real is caused by them. Ineffectual power is simply not power.

Nevertheless, such conclusions as the above do follow from influential modern treatments of the theory of Forms, as quoted above, and this is because modern thought is so inured to seeing everything in terms of separable bits that it fails to see that the Forms cannot be understood except in conjunction with the Principle of Plenitude, which is equally essential to Platonic thought. This principle involves a universal downwards transmission of being and reality, which modern "vindications" of Plato typically ignore. That excludes the notion of a realm of unreality, or *maya*. The procession of different degrees of reality involved in this, furthermore, is compatible with the Christian idea of creation, unlike the position of Findlay and Allen, for example.

I will treat this subject at greater length in Chapter 2, where I shall discuss its implications for personal identity. Without this principle, there would be no answer to the question as to why the Forms should instantiate themselves.

Summary

The concept of personal identity which is to be developed here is that of a unitary causal principle, which is manifest as the individual person. This idea of self is found in traditional ideas of the soul, for which Platonic arguments are here re-examined and developed to allow them greater force.

A solution based on Neoplatonic principles is obtained for the problem as to how philosophies which place reality in universals can support the apparently paradoxical idea that the unique individual is also one of the true realities. By this means, religious and philosophical points of view can be reconciled. The meaning of the self through self-knowledge is examined in relation to an earlier and more general form of the *"Cogito"* argument, as a counterpoise to skepticism about the reality of the self. The relation between knowledge of a real self and knowledge of eternal truths is also brought into prominence by reference to arguments of both St. Augustine and Leibniz.

The soul's self-motive activity is treated as being one of its principles of individuation. Its union of knowledge and self-motion is the key to the causal effectiveness of the person, and therefore to whatever kind of self-realization the individual is capable of. For this purpose, the question of the soul's being an entity separable from the body is taken up, and Platonic answers to the interaction problem are given.

The idea that personal identity is a reality, however understood, is taken for granted in the earlier chapters, but answers to more radical skepticism about it are offered later on. The arguments I use for this purpose are not directed against modern philosophy as such, but only against the belief that it is so superior to what went before that it must have a right to exclude forms of thought which differ from it. Such a belief is not a result of philosophy as such, but comes only from a submission to fashion and social conformity. Therefore, I end by using the theory of identity presented here to explain why a spiritual conception of identity is not generally welcome in the modern world, and the likely consequences of this for the future of mankind are indicated.

Notes

[1] There is the tendency of modern minds to seek a sense of security from materialistic explanations.

[2] *Death of the Soul*, 63–64.

[3] Ibid., 114–115.

[4] Ibid., 115.

[5] Ibid., 113.

[6] *Res Cogitans*, 128–129.

[7] Ibid., 184–185.

[8] Ibid., 185.

[9] *Death of the Soul*, 126.

[10] Ibid., 127.

[11] Max Horkheimer, *Eclipse of Reason*, 66.

[12] Ibid.

[13] Ibid., 95–96.

[14] *Plato: The Written and Unwritten Doctrines*, 208.

[15] Mircea Eliade, *The Myth of the Eternal Return*, 22.

[16] Ibid., 34.

[17] Ibid.

[18] Ibid., 6.

[19] Ibid., 7–8.

[20] E.A. Wallis Budge, *Egyptian Religion*, 193.

[21] *Plato I*, ed. Gregory Vlastos, 167.

[22] Allen, ibid., 168.

[23] *Metaphysics* 987b.

[24] Allen, ibid., 170.

[25] Vlastos, ibid., Ch. 8, v, 181.

[26] Ibid., 183.

[27] Findlay, ibid., 235.

1

Soul as Separable Entity

Some Early Ideas of Identity

T he first philosopher whose ideas are important in relation to personal identity is Plato, whose conception of the soul has had a continuing influence throughout the centuries. Before Plato, there would be reason to consider Pythagoras, were it not for the fact that we have so little direct knowledge of what he taught. His thought is present in Plato as an influence, along with yet earlier influences which are known to us through Homer.

Much of the content of these earlier traditions sounds so strange to us that it is scarcely comprehensible. According to J. D. P. Bolton, the Iliad shows that men of that time had no sense of owning their own bodies, but spoke as though their limbs were other (albeit friendly) persons: "Achilles says he will never forget the dead Patroclus 'while I am among the living and dear (or friendly) knees stir for me.'"[1] While this clearly means "while I am alive and kicking," the "knees," which were a symbol of the body's strength, were evidently not thought of as being owned. More generally, the boundaries between the self and the not-self seem to have been only vaguely conceived. Something of this lingers in French grammar, where one speaks of "the" arms and legs, for example, and not "my" limbs.

What we can gather from Homer in this connection is not very consistent, either. On the one hand, it looks as though Homeric man equated personal identity with the body, however little integrated with the self:

The proem of the Iliad announces the poem's theme, the destructive anger of Achilles, which "sent the souls of many heroes to the house of Hades, but themselves it made the prey of dogs and carrion birds"; the flesh that is torn, the bones that are crunched, are more nearly the heroes' *selves* than the shadowy souls of them. . . .[2]

However, before this, it has been observed that Homer has no word for the body, that is, as a living being:

> Further evidence that this notion of the unity of the self was still only half-formed in the period of the Homeric poems may be seen in the absence from them of any word for the living body. The word which later Greeks used to mean body, alive or dead, in Homer means only "corpse."[3]

This indicates a remarkably defective idea of the body, considering the importance it evidently had as a "self." Attention was directed to outlying parts of it, like the hands and the knees, where one's strength was supposed to reside. While the real man was what was eaten, the living body did not appear clearly at all. Not unrelated to this is the fact that the distinction between the attributes of gods and animals seems to have been obscure as well. Hera, the wife of Zeus, is "mild-eyed" in most translations, but the original words mean "cow-faced"; and likewise Athena, who in the translations is "grey-eyed," is in the original said to be "owl-faced."

Such oddities must have been the despair of modern translators. In Homer's time, they could even have been conventions handed down from yet earlier times; and one is led to draw comparisons to the Egyptian gods, with their heads of animals and birds. The idea of the survival of the self in the hereafter is nonetheless present in these earlier times, but it was only a prospect of gloom, not of hope, which is illustrated by the ghost of Achilles telling Odysseus that he would rather be the lowest among living mortals than king over all the dead.[4]

As Homer is a poet, not a philosopher, we should not expect that he gave anything like a complete treatment of the subject; and this, together with the great honor paid him by the Greeks, may account for Plato's dislike for poets. However, Homer's view of the soul or shade as a vestigial being in Hades, taken by itself, was not peculiar to him, but was much the same as the Jewish belief in the twilight existence of souls in Sheol; besides, the Babylonians and Sumerians also had a similar belief.

The difference between this and the idea of the soul we find in Plato is not simply the result of a progressive change; for although the Homeric and Jewish ideas were ancient, so also was that of the Egyptians, which was always capable of affecting the neighboring cultures. It was a very comprehensive conception, such that the Homeric and Jewish beliefs could well be residual forms of it, since the latter correspond to the Egyptian conception of the Ka, with its ghostly afterlife which remains attached to the phenomenal world. For this reason it had to be propitiated by rites to make it remain at rest, and it was not so much the actual soul or person as a "double" of the person which was left in a subtle kind of matter: "an abstract individuality or personality which was endowed with all his natural characteristics. . . ."[5]

At the same time, the soul in the personal sense of the word, called the Ba, was conceived to be capable of an afterlife which was far more real than that of a ghost, and seems to be little different from that of traditional Christian belief: "It had the power to leave the tomb, and to pass up into heaven where it was believed to enjoy an eternal existence in a state of glory."[6]

This is also much closer to the Socratic idea of the soul as rendered by Plato, as for him it unquestionably constituted the real self, as well as being immortal. This appears in the *Phaedo,* where Crito asks Socrates how they should bury him, to which Socrates replies that they can do so in any way they please if they can catch him, since for him the only *real* Socrates was the one who was holding the conversation. As indicated above, this view of the soul was, in its own time, a revival of an ancient idea, not an innovation; it was maintained three thousand years before Plato: "Already in the Vth Dynasty, around 3400 BC, it is stated definitely: 'The soul to heaven, the body to earth.'"[7] This shows that we should not attach the idea of the separable soul too exclusively to Descartes.

As J.D.P. Bolton puts it, "Whatever it was that was choosing his words and marshaling his discourse, the *reasoner,* that was the real Socrates; not the stark, dumb husk which the poison would leave his friends to dispose of. Socrates' position is the opposite of Homer's, for whom the heroes' true selves were their bodies, not their souls."[8]

The Alcibiades *Argument*

The foregoing is the position which Plato made his own, and from which he never departed. That the real self is the soul is an idea which he expressed in one of his earliest dialogues, the *Alcibiades I.* As its subject lies at the heart of what we are concerned with here, its main argument will be examined as an introductory development. The discussion leads to the point where *Alcibiades* admits that he needs to improve himself (127e–128), upon which Socrates bids him consider what "taking care of oneself" means. Examples are given to show that this expression is usually uttered carelessly, as distinctions between the thing itself and what belongs to it are often ignored, as in the case of the body and its clothing, and the feet and the shoes. But we cannot take care of the essential man, rather than of what merely belongs to him, if we do not know what he is: "And should we ever know what makes a man better if we did not know what we are ourselves? Impossible" (128e).

This leads to a reference to the inscription "know thyself" at the temple at Delphi, and the question as to whether self-knowledge is easy to obtain or not. Socrates begins with a definition of himself as the user of the words with which he is conversing. These words are compared with the tools used by a shoemaker, and with the instruments used by musicians. The physical things used obviously imply the existence of their users *qua* physical or embodied beings, and in the same way the words used are also evidence of their user, embodied likewise.

The analogy is not quite complete, however, because the shoemaker and the musician relate as physical beings to the tools and instruments, whereas words *qua* words, or units of significance, are not physical things. In effect they are non-material things used by a non-material agent. However, for the present purpose this is enough, as the general fact of instrumentality in different things naturally evokes the idea of a user, even though it be centered on physical examples, such as a hand holding a pen or a knife.

The next point made is that the craftsman, who uses his hands and eyes as well as the tools of his trade, thereby indirectly has to use his whole body at the same time. One cannot say that it is the body which is using the hands which are using the tools, because the body differs in function only relatively from the hands. By saying that the man *uses* his body, therefore, we imply that the man himself differs from his body as it does from the hands, or as the latter from the tools. The soul is found to be the only thing which has this kind of relation to the body, and the conclusion is quickly reached that the real man must needs be one of three things, namely, body, soul, or a compound of the two.

The man is by definition the ruling principle, and it is agreed without argument that the body does not rule itself, whence it follows that it cannot be the man. The possibility of rule being exercised by the body-soul combination is also discounted, on the grounds that if either of two conjoint principles is ruled from outside itself, so also must be their combination; one and the same thing can both rule and be ruled, if autonomous, but not in combination. The autonomous being, or self, therefore either does not exist at all or is the soul.

This argument that the soul is the man is said to be imperfect on the grounds that no definition of selfhood in general has yet been worked out (130c). Another possible reason for this reservation lies in the point referred to above, that this reasoning involves a rather sweeping transition from the instance of Agent and Instrument where both are corporeal, as with hand and knife, or the whole body and any form of work, to the instance where neither are corporeal, as with the soul and verbal communication. The intermediate cases of the action of the immaterial on the material, and vice-versa, are passed over as well. It may be reasonable to allow that the agent-instrument relation applies equally to both material and nonmaterial relations, but no proof is offered. Granted that this is so, one arrives at an illuminating result, and it could only be challenged on the grounds that relations between physical or material agents and patients alone are the paradigm of what is involved here, and so might not apply beyond the material.

A counter-argument to this would be that the agent-instrument relation is a paradigm in its own right, instanced equally in material and psychical realities. This position can also be justified on the grounds that it is not from the material cases of agency *qua material* that we derive the agent-instrument relation, because all such cases can be conceived in terms of their component ideas or universals, and not of their materiality. The latter, in itself, need not be supposed to contribute anything to the conception.

Following the conclusion as to self and soul, it is further agreed that one does not hold a conversation with the face of the other person, but with his soul. The body is classed among the possessions of the individual. Doctors and physical trainers therefore cannot achieve self-knowledge through their professions; and still less is this possible for craftsmen whose business is with things apart from the body itself, and so yet further from the true self (131b–d). This argument is the basis of the traditional distinction between the "liberal" and the "illiberal" or useful arts. Only the liberal relate to the essential man and give rise to self-knowledge.

The question as to how we can best take care of ourselves soon arises again (132b), along with the meaning of the Delphic inscription. It is not enough to know that the man or the self is the soul; one must learn more about the soul itself if self-knowledge is to be effectual. Earlier in the dialogue the attempt to discover the essential nature of selfhood was postponed as being too lengthy a business, and then was never resumed. Instead, the discussion turns to individual self-knowledge.

The precept "know thyself" is compared with a fanciful counterpart, "see thyself," addressed to the eye. The eye can only obey this by looking into mirrors or other reflecting objects, such as other eyes. Plato thinks that the eye can see its reflection in the pupils of other eyes, such that its image appears in the most "perfect" part of the eye, the part with which it most directly performs its function.

An analogy is at once made between the eye and the soul in this respect, with the result that the soul must know itself not merely by study of other souls, but through the power in them to which the pupil corresponds, which for Plato is "that region of the soul in which wisdom, the virtue of the soul, resides" (133b); "And can we say that any region of the soul is more divine than that which is the seat of knowledge and understanding? We cannot" (133c).

Something more than an analogy is meant here, because the eye is taken to be a physical counterpart of the mind, manifesting the same principles. This comparison appears again in other dialogues, such as the *Phaedo*: "I ought to be careful that I did not lose the eye of my soul; as people may injure their bodily eye by gazing on the Sun during an eclipse. . . ." (99d–e). This part of the soul is also said to resemble God, who relates to it rather as it itself does to the soul as a whole. For the soul, therefore, to contemplate God and to contemplate its own essence have much the same effect. It is clearly assumed that the soul is an expanded or projected form of its rational essence, so that everything about it is somehow present in that essence.

Thus a concentration on intellect, though impersonal, will give rise to an understanding of the self without even directly aiming at it. A knowledge of the universal gives rise to an implicit knowledge of the particular. This will bear comparison with what will be said in regard to Locke's ideas on identity, where the acquisition of knowledge, by extending the bounds of the self, *confirms* its identity; a greater inclusiveness resolves one the more fully from other beings.

In the last part of the dialogue, this inner knowledge or wisdom is related to moral virtue. Living virtuously is thought to be inseparable from good management of one's own affairs and those of others: "The only real object of all thought, reasoning, understanding, or knowing is our own true and unillusory well-being. . . . Stupidity is ignorance of what will be rewarding in the long run,"[9] as Thomas Gould notes in regard to this argument.

But without deeper self-knowledge, this good management will be impossible, and so also will virtue. The bad and the ignorant are therefore fit only to be governed by others, and an argument for slavery is incidentally presented.

From a common-sense point of view, the above reasoning has at least one paradox about it. What one wishes to know is by definition a person, a unique being, whereas the key to this understanding is said to reside in something impersonal. The individual person, *qua* individual, is indeed not knowable on Platonic premises, for which only the universal is knowable. The solution to this paradox will be found in later chapters,[10] in the context of the metaphysics of the later Platonists, for whom individual beings derive systematically from the gradation of the universals.

As this argument for the soul as the real self will be important for what follows, it should be understood that, despite appearances, it is not an argument for dualism as currently understood, and for two reasons. Firstly, on Platonic premises the difference between the material and the intelligible is not univocal, as it is for true dualism, for the reason explained in the Introduction. Secondly, a full understanding of the human psycho-corporeal complex comprises much more than the basic duo of body and soul, as I shall set out to explain later on.[11]

Why Soul is Thought to be Immortal

A further examination of the nature of the soul is made in the *Phaedo,* where the death of Socrates provides a focal point for reasonings about the immortality of the soul in conjunction with the theory of forms. This subject is significant from the present point of view because the immortal soul and its adoption by Christian teachings is historically the main source of the idea of personal identity which we have in the West. Opinions differ as to how effective the arguments used in this dialogue can be taken to be, especially as there are differing opinions about the theory of Forms. For this reason, it will be best to consider the nature and function of demonstration in this context, before examining its subject.

There are at least two possible functions of demonstrative argument here—one of which would be to induce assent even from those who positively disbelieved in the soul; the other, to remove mental and emotional barriers against it in minds which are at least neutral towards it. Of the two, the former may not be possible for this purpose, for reasons which will be considered later, whereas the latter is a practicable aim, and could prepare the way for something which would amount to proof.

As this subject concerns something about oneself, and can only be proved or disproved within the self, there is a special difficulty about what should constitute proof. The thing to be demonstrated, the one who carries out the demonstration, and the means used to this end are all coincidental in the self. It is hard to see why we should be in doubt about the subject at all. If the soul is mortal, that is, if it is simply a combination of natural forces, why are we not assured of the fact? If it is immortal, why should we need to prove that, either? There are widely differing ways of treating this problem which correspond to the deep divergence between empiricistic and metaphysical thought.

The modern, empirical method takes the mind of the philosopher by itself as a kind of fixed standard, its only qualification being a level of intelligence equal to the problems before it. In other words, it bases itself on the reasoning faculty in a state of abstraction. Platonic thought, however, insists on adding to this role of the intelligence its relations to the dominant desires, aversions, and tendencies of the whole person. This should make the functions of will, imagination, and desire crucial in relation to reason, and if that should seem to mean a denial of the objectivity of reason, the answer lies in the ancillary position of the other faculties.

The need to replace a chair, for example, can make one aware of a number of furniture shops whose very existence one had hitherto ignored. This is not to say that reason is in any way changed in its operation when applied to this purpose, but that the new orientation of will and desire creates a new sphere into which the reasoning function can pour its activity. What we do or do not desire is thus decisive in regard to what the intelligence will do, without this compromising its intrinsic objectivity in any way. At the same time, the desires differ widely among themselves in regard to how far they are conducive to or compatible with reason's own requirements.

This way of regarding the mind's operation has been neglected in modern times, but it is clear that Plato thought it was all-important, as did the Fathers of the Church, who did not accept the idea that there could be metaphysical knowledge without a virtuous direction of the will. As R. E. Cushman has expressed it: "This was Socrates' problem: the prime datum of the human consciousness (i.e. axiological awareness) cannot be exhibited and demonstrated to all and sundry. It requires 'tendence of the soul,' alertness to it, and above all, veracity about its notices."[12]

Plato's position on this issue is the easier to defend, on the grounds that the burden of proof lies more on those who would say the mind is not modified by moral and cultural tendencies than on those who say it is, because the person's activities must fall within the unity of the self.

But here we encounter what might seem to be an inconsistency. Much in the theory of ideas, as expounded in the *Phaedo,* relies on the conception of pure thought attaining its object without any modification thereof by the senses. The more free our thought is from sense-impressions, and the pleasures, pains, and emotions that go with them, the more readily will our thoughts reach the truth. Ideally, the mind would work at its best if it could ignore the body altogether. However, is this consistent with what has been said of the influence of moral character upon the mind?

If we can make choices within the material world which determine the relative spheres in which reason works, we should also be able to make choices which affect our relation to the material world as a whole, not just to parts of it. Such choices can be directed away from the practicalities of the material world as such, in favor of a more subtle reality. In this way, will and character can affect the things reason does, without affecting its intrinsic operation. Reason may be as naturally fitted for a transcendental sphere of operation as for a physical one, but it has no power of its own to place itself in the higher alternative; that is the function of the will and a deliberately cultivated sentiment.

This may give some idea of what is involved when we wish to judge whether a purported proof of the immortality of the soul deserves the name or not. The arguments in the *Phaedo* illustrate this principle because they are related to the imminent execution of Socrates, who begins by comparing the philosophic life to a "practice of death and dying" (64a), on the grounds that the mind's intellectual drive toward truth is a movement of the soul which is of the same general nature as its departure in death. In either case the soul relinquishes sensible things, this being necessary for the pursuit of truth, on the grounds that the senses never give us anything which is strictly accurate. Sight and hearing are the most accurate of the senses, and they are very far from the mind's standard of accuracy.

When we make accurate statements, and state things as they truly are, we reach behind the constantly changing and shifting perceptual manifolds which constitute the occasional causes of our statements. There is therefore no possibility of accurate statements relating with full exactitude to sensible things *per se,* but only to the Forms which inform them. The soul knows these Forms as they are, logically and chronologically prior to their instancing, whence the philosopher's unconcern for externals except where they illustrate universals both results from and is conducive to this kind of concentration: "Then it is your opinion in general that a man of this kind is not concerned with the body, but keeps his attention directed as much as possible away from it and, toward the soul? Yes, it is" (64e). This applies to the soul and to the theory of forms equally, and it extends to our awareness of absolutes like good and justice (65d). The reality of these absolutes is admitted, while it is agreed that none of them is ever known by eyesight, or by any other sense. The means by which the absolutes are known are purely intellectual: "And he attains the purest knowledge of them who goes to each with the mind alone, not introducing in the act of thought sight or any other sense together with reason, but with the very light of mind in her own clearness searches into the very truth of each" (65e–66a).

There is then no need for true statements to be confined to the analytic *a priori* kind, if in fact they are representations of combinations of Forms made according to the ways in which they inherently do and do not combine. The above conclusion could not be either confirmed or disputed by reference to any kind of sensation, as should be the case if the senses give truth. The body would only be conducive to truth when in a passive condition, apart from which "the body is always breaking in upon us, causing turmoil and confusion in our energies, and so amazing us that we are prevented from seeing the truth" (66d).

As the *Phaedo* is a relatively early work, it is sometimes claimed that Plato later moved away from this position. However, in the *Timaeus,* a late work, a very similar conception of the body's relation to soul is presented in the discussion of the newly incarnate soul:

> And so at the moment in question, causing for the time being, a
> strong and extensive commotion and joining with that constantly

flowing current in stirring and violently shaking the circuits of the soul, they seriously interfered with the revolution of the Same by flowing counter to it, and hindered it from proceeding on its course and governing. (43c–d)

Following upon this union of body and soul, the main business of life is to overcome this original state of confusion which, although we are not told so directly, would have been fatal to the soul's pre-life knowledge, if any such pre-life knowledge existed. Only when the "sensations" are stilled will the intelligence be able to resume its proper function. In the *Phaedo*, the conclusion drawn from this is that death could only be an advantage to the man whose quest for truth always required him to stifle the irrelevant clamors of the body.

This relation between the theory of ideas and the immortal soul is then developed further (78b–80b) in the discussion of the difference between things which are changeable and composite, and those which are the opposite. This argument, based on our ability to know the unchanging, deserves to be considered in detail, because, unlike some other arguments in this dialogue, it can, subject to the condition outlined above, be taken for an actual proof of the immortality of the soul, and not just an attempt at one.

From 78b, they consider the possibility that the soul might be dispersed at death, much as the body is. Accordingly, Socrates seeks a deeper understanding of what makes anything liable to dispersal, and what makes it immune from it. The clearest case of the dissoluble is that of a thing we know to be compounded from the different things which have been put together to make it. Conversely, if something is uncompounded, there is no reason to fear that it could dissolve.

An essential feature of the compounded is that it is always changing. The differences between its components are never resolved, and so are always liable to reassert themselves, forming different combinations. From this it is inferred that the uncompounded is also immutable, and appeal is made to the theory of ideas, adduced earlier in the dialogue in support of this. Thus the unchanging Beautiful itself is contrasted with the ever-changing things in which it is instantiated; the Equal itself with its instantiations, and so on. In each case the changeable reality is the one which can be seen and touched, while the unchangeable is the invisible reality, perceived only by the mind.

This distinction is then applied to that between body and soul, with the soul allied to the invisible and unchanging and the body to the visible and the changing. The soul can voluntarily conform its own state to that of the unchanging reality: ". . . then she passes into the other world, the region of purity, and eternity, and immortality . . . and being in communion with the unchanging is unchanging" (79d).

The use of sense perception, on the other hand, is said to be the drawing of the soul into the changeable and the unstable, where it suffers confusion on account of the conflict between this and its own nature, in proportion to the depth of its involvement in the sensible. In this sphere of activity, nothing is really known, every-thing is made up of images, impulses, and opinions, because mate-rial reality is too alien to that of the soul for the highest power of the latter to be effective in the realm of the former. Where truth does appear in the sense world, it is always conjoined with other things which confuse our grasp of it, or distract us from it.

This state shows by way of contrast that

> the soul is the very likeness of the divine, and immortal, and intel-
> lectual, and uniform, and indissoluble, and unchangeable; and that
> the body is the very likeness of the human, and mortal, and unin-
> tellectual, and multiform, and dissoluble, and changeable. (80b)

Because of the soul's relation to the immutable, therefore, we can consciously know truths. When we can say we know something, e.g., that we are alive, or that we do not wish to be deceived, we per-form an absolute mental act—that is, one which is not conditioned in itself by our position in space and time, or by any of the proper-ties of matter currently affecting our bodies.

The subject of what we know may or may not be contingent, but our knowing of it never can be. Joseph Pieper sees this issue simi-larly:

> This very type of demonstration makes it clear to us that what we
> judge as true must be free from all non-mental causality. Even if

someone were to declare that all human opinions without exception have come about as the consequence of mechanically operating necessity...he is still assuming that his own opinion is excepted.[13]

This conclusion is not easily attacked, because the reasoning involved does not depend on any specific known truth, but requires only knowledge *per se*. An objector could claim that he knows that the above conclusion is untrue, or that he knows of grounds for doubting it, but in so doing he too must appeal to the absolute nature of knowing, so as to deny it. However, a less contradictory objection would be that this argument only means that true statements are absolute acts, but this does not mean that there must be an absolute agent to perform them.

This would be like saying that as knowing is an activity, and so distinguishable from the soul's essence, the above proof does not apply directly to the soul. But this would only be justifiable if knowing were somehow not our own act. Otherwise, its relevance for the soul itself follows from the principle that an activity cannot excel the essence it derives from, in which case the objection would be beside the point. As Aquinas expressed it, "Nor can the operative power of a thing be superior to its essence, since power is consequent upon the principles of the essence of a thing."[14]

Another difficulty in regard to the nature of the agent forms the basis for the next main discussion in the *Phaedo*. Here Simmias says that the soul might be comparable to the state of attunement of the strings of a lyre. Everything said about the soul up to this point might also be applicable on the model of attunement: it is invisible, incorporeal, ordered, and exact, whereas the lyre itself is material, mutable, and liable to destruction.

Clearly, the attunement could not survive the destruction of the lyre, for all its immateriality, and similarly the soul would not be able to outlast the body if it were likewise a harmonization of all the body's elements. The first counter-argument to this (92b) relies on the preexistence of the soul, which had already been argued from the premise that knowledge is a form of recollection. The harmonization or attunement must be the last part of the being to be formed, following all the parts of the material structure. But the soul, with its innate ideas, cannot be thought of as being added after the completion of the body, and cannot have any less duration than does the body, although it may have more.

Since an attunement necessarily must follow the structure in which it resides, it is in a wholly dependent relation to it. The soul, on the other hand, is not a mere echo of our physical condition, as apparent from our subjective life, where it is a source of volitions, and selects its experiences. Moreover, an attunement admits of degrees, whereas there is no such variability among souls, each of which is just as much a soul as any other. This identity of kind is not affected by individual moral and intellectual development, even though this may be such as to obscure the soul's essential intelligence. No matter what a soul's individual tendency may be, it has a characteristic kind of activity which defines it irreducibly. All this is inconsistent with what we understand by an attunement, and is consistent with the idea that there is an absolute agent who is the author of absolute acts of knowledge.

Looking more directly at the question of agency in regard to true statements, one cannot designate the author of them as a purely physical being so as to remove the soul from the discussion, because this would be to require that something of a necessary nature should derive wholly from a mere combination of contingencies, a contradictory supposition. Something would have to come out of nothing if necessary truths were to result from our physical being, that is, from the cohesion of a certain number of particles. Thus a soul-agent with the absoluteness of cognition inherent in it cannot be avoided, even if we allow for the possibility of emergent qualities.

When one quality supervenes on another, it is a question of something emerging from something else of essentially the same kind, as when white copper sulfate turns blue with the addition of water. Thus, one contingency can give rise to another; but such examples do not help us see how the absolute could emerge from the contingent, for the very idea of causality requires that like must produce like.

A further advantage of this argument is that it does not depend on whether truths are synthetic *a priori* or merely analytic. That issue concerns the creative potential of our power of knowing, but it is the fact that we know anything, even were it pure tautology, which is the basis for proving that the core of our consciousness is exempt from the contingency of the body and its constantly changing states.

In regard to personal identity, it should be noted that this power of knowing the truth, by which man was designated "*capax verita-tis*" by the scholastics, though crucial for the identity of soul *qua* soul, does not by itself serve to differentiate one soul or person from another. This is because the soul is treated here only in relation to knowledge, and not to will. While souls are differentiated as a class by their possession of intelligence, and are differentiated from one another in an impersonal and quasi-quantitative manner by their different degrees of intelligence, they are also more positively differentiated from one another by being sources of a flow of volitions. That aspect of soul will be the subject of a later stage in this study, where its personal nature is to be accounted for.[15]

What has been said of our ability to know unchanging truth in an unchanging mode should now be considered in contrast to what we know of ourselves as physical beings. It somehow subsists with the latter, which appears to be practically nothing but change when considered at all closely. Physically, we are subject to the effects of changing atmospheric pressure, temperature, and humidity, cosmic radiation, pulse rate, blood pressure, rate of breathing, and our position between sleep and waking, to name only some of them.

Each of these natural conditions varies more or less independently of the others, in combinations which can never recur in a lifetime, though the individual variations recur endlessly, their changes going on continuously in patterns which are all broadly cyclic. Such is the natural, physical basis of our activity as knowers, which must be exempt from them all if it is to be able to arrive at truth. This indicates that there must be a fundamental dualism, not so much between soul and body, as in the soul's own mode of operation: that is, in its being equally able to assimilate to "the intellectual, and uniform, and indissoluble…" and to the "unintellectual, and multiform, and dissoluble," as Plato expresses it. Such is the possibility which implies the transcendence of physical conditions which is intended by calling it immortal, and which is of central importance for the theory of identity articulated here.

The act of knowing has other implications which also place it above the categories of embodied life. In knowing that I am a knower, I know implicitly that there is no intrinsic limit to what I may know, at least within a given range of difficulty. Let us suppose there were such a limit. That would mean that, after having gotten to know a certain number of things, I should have to stop and be unable to know any more, without suffering any natural incapacity. But how long should it be before this happens? If anything can prevent me from knowing, it must effect a change in me, not in the known; so either it is inherent in me from the beginning or the limitation comes into being after a certain time. In the former case, it would prevent me from ever knowing anything at all, and in the latter, my ability to know would be unrestricted unless some contingency were to put a stop to it.

But as I do in fact have knowledge, the former does not apply, while the latter does not entail any limitation in me *qua* knower, only a possible extrinsic one. The potential range of our knowing is therefore unlimited, as though it were naturally the counterpart of the world itself. Thus the soul has a potential and dynamic infinity matching the actual and static infinity of the world. Here again, it has a property which has no parallel in the physical state, and which would therefore defy attempts to reduce it to the latter.

Answers to Possible Objections

The faculty of knowledge is presented here as the means of proving our transcendence in relation to the world we have knowledge of. There must be a non-physical causality, in which our thought is determined solely by the truth of its object, if there is to be knowledge. This would make the soul a separate substance in relation to the body and the material world; but the dualism this involves is not a Cartesian dualism.

This is because Descartes retained a Platonic idea of the soul, which he acquired through Augustine's writings, while ignoring the theory of ideas that originally went with it. According to that theory, the material world has no properties except insofar as it participates in the Forms, which are made present to the soul in a pre-instantial state. In this case, there is no simple answer to the question whether the material world is truly alien to the soul. Under one aspect it is, and under another it is not.

The mode of interaction this involves is therefore one-sided, since this theory allows the soul to be an individual agent, not dependent upon the material realm for its being, while the material is essentially dependent. The world with which the soul interacts has no option but to harmonize with it, because it is made by means of the Forms present in the soul *in potentia*.

However, there is still the question of why our role as knowers convinces so few minds of the conclusion presented above. The answer to this requires further reference to what was said previously concerning the influence of the will and the character. Plato recognized that although man knows he is capable of knowledge, this by itself does not put him under any necessity to *prefer* the activity of knowledge to that of opinion. In practice, human nature feels more at home in a world of experiences which involve only opinions. One accepts the practical necessity for knowledge, while seeing it as just a constraint on the freedom of the will's activities. Given this orientation, the force of metaphysical insights will be lost, and only a "conversion" (*epistrophe*) of the whole person, as it is repeatedly referred to in Book VII of the *Republic*, will allow the "eye of the soul" to function as it should.

There are, besides, more specialized counter-arguments to the idea implicit in the above, that the soul must be a simple and uncompounded substance. In this connection it has been criticized by Kant,[16] specifically in the form given it by Mendelssohn. It should be noted that much more than a mere quantum of partlessness is entailed by the *Phaedo* argument, necessity, exactitude and immutability also being implicit in the soul's function of knower.

Kant presents an argument which depends on a close analogy between the soul and the various kinds of intensive qualities it knows. He does not believe in a spiritual substance, so his argument requires us to equate the soul with its consciousness, just as Descartes does. We are reminded that consciousness, for all its partless nature, admits of degrees, whence there need be no objection to its dwindling down to nothing without the loss of any discrete parts:

"For consciousness itself has always a degree, which may be lessened."[17] If the soul indeed simply *was* consciousness, this would be a problem, but in fact it is something the soul *has*.

This is indicated by the fact that its consciousness actually does dwindle to nothing every night when we go to sleep—but this has never been thought to hinder its continued existence. Kant is in fact confounding the soul with the conscious activity by which we know it, besides misunderstanding the meaning of the fluctuations of consciousness. Consciousness depends on the soul, but the soul does not depend on consciousness, as Kant's argument seems to imply.

What we have inferred about the soul applies directly to its cognitive activity, but only indirectly to the soul itself. No amount of variability in the soul's activity can invalidate the inference in this case, any more than in other cases. For example, we infer that someone is honest if we find him to be so on a number of occasions, and do not find him to be otherwise on other occasions; we do not need his whole life to be one long honest action in order so to know him. In general terms, quantitative variation does not affect the question as to what is qualitatively present in the subject.

Kant's argument should also involve a question of empirical evidence, for what he calls the "elanguescence" of the soul must happen to it of itself, i.e. without any causality from the body. In that case, it would not always have to wait for old age before this happens, and so it should be frequently observable at any stage during the lifetimes of individuals. It should be noted that cases of insanity or senility do not meet this condition, because they are dependent on physical factors. In this case, conditions very like insanity and senility would have to occur in persons who were organically entirely sound. The fact that no such cases are known implies that this supposed decline of the soul does not in fact take place before death, although it would be bound to do so in a certain percentage of cases if it were a reality.

Where there is a real decline in the faculties, as for example in the eyesight, it can be shown that this is not owing to any failure of the soul. Thus, if the sight has grown dim because of cataracts, the faculty of sight can become as good as ever if the eyes are treated with the appropriate operation. The same is relevant for all the other organs, even where no physical correction is practicable, as with the brain. Aristotle reasons about the soul in just the same way, concluding that "Old age consists not in something having happened to the soul, but in something having happened to that in which the soul resides, just as happens in intoxication and diseases,"[18] for "If it [mind] could be destroyed the most probable cause would be the feebleness of old age, but, in fact, probably the same thing occurs as in the sense organs; for if an old man could acquire the right kind of eye, he would see as a young man sees."[19] The decline of the physical instrument of consciousness merely causes the soul's powers to become increasingly imprisoned within it, without these powers being affected in themselves. Kant's personal motives for introducing his argument against the soul may be relevant here, because, as with Bradley in his *Appearance and Reality*, a philosopher may be tempted to create the appearance of as much destruction as possible, so that the reader will feel the need for the remedy which is being offered him.

In my account of the main argument of the *Phaedo*, I draw a hard and fast distinction between natural causes and purely mental or intellectual ones. This means that, for that stage of the argument, I ignore the realm of the emotions, which is in some sense a mean between the two types of cause. Nevertheless, it is only a mean under a certain aspect, because it shares fully the phenomenal nature of the physical, while sharing in the intellectual only in a derivative and quasi-symbolic manner.

On the one hand, an emotional state is an organic entity like a physical pain, but on the other it is to some degree referential, or "about" something, in the manner of a proposition, extrinsically, by association with statements held to be true. For example, one's anxiety over the destruction of the ozone layer depends on the knowledge that this layer is in fact being destroyed, but its relevance to this knowledge still does not bring it any closer to being a form of knowing.

There is also the objection that this argument for the immortality of the soul does not allow for the possibility that intelligence might be an emergent characteristic, deriving from the material level. It should be noted that part of the role of mind is to determine the nature of phenomena as such. As it comprises the criteria for their being phenomena at all, one could not seek to derive it from the latter without making a category mistake; mind knows phenomena, but phenomena know nothing.

If a set of contingent things were supposed to give rise to logical necessity, the difference between cause and effect would go far deeper than in any physical cases of emergent qualities. An essential property of logical necessity is that it is "unbegun," so that to speak of it arising *per se* from a temporal change would be contradictory. It cannot begin to be true or cease to be so on the same premises. There is, of course, a harmless and rather trivial sense in which logical truth arises at moments in time, owing simply to our awareness of it, as the view seen through a doorway could be said to result from our opening the door. But the view of intelligence as emergent would, on this comparison, amount to an absurd claim that the act of opening the door actually generated the view seen through it.

To say that logical truth is not contingent or temporally derived is to say that it is self-constituted, and self-constitution is a property treated by Proclus:

> All that is self-constituted is without temporal origin. For all that has a temporal origin is perfected by another, which brings into being that which as yet is not. . . . But whatever produces itself is perpetually complete, being perpetually conjoined with—or rather, immanent in—its cause. . . .[20]

Here it may make it seem as though the soul is being confused with God, although its essential mutability and the finitude of its powers exclude such a supposition. Nevertheless, its intelligence shares in some of the divine attributes, like those of being self-constituted and of being without temporal origins; but the attributes of the intelligence do not necessarily extend to the soul as a whole. It is for this reason that Aristotle restricts its immortality to its impersonal reasoning part. Nevertheless, this is to ignore the possibility that the diverse elements of the soul could become integrated with its intellect sufficiently for them to participate in its transcendence in a quasi-natural manner on their own level.

The properties of the soul's non-intellectual nature vary immensely from one person to another, and also within the same person over a period of time. Because of this distinction, the soul can be conceived as a compound of an intellectual nature with another more contingent nature which depends largely on the individual's habitual conception of himself and his conditioning influences. There is no necessity for these components to agree or be consistent with one another. The range of options resulting from this condition, whether for good or ill, may well be essential to the possible immortality of the soul as a whole, when conceived as needing to be realized.

This would be consistent with what Plato says in the *Phaedo*, where he does not seem to make the soul's immortality unconditional, but rather attaches it to an ability to turn its energies inward so as to bring them more directly under the influence of its reason. While all its possible conceptions of itself cannot be equally valid, they are nevertheless all creative acts which tend to the realization of what they contain, whether they are true to one's essential nature or not. Thus the immortality of the soul, apart from its intellectual center, would, when fully personal, be a potentiality in need of realization.

This would involve a kind of assimilation of the soul to the nature of what was called the "eye of the soul" in the *Alcibiades I*. Another way of expressing this would be to say that it depends on a point of contact between soul and spirit, within a tripartite conception of the person conceived as consisting of body and spirit, with soul mediating between them. Here again we encounter the apparent paradox of a personal self-realization resulting from an assimilation to a reason-principle which is not personal. It points to a deep difference between cause and effect, comparable to the way Being is the formal cause of all existences, while not itself existing. This assimilation is *inter alia* an assimilation to something self-constituted and incomposite, and this is the ground of soul's being a separable entity. Its capacity for knowledge similarly indicates a transcendence of the natural level, which also enters into the conception of separability. The question as to what the soul could be in isolation, and what the contribution of the body to the whole being would be, will be considered in Chapter 2.

Another way in which the soul stands out from the natural order lies in its capacity for the universal and the infinite. The main argument in the above, based on capacity for knowledge, is not tied to any special kind of knowledge; but there is at least one field of knowledge the nature of which provides a significant extension to this argument, this being knowledge of the universal. According to the Aristotelian and Scholastic principle, "*Anima est quodamodo omnia*"—the soul is, in a certain sense, everything, as it relates equally to all things:

> The spiritual soul, Aquinas says ... is meant to fit in with all being.... "Every other being takes only a limited part in being," whereas the spiritual being is "capable of grasping the whole of being." ... "The whole of reality" and "spirit" are corresponding conceptions.[21]

For a purely natural being, this would be contradictory, as a natural being is by definition relative and partial from every point of view. The fact that soul can grasp the world as a whole implies that it grasps the *essence* of all things, and through this the actual world, as there is no question of its having to exhaust an infinity of particulars in order to know the world as such. This relation to totality is relevant as much for the possibility of philosophy itself as for the existence of the immortal soul. There is a deep and necessary relation between these two issues.

The Principle of Self-Motion

Another aspect of soul which seems unrelated to the foregoing is its role as source of dynamism and life. This too has been made the basis of arguments for its immortality, or for its transcendence of all physical conditions. One such argument, based on its motive power, is to be found in the *Phaedrus* and Book X of the *Laws*, in the latter of which it is presented as an antidote to atheism.

The essence of the argument is very simple. Something which is always in motion is by that very fact immortal (*Phaedrus* 245c) and the converse is that the mortal is that which only has motion imparted to it, and which it gradually loses. A being which is self-moved is an ultimate motor-principle, not something moved, and so its motion by definition can never cease. The question is how to identify this with the soul. It is correct within the definition to say that "a first principle cannot come into being" (245d), for otherwise it would itself be in need of a first principle. What does not come into being must therefore be imperishable as well.

There then follows a rapid transition from this to the soul, which is found to answer to this very property, by an act of intuition. One would prefer to find some intermediate reality by which to effect this transition, but it seems that one simply has to see it to be so. However, it is possible to see a connection between this dynamic power and the self-reversion which has been attributed to the soul's intellective powers in the above. In either case, the decisive factor seems to lie in the almost unrestricted degree of access to itself as a whole, by itself as a whole, for which it is noted. Self-reflective knowledge and self-motion could equally well result from this property, though this is not referred to in the text.

According to Plato, not only is soul that which is self-motive, but the statement can be reversed such that whatever is self-motive is soul. It has been pointed out that this argument may apply only to the immortality of the soul in general, and not of the souls of particular individuals. The soul's conservation of its own motion need not mean that it will also continue as the same person unless some other factor intervenes, such as the continuation of some specific quality of the motion.

But something more than the individual is involved here. One can say that Plato has an intuitive grasp of what we know as the Second Law of Thermodynamics, since he sees that a world composed wholly of alter-motive beings could only decline into a state of universal immobility: "were it otherwise, the whole universe, the whole of that which comes to be, would collapse into immobility, and never find another source of motion to bring it back into being."[22]

The world must be supposed to have had already an infinite time for this to happen, and the fact that it has not yet done so could be explained on the basis that there is a motive force of a wholly different kind in it, namely the self-motive.

This conception can be seen to derive from the four *a priori* combinations formed by the functions of moving and being moved: (a) that which is moved by other things but does not move anything else; (b) that which is moved and moves other things; (c) that which moves other things but is not moved by them because it is self-moved; and (d) that which moves other things without being moved, either by itself or by other things.

Plato's alternatives treat only (b) and (c), the second and third possibilities in the above, which are the most clearly manifest forms of motion. The first, (a), would in fact be matter, rather than material things; and the fourth, (d), would presumably be God. If we accept Aristotle's idea of God as the Unmoved Mover, and that He moves all the alter-motive contents of the world, we cannot logically avoid the intermediate function identified by Plato, the self-moved. Conversely, if we start from the realm of things moved, and try to deduce from it a universal Mover, the transition to such a mover cannot be fully carried out without including the self-moved. Like material things, the latter is subject to motion, and, like God, it is not passive to the action of other things that have been moved.

Without the self-moved, there would be a hiatus in the range of possibilities of motion. This would be contrary to the Principle of Plenitude, which will be considered in detail in Chapter 2, where it will be shown to be essential to this form of philosophy. However, that Aristotle rejected the self-moved is clear from *De Anima* I, iv, 408: "But of all the unreasonable theories about the soul, the most unreasonable is that which calls the soul a number which moves itself. In this theory there are inherent impossibilities. . . ."

These impossibilities seem to lie mostly in supposedly trying to move an arithmetic unit (which is obviously non-spatial), as though Plato meant a mere numeral and not a number-*eidos*. Thus by this *ignoratio elenchi* Aristotle invites one to ignore a fundamental possibility, as if one could ignore one of the four combinations made by Hot, Cold, Moist, and Dry. This appears to be a deliberate incoherence in the interests of a preconceived naturalistic agenda.

Plato develops the same idea in more detail in *Laws* X, where he declares it to be a doctrine of the soul of which the great majority are ignorant. Soul is held to be one of the "primal beings," being anterior to all material things. All that is akin to soul must share in this primacy—"judgements, foresight, wisdom, art, and law," which are prior to "hard and soft, heavy and light."[23]

This implies that works of art will be the "grand primal" works, while those of nature will be secondary and derivative; and here Plato inverts the common-sense order, just as his theory of ideas does, where it makes particulars derive from universals. Thus where "natural" means "truly original," it will be the existence of soul which is the natural to the highest degree. But how to establish the anterior nature of soul? The key to this is found in motion. Some things are in motion, while others are at rest, both kinds equally occupying space. Those which move are subdivided into two classes: those whose movement takes them from place to place; and those which move in one place only, that is, those which rotate.

Motion as change of place is analyzed under various headings, such as colliding without change, and colliding with change, the latter divided between cases resulting in aggregation and those resulting in disintegration. In all, ten kinds of motion are deduced from five dichotomies, which are all subject to the one "which can set other things in motion, but not itself" (894b), while the tenth of the moving powers is a self-motive cause of motion, setting itself in motion as well as other things. The latter is involved in every kind of motion, because it is reckoned to be the most powerful of all the different kinds of movers, and is the only conceivable kind which can mediate between the moving and the motionless by properties common to both. (The ninth kind, on the other hand, is the one which moves other things because it itself is also moved from without.)

The numerical order is then reversed, so as to make the self-motive the first, because it would be contradictory for any motion which depended on external impulses to be taken for the first (894e). That there is such a thing as a mover which is also a self-mover is accepted without direct argument, apparently on the strength of its logical possibility, together with the idea that this must imply actuality, according to the Plenitude principle referred to above. This kind of mover is identified with the soul without further ado, as in the *Phaedrus*, on the grounds that self-motion is one of the things it is known by. The option of seeking something which would be solely a source of self-motion and nothing else is not considered; rather it may be enough that the soul has this property among others.

If all things were at a standstill, motion would only be able to begin from something which was able to move itself. For this reason, self-motion is said to be the "earliest" and the "mightiest" kind of motion, while all those that consist in merely transmitting motion are secondary (895b). So important is self-motion that it is presented as constituting a definition of soul, but no attempt is made to see how this relates to what has been said in other dialogues about the soul as a knower.

The question as to how the soul interacts with the material things it moves is not considered either in the *Phaedrus* or in the *Laws*. That it has an ontological primacy over the material elements is felt to be enough to ensure its power to move them. One might say that just as they are in a dependent relation to soul as regards being known, so they are also in regard to motion. If "being-moved" is part of the definition of material things, and "imparting motion" is likewise that of the soul, the matter is settled within certain limits.

The world as a totality is said to be governed by a soul commensurate with it, guiding and sustaining its motion in a positive way, which is interpreted as circular. This motion is held to be wholly benign, and so cannot account for the evil in the world (896e). Accordingly, Plato takes the option of positing a second world-soul, which produces motion of a rectilinear kind, which though not evil as such makes forces of destruction possible. Within the individual it would correspond to the dark, intractable horse in the *Phaedrus* chariot-myth, and is Plato's nearest approach to belief in a devil.

In the *Timaeus,* there is said to be a certain residue of energy which is not due to the rational soul, and of this, T. Gould says:

> Plato corrects this inconsistency by the obvious, though rather desperate, expedient of declaring that there are two kinds of *psyche*. One is self-generating circular motion, like all of *psyche* but for the "mortal parts" in the *Timaeus,* and the other is self-generating rectilinear motion, characterizing both the tendencies of bodily nature as such and the irrational parts of human and animal *psyches.* This astonishing idea is the extreme, but logical, development of Plato's later thought.[24]

If all causal power is to be confined to soul, and not to matter, we cannot evade the idea of a soul which is in some way evil; and it is noteworthy that for Christian doctrine also, evil is attributed strictly to the souls of men and fallen angels, not to the material world. One general consequence of this is that when things are explained in a theological manner in terms of striving, hostility, hope, fear, and so on, something more would be involved than mere anthropomorphism. The relations of finite souls to their parts of the world would simply reflect the cosmic rule of the world-soul over matter.

In this way, Plato inverts the evolutionistic order which would derive the higher realities from those of matter and material motion, which Plato took to be the main source of atheism, "because it involves the belief that *psyche,* and thus art and intelligence, are accidental side effects of valueless processes."[25] His order of priorities is not unreasonable, because there is no more reason why the physical elements should be *a priori* primitive and causal than why soul should be. In favor of the soul theory it can also be argued that the only experience which is primal and un-hypothetical is that of thought. Even the simplest material object is in fact a construct which we once had to learn, however habitual it may have become since. This order of priority may well reflect degrees of reality.

Self-motion, although we are not told so in *Laws* X, comprises an additional argument for the immortality of the soul because it involves an uncompounded nature. By contrast, the apparent self-motion of a machine can always be traced to the action of one part against another, it being in fact a series of alter-motive instruments acting in a repeating cycle. But with true self-motion, there is no one part moving another; moved and moving are strictly coincident, and that rules out all physical parallels, and signifies the spiritual nature. Self-motion is in any case a fact of experience which is part of us like rational consciousness, and is a vital clue to the question of what we essentially are. Should our self-motion in practice be only partial, owing to the number of factors acting directly and indirectly on our wills, that need not exclude an element of absolute self-motion.

This conception is also of importance for the question of individual as well as generic identity, because it leads naturally to a factor which individuates the soul—this being the continual flow of its acts of volition, which will be considered at greater length in Chapter 4. Only a small adjustment is needed to identify the soul's self-motion with its volition without compromising the essential idea. If the connection between the self-motive power and that of cognition is a little obscure, it is no more so than that between cognition and volition, and we may reasonably equate these two relations. In this relation, we shall be able to see later that Leibniz, in the *New Essays*, could be said to have revived, whether intentionally or not, Plato's idea of soul as the self-motive principle.

The principle involved here unites a number of theses important for our present purpose, namely the immortality of the soul, the identity of the individual, and the mind's ability to defy the Second Law of Thermodynamics and spontaneously create new order. Because all other movers in nature are alter-motive, it is necessary that they must use up the energy imparted to them, and eventually lose the identities they once had. Such is the reason for the universal downward tendency to disorder in the realms treated by physics and chemistry; and this is precisely what a self-motive being is by definition exempt from.

There is a necessary connection between the tendency toward disorder and the inability of natural things to conserve motion imparted to them from without. The continual lessening and dispersal of motion means that nothing in the material world can remain the same. On the other hand, self-motion implies not only an independence of external sources of order, but also the ability to sustain and renew order and act with free will, that is, a will not bound wholly by universal physical conditions. In this, we can identify the basis of the Platonic conception of free will, since there could be no such thing for a being which was not self-motive. This may not have mattered to Aristotle, with his naturalistic point of view, but it should have mattered to Aquinas, whose doctrine so largely depends on it.

The souls of animals, *qua* souls, must also have self-motion, but this does not imply free will in the absence of intelligence. Without the latter, self-motion has no principle of its own by which to guide itself, such that it must be wholly at the disposal of external pressures. Conversely, in rational beings, it could be said that God moves even the self-motive among them by means of mental perceptions of values such as goodness and truth. On this basis they can transcend the Second Law, which could well be called the law of alter-motive natures.

Criticisms of Self-Motion

Aristotle's denial of the self-motive nature of soul was to be an important influence on Catholic theology once the latter became committed to Aristotle, and for this reason his objections to self-motion appear clearly in the works of Aquinas. In this connection, Aquinas appeals to the idea that man is "unqualifiedly one," a phrase he uses several times, which, if true, would seem to rule out the conception of a separable motive principle acting on the body.

However, if this unity were a reality, man should not be mortal at all, but should rather be indestructible and everlasting. One might question whether anything in this world can be "unqualifiedly one," apart from arithmetic unity and the geometrical point. The main question as to the nature of the soul is presented as a choice between two sides of a dichotomy, one of which is that the soul is in the body "as form to matter" in the manner of a Form, without a subsistent reality of its own; while the other is that it is in the body "as a sailor is in a ship,"[26] this latter expression being used to express Plato's position in regard to the soul as mover of the body.

To maintain that man is unqualifiedly one in this context, and use it as a presupposition, is practically question-begging. Even unity in general is hard enough to attribute precisely, as it can mean the unity of a complex structure like a clock or a calculator, or that of a simple entity like a stone. If man is a unity in the former sense (which is almost certainly the case), it is of no use for the argument against the separable soul; it can only serve this purpose if one thinks in terms of the unity of the stone.

The reasoning used here is also mistaken in that it ignores the fact that the soul is not the kind of being which can be characterized unequivocally by expressions of spatial location like that of the sailor in the ship. If it could be, it would not be distinguishable from a spatial object, and indeed it could almost be treatable as a body. It is essential to the idea of soul that it should transcend the dichotomies which govern physical things. Only aspectually can it be said to be in the body as the sailor in the ship, and only aspectually can it be said to be consubstantial with the body. These aspects are necessary for a knowledge of it, rather in the way that two or more two-dimensional planes serve to express a three-dimensional object from different points of view.

By confounding a complex unity with an inert or elementary one, the Aristotelian position is made out to be starkly in opposition to the Platonic, instead of being complementary to it, as the Neoplatonists understood it.[27] Aquinas further argues[28] that the real man cannot be the soul directing the body because "animal and man are sensible natural realities." This is also said as though it were self-evident, although it is open to an obvious criticism. The difference which death makes to the sensible and natural aspect of animals and men is little or nothing, to begin with, at least, but for all that they are then no longer there at all *qua animals* or men, since these consist primarily of life and consciousness, which are not sensible.

The fact that they are not sensible does not mean that there is no way of perceiving them, however, since they are perceptible in an indirect sense, as when we say a person is visible to us when we actually see a face and a collection of clothing. Such things "are" the person in the same ambivalent sense in which a portrait of him also "is" him. But this sense in which we can say that a person is a sensible reality is, however, of no use to an argument for the exclusion of a separate soul, because that would require that the person should be their sensible appearances and nothing else, rather than the invisible cause of those appearances.

Here again we encounter a false dichotomy, namely that the body be univocally the person (apparently Aquinas's view, if taken with the idea that the person is unqualifiedly one), or that it be univocally not the person (Plato's view according to the Schoolmen). But the facts do not compel us to make any such choice, for the relations they involve are not nearly simple enough. Person and body are not related reciprocally. While it is true to say that the body of John Smith (if he is alive) is John Smith, it is not true to say that

John Smith is John Smith's body. In other words, there is no unequivocal way in which a person can be either sensible or non-sensible, whence we cannot trust arguments which ignore this. A more truthful idea of the body as "not other than" the person would be perfectly compatible with the Platonic idea of soul and body.

Aquinas gives a direct argument against the soul's being the self-moved mover of the body utilizing *De Anima* II.5.[29] In the latter, it is said that "sensation consists in being moved and acted upon." From this it is argued that an individual is "passive in sensing," and that one's soul is in effect moved by the sensations that come to it. This passivity would mean that the soul has no function as mover in perception, and so could not be "diverse from the animate body."

It is not hard to test the truth of this. If Aristotle was right, and the soul or conscious being really were passive in sensation, lapses of attention should be impossible, and we should all enjoy sensorial infallibility, provided only that we be present in the right place at the right time. Besides this, we should be able to master any text, however difficult, merely by staring at it, if the activity really were external to us. In reality, our senses are constantly receiving masses of material which we do not really perceive, simply because our interests are directed elsewhere, as in seeing a clock without reading the time by it because one is having a conversation.

This means that only the physiological infrastructure of perception is really passive to the input in the way Aristotle describes, whereas the soul, the conscious perceiver, is not. Without the activity of the latter on the sensory input, the passively acquired sensation is never turned into a conscious experience, and so might as well not be there. Consequently, the passive element in sensation is of no use for proving a passivity in the soul, whence its function as mover cannot be compromised in this way. The statement quoted from Aristotle is in any case too general to support the weight of argument put on it by Aquinas.

Aquinas offers a more technical objection to the Platonic idea of the soul (Ch. 57, 6) on the assumption that body and soul have many operations in common (e.g., sensation, anger, and fear). Aquinas argues that, because of this, body and soul cannot be separate things: "It is impossible that things diverse in being should have one operation." This is supported on the grounds that there is a distinction between "that in which the operation terminates" and "the manner of its issuance from the agent."

In the former case, it is only too clear that diverse agents *can* have one operation (e.g., decisions made by committees). In the other case, however, much depends on whether the "issuance" of the operation from the agents is really diverse or not. For example, there is the case of a hand and the pen held by it. It would be futile to ask whether the writing is done with the hand or the pen, as it is clearly done with a combination of both. Their operations are clearly one in the action in which they "terminate," and they are equally inseparable at the stage of "issuance" because this comes from the combination of hand and pen, and not from either of these two things separately. The distinction which this argument relies upon is therefore rather dubious.

Furthermore, this argument presupposes that the body is also an "agent" along with the soul, and that there are "operations of soul and body together," evidently in the sense of two horses harnessed to the same carriage. In this case, there could well be problems in the coordination of these agents; but this supposition is in fact nothing more than a dogmatic denial of the idea that the soul is always the mover, and the body always the moved. If the body was, after all, as much an agent as the soul, then the soul would indeed not be its mover. But this is practically question-begging, and makes the rest of the argument redundant. Aquinas directs a further argument against the role of the soul as mover, which is also based on the dubious dichotomy between form-of-body and separable agent referred to earlier. This appears in the contention that "if the soul is united to the body *merely as mover to movable*,"[30] then the soul should be able to separate itself from the body and reunite with it as and when it pleases.

If it were true that the relation of soul to body was practically as external as that of a man pushing a handcart, as this implies, the conclusion would no doubt follow; but there are no grounds for thinking that Plato ever entertained such an idea. This argument clearly depends on the soul's being *merely* a mover, which arbitrarily restricts our conception of it, making its action too much like the action of one body on another.

That the functions of mover and Form-of-the-body combine in the same entity will be made more apparent when it is shown how soul is a special case of Form in the Platonic or transcendental sense of the term,[31] that is, a Form whose properties include motive power in addition to the more usual one of quality.

What have been examined above are some of the classic Aristotelian arguments against the soul as a separable agent exerting motive power over the body, and it seems that none of them is effective, let alone decisive. Besides, they typically rely on attributing to Aristotle's position an exclusiveness which probably not even Aristotle himself would have claimed for it. This would be a case of being Aristotelian for its own sake, not for that of the problems solved by it, because Aquinas himself acknowledges that the concept of self-motion is ultimately indispensable where free will has to be discussed, as in accompanying chapters: "Now the animal is a *self-mover*, and the mover in it is the soul and the body is the moved,"[32] and "those alone move freely which in judging *move themselves.* . . . So only things that *move themselves act* freely."[33] This is a case of an idea which is treated as valid in one context but not in another, because of an external agenda.

I have quoted from medieval discussions of self-motion because this conception ceased to have much place in philosophy after those times. Not only has it been neglected in recent centuries, it has played little part in the thought of philosophers who have belonged to the Platonic tradition. That this is unfortunate; and the actual importance of this idea in relation to the better-known Platonic ideas is the subject of the next section.

The Two Accounts of the Soul;
Their Inner Relation; Circular Motion

The psychical self-motion is also said to be "circular," but the neglect of this aspect of the subject concerns philosophies of the soul, of course, and not the cosmological applications of it developed by Aristotle and his successors. These applications were so influential that they could be said to have flogged the idea to death before it was superseded by the Copernican theory. As a result, this idea was abandoned, although the more rational response would have been to return to its source. Had this been done, our understanding of the nature of the self would have been much better founded.

So far, two forms of the theory have been presented, one deriving from the *Phaedo* and the other from the *Phaedrus* and the *Laws*, though the relation between these two versions is far from clear. In the dialogues they likewise appear isolated from one another, with no indication that Plato ever thought of relating them. However, the idea of self-motion can be shown to be the counterpart to the argument from knowledge. In that argument, it is stated that our grasp of truth and our ability to form true statements result from a kind of causality which owes nothing to physical causes.

Although this argument is complete in its way for the purpose to which it is put, we are not told how this non-physical causality operates. Mind or soul connects with truth and reflects the relations between the Forms. The power of self-motion involves something which is, in its own way, just as much beyond the scope of natural forces. It involves the action of the whole being upon that whole being, unlike the motion of machines, which depends on certain parts acting on one another in a sequence so as to move the whole. Self-motion truly so-called implies that the being is, in Proclus's terms, "converted to itself," or "reverted upon itself," a property which is more often considered in relation to knowledge.

Only self-motion, with its transcendence of natural forces, meets the conditions for what we know of intellectual activity. This relatedness also throws light on the deep relation between intelligence and free will. Besides, the relation, or rather the lack of it, to the Second Law of Thermodynamics is the same for both the self-motive principle and for the order-creating power of the intellect: the former because of its freedom from the natural dissipation of energy, and the latter because it works in a sense opposite to that of the rising entropy in nature, by creating new order.

This relation between the *Phaedo* and *Phaedrus* arguments has apparently not been seriously considered in philosophy before, either by commentators or even by the major Neoplatonists. While the *Phaedo* argument remained in continuous use, both in Platonism and Scholasticism, the self-motion argument of the *Phaedrus* and *Laws* has been long since undeservedly relegated to the category of outmoded scientific speculations because of its association with Aristotle's cosmology.

Another problem associated with this latter argument is that the psychical self-motion is identified in *Laws* X with circular motion. The mere fact that it is thus given a geometrical form is taken to mean that it cannot be more than a figure of speech. However, the circulation is capable of admitting more subtle meanings. When soul is conceived as having essential motion it is only natural that this motion should itself be conceived as the kind which unites the mobile with the immobile, corresponding to the soul's function of mediating between the individual and the eternal, the changing and the eternal:

> It is a motion proper and similar to the turning (*periodos*) of reason. What do circular motion and rationality have in common? Both move steadily, consistently, with order and due proportion.... But the motion related to the absence of all intelligence (*anoias apases syngenes*) is rectilinear ... of all Plato's ideas, this one was the most influential in the succeeding centuries ... a mean between the motionless Forms and the flux of the sensed world.[34]

Circular motion resolves the duality between the unmoving center and the moving periphery, then; and this may well be relevant to the duality already remarked in regard to the soul's ability to assimilate its activity to changeless truths as well as to things in a state of change. The problem with this is that it seems we are only speaking of an analogy and not of the actual reality. The natural phenomenon which would give the clearest image of it is a vortex, such as a whirlwind. But since the soul is not literally any kind of phenomenon, there may be no point in relating its epistemic functions to physical and spatial models.

For most philosophies this objection could well be insuperable, but the theory of Ideas allows an answer that avoids the conclusion that the circulation model is a mere figure of speech. It does not take any phenomenon to be merely a phenomenon, but rather to be an instance of a Form which comprises all its reality in a transcendent permanence. Thus the vortex would have its Form, like anything else in nature, only with the difference that this particular Form is instantiated in the soul as well.

Given some such higher-order instantiation in the psychic substance, then, we could have a real basis for the analogy. Plato does not explicitly say that there must be a Form of circular motion, but the whole tendency of his thought implies it, and he may well have taken it for granted. Such a Form would also support an answer to criticisms of his later theories, according to which his metaphysics would have to depend on a rather dubious kind of physics, as the literal sense of the texts would imply.

As Gould says, "That Plato believed in the equation of intelligence and circular motion is beyond question";[35] but to take this literally would be to father on Plato a materialistic idea which would destroy the coherence of his thought. If his "circular motion" were anything less than the Form of Circulation, he would have ignored an obvious case of self-contradiction, given his premise that the Forms are the primary realities.

Whether there is such a thing as self-motion and whether it can be called "circular" are certainly not the same question, and the relation of self-motion to intelligence has been shown to exist without it; but for all that, the properties of circular motion express what is involved in the application of intelligence to its objects with a correspondence which is too close for it to be a contingency.

Notes

[1] *Glory, Jest and Riddle*, 5.
[2] Ibid., 54.
[3] Ibid., 8.
[4] Ibid., 16.
[5] E. A. Wallis Budge, *Egyptian Religion*, 189–190.
[6] Ibid., 191.
[7] Ibid., 193.
[8] *Glory, Jest and Riddle*, 68.
[9] Thomas Gould, *Platonic Love*, 71.
[10] Chapter 2, X.
[11] Chapter 2, XI, XII.
[12] *Therapeia*, 25.
[13] Joseph Pieper, *Death and Immortality*.
[14] *Summa Contra Gentiles* II, Ch. 56.
[15] Chapter 4, 144–48.
[16] *Critique of Pure Reason*, Of the

Paralogisms of Pure Reason.
[17] Ibid.
[18] *De Anima*, I.iv.
[19] Ibid.
[20] *Elements of Theology*, Prop. 45.
[21] Joseph Pieper, "The Philosophical Act," II, 115.
[22] *Phaedrus*, 245d.
[23] *Laws*, 892b.
[24] *Platonic Love*, 130.
[25] Ibid., 133.

[26] *De Anima*, I, iii.
[27] *Summa Contra Gentiles*, II, Ch. 57, 2 & 3.
[28] Ibid., Ch. 57, 5.
[29] Ibid., Ch. 57, 8.
[30] Ibid., Ch. 57, 13.
[31] Chapter 2, X.
[32] Ibid., Ch. 65, 5.
[33] Ibid., Ch. 48, 3.
[34] *Platonic Love*, 135 and 137–38.
[35] Ibid., 137.

2

The Psycho-Physical Complex

Personal Identity in Neoplatonism

Plotinus provided a number of additional arguments concerning the nature of the soul in the Platonic tradition. Unlike his predecessors, however, he went on from this to a theory of selfhood, and to an account of the relation of the individual person to the whole of being. Accordingly, this chapter will proceed under these general headings, in the same order.

Plotinus's theory of the soul occupies the whole of the Fourth *Ennead*, besides appearing in numerous passages elsewhere. This is where we find the Neoplatonic conception of identity. The person is conceived to have a real identity through the immortality of the soul and its transcendence of matter. *Ennead* IV, 7, which deals with this most directly, attained a special historical importance: "Plotinus's early, very 'scholastic' treatise IV, 7, on immortality, whose arguments, repeated with relatively little change by Augustine and others, thus became the common property of the European metaphysical tradition."[1]

What is discussed here is not the survival of some ghostly part of the self, but rather that of the "man himself" or the "true man" (*aner estin autos*), which Plotinus identifies with the soul—this being, however, a more complex entity than conceived by Plato. This is made even more explicit a little later, where it is stated that

> The sovran principle, the authentic man, will be as form to this matter, or as agent to this instrument, and thus, whatever that relation be, the Soul is the man [*to de kyriotaton kai autos ho*

anthrōpos, eiper touto, kata to eidos hos pros hulen to soma he kata to chromenon hōs pros organon, hekateos de he psuche autos].[2]

Thus from the start it appears that Plotinus is following Plato's idea of man as body ruled by soul given in the *Alcibiades*: "But we are agreed that that which rules the body is the man?"[3] This is also a position which was accepted by Aristotle, who was another important influence on Plotinus: "For though this is a small portion [of our nature], it far surpasses everything else in power and value. One might regard it as each man's true self, since it is the controlling and better part."[4]

However, it should be noted that Plotinus's statement is the more complete in that it combines the Form-matter relation with that of agent-instrument, reflecting his work's nature as a synthesis of Plato and Aristotle.

Soul and Matter

The question, then, is how to determine that this ruling principle is not material, and is therefore free from the laws of material composition. But before examining these arguments, we need to clarify another question which is not really brought into the open in the *Enneads*. Plotinus confidently states that life cannot result from matter:

> For very certainly Matter does not mould itself to pattern or bring itself to life. It becomes clear that since neither matter nor body in any mode has this power, life must be brought upon the stage by some directing principle external and transcendent to all that is corporeal.[5]

Plotinus makes no attempt to prove this statement, as he feels it to be almost self-evident. However, to modern minds, this can look like question-begging, because, if it is granted, the arguments for the immortality of the soul which follow from it will be made too easy. Too much depends on what is assumed about matter here for it to be taken for granted, since materialists could object that the existence of organisms or animated matter proves that matter in fact *does* produce order and life.

The Psycho-Physical Complex

When we consider matter as naturally found in embodied forms, and not as a metaphysical category, we will not understand it unless we focus on what is truly essential to it. In the clearest examples of it, there is solidity, homogeneity of composition, hardness or impenetrability, and weight and extension. Obviously, not all physical things exhibit these properties to the same degree, and for this reason we need to relate their properties to the *eidos* of corporeality as just characterized, which points inevitably to the conclusion that the material bodies which most clearly possess these determinations of mass, hardness, uniformity, and so on, are the truest and most representative of their kind.

These would include most metals, rocks, crystals, and glass, and on the above reasoning it is on them that we must base our conclusions as to what matter can and cannot do: "Life and consciousness emerge where the creative penetrates its own creation. Characteristically, this penetration does not occur at the higher levels of the mineral kingdom, but at its lowest; dirt and slime being closer to life than pure metals and precious stones."[6]

Given this paradigmatic conception of empirical matter, the bodies of living organisms are material bodies in only a rather ambivalent sense. Their solid content has only a very low degree of cohesion and purity, and is drawn from the detritus of the material order—not from anything that manifests its type, but "from the dust of the ground," in the biblical expression. Organic bodies are also composed of a very high proportion of water, such that they are nearly as much liquids as bodies or solids.

Life and inorganic matter possess mutually exclusive forms of self-organization, because life's structures require growth and assimilation, while matter's structures are rigid, as in the above examples. For this reason, the structures needed by life can only be formed from matter by means of a destruction of the form of order peculiar to matter, that is, its reduction to dust and slime.

All this is consistent with organisms having resulted from matter coming into relation with something profoundly alien to it, and not from matter alone. Given the disparity of natures between it and the living soul it is united to, it would be surprising if it could retain much of its essential nature while in this combination. Organic bodies would therefore not be acts or productions of matter *per se*, in accordance with what Plotinus says in the passage quoted above.

However, this idea of matter is not exactly that of Plotinus, and some adjustment of it to his conception is necessary. For Plotinus, matter is entirely passive and without properties, except only that of receiving instances of the Forms. Such a matter as this would *a fortiori* be unable to "mould itself to a pattern," but if we conceive it in the same manner as above, the only difference is that there Plotinus's inert material substrate is combined with a very limited group of Forms instanced in it, i.e. the hard, the solid, and the extended. Although these qualities are above the purely material level in this metaphysic, they are all of a kind which is positively opposed to penetration by life and consciousness, rather than just negatively, as with the material substratum or *material prima*. This reasoning gives adequate grounds for denying that there is any effective continuity between matter as such and life.

It should be noted that this argument, based on the distinction between the natural state of solid matter and its detritus, is not affected by scientific theories about the constitution of matter. For scientific purposes, solid matter is made up of atoms or molecules in fixed patterns or lattices in direct connection with one another, and in the other case they have only loose and weak connections and do not form any fixed combination.

Some Plotinian Arguments

Soul and embodied natures are said to be distinguished by reference to the different ways in which the Forms function in them (IV, 7, 4). Where Forms are instanced in bodies, they act in an exclusive manner, as, for example, where coldness and heat are present the entry of either of them entails the removal of the other; and likewise for all the various colors, and all other qualities. Similarly, there are things like fire and ice which manifest one predominant quality, from which they are inseparable.

This contrasts with the soul, which can receive any number of Forms without their expelling one another or affecting one another at all. It can just as easily combine in itself Forms which are in principle inimical to one another, and are effectively so when materially instanced, as combine Forms which are always compatible. In this way it is not bound always to produce the same effect in its actions, but can produce contrary ones as and when required. This is an argument which has been recognizably taken up by Aquinas: "in the intellect, things even of contrary nature cease to be contraries. Thus white and black are not contraries in the intellect, since they do not exclude one another; rather they are co-implicative. . . ."[7]

Here, this is presented as proof that the intellectual substance has no contrary, as it transcends such things; and, having no contrary, cannot be corruptible, since corruptibility comes about through the action of contraries. This is an argument which is relevant for the immortality of the soul and for free will equally, since the soul cannot be determined by any of the Forms exclusively, as it comprises them all on an equal basis. Material things, on the other hand, are, so to speak, "owned" by the Forms instanced in them, and hence determined by them.

What Kant calls the synthetic unity of apperception is made the basis of Plotinus's next argument[8] for the soul's immortality, on the grounds that it constitutes a "unitary percipient [*en auto dei einai*]" to which all the separate senses report, and without which the unity of the object could never be perceived. This is illustrated by a comparison frequently used by Plotinus, that to the center of a circle. The central point common to all radii is the condition for all the points on the circumference to be each a part of the same circle. Their multiplicity is in effect a projection of but one point in many directions. A visual object, such as a face, must correspondingly have all its separate points brought together into one, where each is equally related to all the others, as all the radii have one point in common. Otherwise, there would not be one thing, one face, at all. If objects with an extended group of points were to impinge *per se* on the perceiver who had a corresponding number of points to receive them, there would result an equivalent number of unrelated perceptions, in the absence of any overriding unity. The fact that even the largest objects are taken in through the pupil of the eye is seen to manifest this reality on the physical plane.

If, indeed, there were anything material about the impact of objects upon consciousness, like that of a seal on wax, later impressions would be constantly spoiling and obliterating earlier ones. Either, then, there would be no memory, or if there were memory it would bring to an end the sequence of impressions, as the price of its own survival. This form of argument is essentially the same as the Kantian argument concerning the unity of experience, which will be considered later.[9]

The next argument (IV, 7, 7) is based on an introspective examination of pain. It is designed to show the soul to be an "all everywhere," which must rule out its having a material nature. The example used is that of a pain in an extremity, like a finger. This experience shows that if the soul were extended through the body after the manner of a physically extended thing, the sensation would have to be transmitted from each one of its elements to the next in a series, from the finger to the center of consciousness. If anything like this happened, the transfer of the pain in this way would entail *its* repetition at every point, such that it would be multiplied an enormous number of times. One pain would mean many pains in as many different places. Moreover, the center of consciousness would only be aware of the pain in the element adjacent to it, and so would not know its real location.

On a material basis, the finger might suffer its pain in isolation, or there might be a sense of pain at the center of consciousness but without any sense of position. But in reality, the pain exists in both the peripheral and central modes at once, and for this, "one must suppose the perceiving principle to be of a kind as to be identical to itself at every spot [*dei toiouton tithesthai to aisthanomen, oion pantachou auto eauto to auto einai*]; this property can belong only to some other form of being than body."[10]

Elsewhere in *Ennead* IV, he says that we cannot question the possibility of a thing being "at once a unity and multi-present," or "one and many, parted and impartible."[11] The presupposition behind this thinking is that consciousness of pain requires the activity of some kind of unitary, active entity, however much its properties may differ from those of things which we can see and handle. Modern thought is not willing to adopt this approach because of a counter-assumption that the idea of thinghood ought not to extend to things not perceivable by the senses. This is due to the influence of the scientific method of explanation, which will be examined critically later on[12] when alternative conceptions are considered. The Plotinian position explained here is, however, what later discussions in this book are intended to support.

An Anticipation of a Kantian Argument

After answering the objection that the soul might perish through being subject to some kind of material division and dissipation, Plotinus proceeds to another argument against it which is essentially the same as that of Kant in the Paralogisms, already discussed in Chapter 1, Section IV, and which seems to have been ignored in the intervening centuries: "But it will come to destruction by qualitative change [all' alloiōtheisa exei eis fthoran]," where alloiōtheisa corresponds to Kant's term "elanguescence."[13] He answers this by saying that a destructive qualitative change presupposes a compound of Form and matter, so that the Form principle can be withdrawn from it. Yet the soul is not a compound of Form and matter, but is without any material admixture.

Conversely, the fading of a color in a material and the dying-away of a sound in the air both presuppose a material substratum in which the visual or auditory quality inheres. Aristotelians may object that the soul in fact is a qualitative form inherent in the material of the body, and there is indeed a psychical reality corresponding to this, but Plotinus is speaking of the soul *qua* source of motion and intelligence, something for which the Scholastics themselves have to posit a separate "intellectual substance."

The crux of Plotinus's brief argument here is that quality is immutable in itself, and that the only way in which it can be made to appear to vary is for a material thing to be more or less receptive for the instancing of it. The soul, being of like nature with the Forms in their intrinsic, unparticipated state, by definition must therefore not be capable of any sort of qualitative increase or decrease. It is unaffected by phenomenal changes, as whiteness itself is unaffected by instanced white things becoming more or less white.

Nevertheless, the soul is not wholly accounted for in terms of a

Form instanced in matter, as consciousness is also "in" the soul in a similar manner. (The Forms can be in either material or psychic substances in the manner appropriate to each, as noted on page 90 of this book.) In other words, the soul is an example of a noetic reality which is in the physical world *per se* amidst the instantial realities, which implies that the sum total of the real is more complex than a simple two-world system, one of which would consist wholly of Forms and the other wholly of instantiations.

In *Enneads* IV, 7, 8, Plotinus presents at greater length an argument which has already been found in the *Phaedo*. This concerns the possibility of knowing as distinct from perceiving. If the soul were corporeal, it should not be capable of anything but sensation. Thinking has to be independent of the body, because it involves so many things for which there is no bodily counterpart. For example, it can conceive things which have no extension, whereas the corporeal cannot be other than extended. The operations of arithmetic, logic, and music have no spatial meaning, and so could not be functions of a being whose essence was material and therefore spatial. As Plotinus says: "How then will something which is a size think what is not a size and think what is partless with something which has parts?"[14] W.R. Inge identified this idea as essential to Platonism, which has further consequences when we consider the implications of our knowing eternal truths:

> This law of correspondence and mutual dependence of subject and object holds good all down the scale. *Like alone sees its like. . . .* It is found in Plato and Aristotle; and in Empedocles, whom Aristotle quotes as the author of the canon: "*he gnosis tou homoiou tō homoiō.*"[15]

It could be argued that even our experience of size itself depends on something in us which transcends size, or else we should not be able to perceive any sizes greater than our own. As it is, one perceives the heavens without having any common measure with their size. If it were said that the soul, having parts, conceives partless realities with some part of itself which is partless (*Enn.* IV, 7, 8, 15), it has to be conceded that that part at least is not material. But in that case, this alleged part will suffice, while all the others will be irrelevant.

Mind, it is said, has the power of detaching Forms from bodies in an immaterial manner, in order to know them. It can separate "circle," "triangle," and "line"—although this does not mean the withdrawal of their instantiation—and this cannot be done by a material agent since the operation in question is specifically immaterial. Maritain has remarked upon this from a Thomistic point of view:

> No type of material union can attain to the degree of union which exists between the knower and the known. If I lost my being in something else in order to be united with it, I would not *become* that other being; it and I together would make a composite, a *tertium quid,* instead of the knower's becoming the known itself.[16]

On any material basis, then, no kind of fusion is possible without a merging of the identities of the things involved. But knowledge functions like a form of fusion in which subject and object nevertheless retain their identities, rather as contrary Forms like Great and Small exist together in the same mind, and this evidences the non-material nature of knowing. The power of the knower to become immaterially something else while remaining himself is also related to what Plotinus says of the soul's ability to be "at once a unity and multi-present" in the body, "one and many, parted and impartible" *(Enn.* IV, 1, 2, 40). In this connection, the transcendent activity of the soul could be said to be deployed in an aesthetic manner for sensory knowledge, rather than for conceptual knowledge, but the transcendence of its material alternatives of oneness and many-ness is the same.

Soul and Infinity

Although Plotinus does not say so directly, this attribute of being effectively whole in every part implies that the soul comprises a real degree of infinity. The above example of physical pain shows that soul is able to act as a whole no matter where it is active—whether in the body or elsewhere. What corresponds to divisibility in it is its presence at every point in the object of attention, while its indivisibility is evident directly both as a conscious unity and as an ability to be present as a whole in connection with divisible things.

This property, which is not possible for material entities to possess, is undeniably a property of infinity, besides having an application to our picture of soul-life. The connection between the two can be illustrated by a well-known property of infinite series. If we take a part, one half, say, of the natural-number series, we could express it by the series 2, 4, 6, 8, 10,…; and if we were to take one-tenth of it, that could be shown as 10, 20, 30, 40,… Now, if these parts or fractions of the full series are set alongside it thus,

$$1, \quad 2, \quad 3, \quad 4, \quad 5$$

$$2, \quad 4, \quad 6, \quad 8, \quad 10$$

$$10, \quad 20, \quad 30, \quad 40, \quad 50$$

it is clear that if these are all infinite series, then the "fractional" series will always be able to continue as far as the complete one. In other words, it is a property of the infinite that the relation of part and whole no longer applies in its normal form, but that every part has an effective equivalence to the whole

The application of this to the soul supposes that there is an infinity *eidos* which can be instantiated in quite different things, including souls and number series. The value of the numerical example is that it clearly shows what is involved. Plotinus himself does not present this conclusion about the soul explicitly, though he sometimes seems about to do so, for ancient and medieval philosophers had only a rather vague idea of the infinite, and they usually did not distinguish it from the indefinite. Awareness of creation's share in the infinite was blocked by the idea of its enclosure in Aristotelian spheres. They never arrived at the idea of a being which is infinite under one aspect while being finite in all others, although the possibility of such a thing is quite clear from the properties of space. Thus a line of infinite length can measure the span of an infinite surface without being in any sense equal to it, and likewise an infinite surface can similarly encompass an infinite volume.

What we know of ourselves as finite beings in the scope and number of our faculties does not therefore necessarily conflict with our possession of a real infinity as well. It is strange that the ancient philosophers were not more clear about this, because they mostly held that man can in some sense know God, though that could not be expected of a being who was finite in every respect, especially in view of the principle that only like knows like.

On this basis, the real difference between God and created spirits in regard to infinity would be that God is infinite under an infinite number of modes, while creatures are infinite only in finite numbers of modes. Aristotle came near to realizing this, with his idea that "the soul is, in a certain sense, all things." Besides this, the Scholastics at least had the idea of the infinite as an *a priori* constituent of human knowledge, on the grounds that all our knowledge of the formal limits of things comes to us in a purely *post facto* way. They held the infinite to be "of all things the only first and most necessarily known," and to be assimilated to the essence of the soul as the basis of its capacity for knowledge of infinite realities.

Given its infinity, therefore, Plotinus is entitled to be speaking literally where he says that the soul is "both one and many," that is, a unity within a plurality, as distinct from the instanced Form, which is "many and one"; or, more correctly, a many within a unity, and distinct from bodies which are "exclusively many," and from the Supreme, which is "exclusively one" (IV, 2, 2). This text shows how the soul is conceived to occupy a place in a hierarchy which is defined in terms of discrete orders of unity. Plotinus relates this idea of the soul to Plato's idea that it is produced by the blending of the eternal and indivisible with the material and divisible (*Timaeus* 35a).

The Concept of Self

Plotinus's idea of the soul was linked to a conception of selfhood which is the subject of a study by G. J. P. O'Daly,[17] who analyses his conception of it in relation to the Soul, the *Nous,* and the One. The terminology involved owes something of its nature to an absence of a vocabulary relating to the will. The reality in question is said to have

> the mean or middle position . . . between sense and intelligence, a position later referred to explicitly when the self is described as "the

mid-point between two powers, between the sensitive principle, inferior to us, and the intellectual principle superior" (V, 3, 3).[18]

Plotinus begins by accepting the Platonic idea of the self as soul, as expressed in the *Alcibiades*, and then proceeds to analyze it in terms of the embodied self or "composite" and the intellect. Besides soul, *psuche*, he treats identity under the terms "self," "man," the "we" [*autos*], as he enters into its complexities.

This complexity is compounded by the conception of the "mid-point" or volitive center of the soul, which can merge its energies with different orders of being as it chooses. Thus the soul's mode of activity also creates a *de facto* identity according to its chosen sphere. In keeping with his psychic infinity, man is taken to be an epitome of the world, and so as having its different levels of being within him. But this does not mean that the *de facto* identity is a mere accretion, because the realization of possibilities is essential to the dynamic aspect of identity.

Within certain limits at least, what we really are consists in the ability to become various things. This is expressed by our being "amphibious," as O'Daly quotes the expression, from whence "the entire being, man, takes rank according to that which dominates in him."[19]

What we are is inextricably bound up with what we are capable of becoming, as the "mid-point" assimilates itself to different ruling principles.

This property is held to be relevant to the fate of the soul after death, as it is then obliged to resume the kind of life which it lived most intensely in this world. In this life, the level of one's being is said to be freely chosen, for the reason referred to above: "for the soul's nature includes many things, indeed everything, the higher and the lower, insofar as life in any form exists," and it contains "a subordination of various Forms like that of the Cosmic Soul."[20]

What we are is said to result from a fusion of a primal, archetypal being with a temporal being, the "self of the realm of process."[21] The latter is the instantial counterpart of the former, and its purpose in existing is to make itself adequate to its Form or formal cause. One problem which this raises is that the "primal Man" in this connection must be the same as the Form of the individual, with the lower or material person as its instance, in which case we might have to seek a new Form for the combination of the two, if that combination were our true being. However, the physical being, or "self of the realm of process," does not comport any *essential* difference from the Form. Where it differs in actual fact, this difference is due only to its failure to correspond fully to the Form. Consequently, no secondary Form is implied.[22]

Memory and the Temporal Person

The consequences of man's "amphibious" nature are next worked out in regard to memory. The higher and lower selves which derive from this property imply higher and lower souls, consistently with the principle of assigning psychic functions to separate agencies. This may look like assigning separate souls for imagination and reason, but it is really a question of a lower soul which is an integral image of the spiritual, personal soul, which is conceived to be necessary to fill all the degrees of being between the latter and the body. Its function as mediator between soul and body by sharing certain properties of both is a factor here, because of man's being conceived as a microcosm or epitome of all levels of being.

The lower soul is sometimes referred to by Plotinus as the "conjoint principle" or the "image" (*eidōlon*), and memory is said to reside in both the higher and lower souls, according to their several properties. As they are united in one and the same person, the duplication of the memory in this way is not experienced as such during life, but this unity does not persist after death, whence various psychic phenomena may result.

In the afterlife, the higher personal soul is said to retain the memories in *its* own manner while the lower, the (*eidōlon*), will do so in another. The latter, we are told, appears among the shades in Hades, comprising a residue infused with the memories of the deceased, which is not the actual person any more than the body is. Plotinus can be said to make the same distinction here as was made by the Egyptians between the Ba and the Ka referred to earlier (pp. 26–27), the former being the spiritual soul and the latter a sub-personal soul which is not strictly separable from matter.

The role of memory in the hereafter as it resides in these different forms is also examined by O'Daly, who seems to believe that Plotinus taught that it largely ceases in the "characteristically human" soul: "Nor will he have any memory of his personality. . . ."[23]

But in accepting this interpretation, he is ignoring its implications for this kind of philosophy, and still trying to think within the very limitations it transcends. If the soul is said to leave the body and return to the realm of the intelligibles, it will by definition be returning to the archetypal realities of which life's experiences are as shadows or images. In that case, it can hardly be a major issue whether the soul brings with it more or fewer memories, which are only images of those images. Our memory is a manifestation of a mental power which is necessary only because we are subject to the passage of time, which is not supposed to apply to the hereafter. When one goes to live in another town, a collection of badly focused snapshots of it would hardly be essential luggage.

From what Plotinus says of memory elsewhere, it appears that for him it consists essentially in the unhindered activity of the soul: "Must we not conclude that the basis of memory is the soul-power brought to full strength?"[24] In this case, it is hard to see why *post mortem* conditions should make any difference to such a memory, since it differs so completely from the collection of impressions which appear to constitute memory in the passive conjoint principle, or *eidolon*.

In the light of the distinction between memory in the personal soul and in its lower counterpart, it appears that the latter is lost to the self in the long run, because it is inseparable from the physical world. All it can do is transfer the life-impressions of one person to other persons after them, perhaps by adding its content to a collective or racial memory. This duplication of the soul on a quasi-natural level could be of interest to those who wish to explain psychic phenomena which show traces of personality especially where there is apparent evidence for reincarnation. The truly separable soul is practically identified with its central volitive and intellective faculties, while the mortal individual would be as a kind of shadow cast inevitably by the soul in whatever medium it resides in.

Because of the psychic duplication which this philosophy entails, therefore, the memory is both a spiritual faculty of the person and a qualitative condition of the mortal nature. While the latter is not thought of as transferable from this life to the next, the former would be so if we accept the arguments for the immortality of the soul. However, the question of the preservation of our personal memories in the hereafter is made less important by reason of the observation I made, that memory as we know it should not be essential if we go from a temporal to a non-temporal state, something which does not seem to have been noticed by commentators on Plotinus.

Soul-Body Interaction

In Plotinian terms, this question is one of how the soul can exist simultaneously in the realm of intelligibles and in the world of sense, or how the historical personality can exist in the true, spiritual self. Plotinus argues that the real Man and other living beings exist in the intelligible "insofar as they have Being."[25] All living beings, *qua* living, are said to exist in it. This assertion makes it necessary to explain how the senses, which seem to be simply the *accidentalia* of the historical person, can reside in the intelligible realm so as to have any kind of interaction with it. It might rather seem that such temporal properties should be excluded from the true man.[26]

This problem is related to the question raised in the *Parmenides*, whether there are Forms of inferior things. Plotinus originally thought there were not, but later adopted what is called the "principle of total presence."[27] The completedness of the person is the effect of the Form of the individual informing his material substance, and this relates the historical self to the intelligible, as an effect can be said to be in its cause. On the other hand, there is a Platonic position which is nominally opposed to this one, which holds that the soul's embodiment is simply a fall and a corruption of it, which throws its true nature into confusion. (This view of embodiment is evident in both the *Phaedo* and the *Timaeus*.)

Such a conception does not apply here because Plotinus is not content with a simple dichotomy of body and soul. The definition of man as soul in *Alcibiades I* is set aside as too simple to express the essence of identity, for all that its greater simplicity should imply a greater universality. This essence is seen in the light of the elective or assimilative power referred to above as more in the nature of an act than any static entity is, that is, an "act of the soul in its modified phase."[28] There is a distinction here between the soul and the man, in that the manifest man is a projection of the soul's powers.

The Plotinian concept of *logos* is involved here, since this personal identity can be said to be the "*enhylos logos*" ("enmattered principle") of an individual soul. This function of *logos* lies in transmitting the creative Forms from the intelligible order, as part of the creation and maintenance of the universe. Man as *logos* is a channel between the intelligible and the sensible realms; that is, Forms enter the cosmos through his soul, as shown by man's power of reducing disorder to order and realizing new order where there was none before.

The question still remains, however, as to just how this communication between such disparate realities is effected. It is not enough to say that only one part of the soul descends into the material world, while the other remains "undescended." The meaning of this apparent division of the soul must be clarified. Both intellectual activity and sensation have some common basis. The cognition of intelligibles is expressible as the sensation of *aistheta* in a manner suited to the intellectual level; and conversely, the perception of sensibles is an instantial act of intellection on the physical level. The act of cognizing the Triangle itself and the sense perception of a material triangle differ as much and as little as do this Form and its instances. Plotinus sums this up by saying that "perceptions here are Intellections of the dimmer order, and the Intellections There are vivid perceptions."

Owing to instantiation, then, there is a "pre-established harmony" between these two orders; and this "subsumption of the sensible into the intelligible" is the key to the Plotinian solution of the problem of how body and soul interact. The body-soul duality of Platonism can thus be partially resolved to the extent that it no longer involves a relation between completely different substances. Moreover, this resolution is carried out on Platonic principles, that is, with body as instance, and soul as Form.

Forms and souls are normally separate categories; the question of how and why the soul could be capable of this function will be the subject of a later part of this chapter. For the present, one may say that the body "is" the soul in the sense that a photographic image of someone "is" that person. The soul's power to move its body is not exactly like the body's power to move its image in a mirror, but is much more like it than an abstract concept supposedly moving a material object. It is not a case of an abstract entity supposedly moving a concrete one, because bodies are only concrete in relation to other bodies. In relation to the soul, their concreteness is simply a projection of a concreteness which the soul possesses primarily.

This approach to the problem of interaction invites comparison with that of Leibniz, who used the idea of pre-established harmony in the sense generally understood, which is weakened by not being based on the concept of Form and instance. As a result, it means for him only a synchronization which exists *de facto* among physical entities, and between these and our thoughts. Such a theory can be seen as a truncated form of the Plotinian conception outlined above. It has to be so, as he accepts the Cartesian idea that mental and physical things are different kinds of things purely and simply.

It has already been observed that personal identity is conceived here largely in terms of activity, which concerns the soul's nature as a *logos*. For Plotinus, a *logos* is a particular agency of the *Nous,* the cosmic intellect and Second Hypostasis,[29] and the essence of this agency lies in communication between the intelligible and the sensible in the manner ascribed to the soul:

> In terms of the dynamic of Plotinus' system, this seems to mean that *logos* can be understood first as a creative force deriving providentially from the higher soul (and ultimately from *Nous),* and secondly as the opposite force to the creative procession, namely the return of the emanated products to their source.[30]

A Plotinian illustration this logos-function is quoted by O'Daly, this being a sense-perception of fire being matched by a parallel cognition of Fire in the Intelligible:

> But how can that higher soul have sense-perception? It is the perception of what falls under perception. There, sensation is the mode of that realm: it is the source of the lower soul's perception of the correspondences in the sense-realm. Man as sense-percipi-

ent becomes aware of these correspondences and accommodates the sense-realm to the lowest extremity of its counterpart. There, proceeding from the fire here to the fire Intellectual which was perceptible to the higher soul in a manner corresponding to its own nature as Intellectual fire.[31]

Through this perception, the instantial fire is in a sense "returned" to its source. In this capacity, the soul would be a *logos noeticos*, as opposed to being a *logos poieticos* when it acts creatively or constructively. The interplay between sensation and intelligence is possible because the sense-world is formed wholly according to the order of the intelligible world. That they are thus both separate realities and related in this manner appears as a datum from reflection on them. For this reason, objections to the Platonic "two-world" conception would destroy the dynamic and creative interaction between intellect and sense.

There is one aspect of this treatment of the soul-body relation which may strike some readers as familiar. If so, it is because the real inspiration behind it is Aristotle's conception of the soul as the "form of the body," with "form" understood in Aristotelian terms, of course. Plotinus was familiar with this idea, and recast it such that it was a *Platonic* Form which was made Form of the body. This, as the foregoing theory shows, involves greater complications, as the Platonic Form has an independent and separable subsistence, besides a self-motive power.

The idea that it should also serve as Form to the body is in any case an essentially Platonic conclusion, for all that Aristotle first drew it. The theory of the *enhylos logos* or "enmattered word" (recalling "Incarnate Word") used in connection with it shows how effectively Plotinus made a synthesis of Platonic and Aristotelian thought. But Plotinus nowhere states explicitly that he has done this, with the result that his achievement was largely ignored, so much so that a thousand years later one sees the Scholastics discussing the conflicts between Plato and Aristotle as though no solution of them had ever been dreamt of.

The Plotinian synthesis has been equally ignored in modern times, and very few modern commentators draw attention to it. The effect of this must be to lessen the authority of the philosophies which treat the soul on the basis that the Platonic and Aristotelian positions are mutually exclusive. However, one is speaking here of a wisdom which may well be inconvenient from both narrowly fideistic and materialistic viewpoints, in which case one should not expect to see many attempts to apply it or reaffirm it.

Intelligence and Individuation

Having considered the functional aspect of the self, we must now turn to the question of what makes the self an individual, given these principles. For this purpose, we may refer again to O'Daly's account of the self, this time in relation to the *Nous*. This seems to concern only the nature of intellection: "self-conversing, the subject is its own object. Thus while being a unity, it [the self] becomes in the process dual."[32]

The fundamental condition of the intellective act is this "duality in unity," and it will appear as an equally fundamental source of individuality, similarly as in Maritain's remark concerning the individual and the union between knower and known. For our individuation to derive, at a certain level, from the reflection of intelligence on itself is a far cry from pantheistic and even Scholastic notions of individuation, on which it would seem to result only from the material unity of the body. Of course, bodily unity, however relative, is at least to some extent a source of individuation, though much less so than it is for common sense. It is more an *effect* of our individuation than a *cause* of it.

That self-knowledge by the intellect is individuating is shown a little more fully in the same text: "intellection is described as proceeding from an initial unity which *dualizes* itself intellectually."[33] It should be noted that neither the senses nor the emotions nor the imagination is capable of any such self-conversion, as they are all by definition conversive only to what is external to them. According to O'Daly, "One may say that all intellection implies self, precisely because it is only in the act of reflection, which presupposes a subject, that intellection occurs."[34] O'Daly then points out that the self-intellection of the dualized self does not lessen its unity, since its self-reflection depends on that unity. No matter what the intelligence may focus itself upon, the precondition for its doing so is thus a power of focusing upon itself, from which the unity of the self is inseparable.

This, however, apparently conflicts with what a number of philosophers say to the effect that the intellect works best when we are so absorbed that we cease to be self-aware. Plotinus is one who states this position, though it is not too consistent with his other claims. Firstly, the fact that we are not always self-aware while concentrating does not detract anything from the self-reflexive nature of this act, and secondly it does not prove the superiority of thought which happens to take place without conscious self-awareness. All it means is that the power of concentration, as man possesses it, functions like a torch which emits only a narrow beam of light, and which can therefore only illuminate one thing by ceasing to illuminate another. The alternatives imposed upon us by this natural limitation may not exist, say, for an angel, whom one could imagine concentrating on many quite disparate things at once. Such a being would not be able to understand the claims of some philosophers that intellection should be perfected by becoming blind to one of its own essential spheres of operation. Possibly a need to make a virtue of a necessity is involved here.

Moreover, if we get to know something while in a state without self-awareness, we cannot subsequently assure ourselves that we learned it without first knowing that we know it, which shows the self-referential nature of knowledge, which obtains whether self-awareness lapses or not. Likewise, it should be noted that the individual and individualizing nature of intellection is not affected by even the most exalted kinds of object.

The latter point is significant where the relation of the individual to the universal is concerned. Universal realities owe the character they have for us to the conditions imposed by an individuated act of cognition. The universal could not be supposed to retain its quality if the individual nature did not also remain the same. A self-transcendence which obviated the individual nature would therefore also obviate the reality for the sake of which this change was made, if there were a question of such a change.

Because the idea of individuality in this context is bound up with intelligence, it is said to reside in the highest part of the soul's activity: "the We [*hēmeis*] is the Soul at its highest, the mid-point between two powers . . . the sensitive and the intellective."[35]

This does not agree very well with other passages where the "mid-point" refers to the center of the soul's own activity. However, it is not clear whether this is Plotinus being inconsistent, or whether man's identity itself contains an ambivalence along these lines. This may be seen reflected in man's physical form: his brain is situated higher than his heart, but its superiority of position is offset by its peripheral position on a circle which has the heart at its center. The complexities involved in this are evidently not reducible.

Finally, the individuation resulting from the self-reflexive nature of intelligence does not suffice for anything like a full personal identity, even though the latter necessarily includes individuation. By itself, it suffices for individuated being in general, not for a unique person, rather as the ways of proving the immortality of the soul discussed in Chapter 1 suffice only for immortal soul in general. The development necessary for a strictly personal identity will occupy the following sections.

Can There Be a Form of the Individual?

The subject indicated by the heading of this section, which can sound rather like a self-contradiction, has been treated by A.H. Armstrong under the heading "Form, Individual and Person in Plotinus,"[36] where he points out that Plotinus does not make it clear whether there really can be Forms of individuals, in addition to Forms of universals. On the one hand he affirms that there are Forms of individuals, particularly of individual human beings (*Enn.* V, 7, 1), whereas elsewhere (V, 9, 12) he states that ideas are of universals, that is, "not of Socrates, but of Man."

But in the latter passage, the possibility of a Form of the individual is also referred to, while the discussion chiefly relates to how far the individual nature is due to the eternal idea, and how far to the peculiarities of matter. This means that the latter passage is only a qualified denial of what is said in V, 7, 1:

one Reason-Principle cannot account for distinct and differing individuals: one human being does not suffice as the exemplar for many distinct, each from the other, not merely in material constituents, but by innumerable variations of an ideal type.

Plotinus then endorses the idea of Forms of individual persons as follows: "There is no need to baulk at this limitlessness in the intellectual; it is an infinitude having nothing to do with number or part."

According to Armstrong, one way of settling the question of Plotinus's meaning is to consider the kinds of individuals referred to in each of these passages. In *Ennead* V, 7, they are specifically human individuals, besides whom, as he points out, Forms of *daimones* and gods, whether embodied or not, are also covered by the affirmation in this passage. There is in any case a sharp distinction between the higher and lower parts of the personality, the higher part being "part of the intelligible world, not separated or cut off, belonging to the whole" (VI, 4, 14). This distinction is not modified by the conception of a Form of the individual person. The suggestion is that the self in the intelligible world is too complex a reality for anything like all of its properties to be manifest in one human life. This accounts for the statement at the beginning of V, 7 about the soul of the individual containing "the Reason-Principles of all it traverses," similarly to what Leibniz says of the monad with its future *in potentia*.

The correspondence between the knower and the field of the knowable is, in Plotinian terms, the principle that "every soul contains all the reason-principles that exist in the Cosmos."[37] These properties of the soul can be taken as a sign that it has other personalities latent in it, which would account for the statements in Plotinus signifying reincarnation. A complication also arises from the distinction between soul and the whole person, because, as Armstrong points out, "for Plotinus, or for any Platonist, the belief that souls are eternal, and belong to the authentic world of intelligible reality . . . is independent of any belief in Forms of individuals."[38]

The soul is not the whole person, despite its *logos* function, and the question here is whether this theory can account for any enduring meaning for it which would correspond to the Christian idea thereof. According to the conception of soul which we have here, therefore, Socrates would not wholly cease to exist on attaining the highest state, even if there were no individual Form of Socrates. The question is how fully the empirical personality manifests an eternal identity. An apparent denial of individual Forms appears in V, 9, 12, already quoted above.

Armstrong demonstrates that the statement "not of Socrates but of man" refers only to the logical conditions for making these statements, and he also points out that for some reason Plotinus does not use the Platonic argument that if individual persons are known at all, they must also be universals, since on the normal Platonic-Aristotelian view, knowledge is only of universals.[39] This would have been appropriate from the nature of this philosophy, taken together with the fact that no one is likely to deny that they know other persons.

Concerning Forms of individuals, Plotinus in V, 9, 12 relates the question to physical attributes like those of being aquiline-nosed and snub-nosed. According to Armstrong, he uses this illustration to explain individual differences in an Aristotelian manner as specific differences in the Form of Man, which are simply due to the indefiniteness of matter. However, Plotinus actually says that matter affects only "the degree of aquilinity," so that it cannot be said to produce the thing itself, whence this text can really be consistent with individual Forms after all. In this respect he cannot be regarded as following Plato, who never taught that there were Forms of individual men. On the other hand he did not regard them as mere ephemeral instantial entities, but rather as knowers and lovers of intelligible reality. Because of this relation to the eternal intelligibles, man *qua* knower is himself a member of this everlasting realm.

This concept of man is always given full weight by Plotinus. His idea of Forms of individual persons is by no means a substitute for this concept, but rather an attempt to complete the picture by working out some of the deeper consequences of the theory of Forms. Again, he links the individual person to the Intellectual Cosmos by a restriction of the two-world idea, inasmuch as the soul exists in both worlds at once. Things such as "rightness" and "moral wisdom," as well as the soul itself, "are no images or copies of the Supreme as in the sense-world, but actually are those very originals in a mode peculiar to this sphere."⁴⁰ Thus the material world can be said to transcend itself in certain of its contents, and a kind of continuity is thereby created between the eidetic and instantial worlds. The Absolute Soul is part of the system, and this, Armstrong claims, confirms the idea that individual Forms do not exclude the "higher universal Forms, of Man and of Soul, in which the lower Forms participate."⁴¹ All this is conducive to the idea of individual Forms which is presented as a possibility in *Ennead* V, 7.

This clearly does not yield a necessary conclusion, and there is much else in the *Enneads* which could be taken to mean that the individual person might result from the combined action of a number of species' Forms, and not that of a single Form. The answer is to be found, not from collecting statements pointing in the one direction or the other, but in deducing something about the essential nature of this kind of philosophy that makes the Form of the individual rigorously necessary, and not merely possible. This philosophy is clearly founded on the theory of Forms, which considered by itself will never enable us to conclude this matter. However, it has another foundation, one which has almost entirely escaped the notice of modern commentators, and which has been so little understood in this context that the only name we have for it is one coined by A.O. Lovejoy, namely, the "Principle of Plenitude."

This is well-enough known in connection with theodicy, where it concerns the way in which the Creator is conceived as maximizing the range of his creation; but its key role in Platonic metaphysics seems not to be known at all, even though it is the means of explaining why the Forms do in fact instantiate themselves. Without it, the *eidos*-instance relation could seem more like magic than philosophy. The connection between the theory of Forms and the Principle of Plenitude appears in the fact that the Forms comprise an order of intelligible realities which, though all are universals, differ very greatly among themselves in power and in degrees of universality, these differences being reflected in the numbers of instances they have.

Some of them, such as Being and Unity, are instanced in everything, whereas the Form of Goldfishness, for instance, is instanced in relatively few cases. There is a gradation in order of universality from the highest Forms like Good, Beauty, and Truth, to those like Plant, Animal, and Soul, and then from each of these to all their component species. Likewise the Form of Humanity is followed by those of all *its* different races, and the latter by the Forms of their different nationalities. (The Biblical idea of an angel being assigned to each nation seems to echo this idea.)

It should be noted that there is no point at which one could logically cease to add any further Forms in descending order of universality—yet is it strictly *necessary* that they should extend in this way, comprehending all possibilities? The answer to this lies in the Principle of Plenitude, for which every lesser degree of any possibility is necessary after every greater one.[42] Plotinus was fully aware of its importance, and wrote extensively about it, which makes it all the stranger that modern vindications of Platonism are so silent about it:

> "The outgoing process could not end with souls, their issue stifled; every kind must produce its next; it must unfold from some concentrated central principle as from a seed, and so advance to its term.... To this power we cannot impute any halt, any limit of jealous grudging; it must move forever outward until the universe stands accomplished to the ultimate possibility." (IV, 8, 6)

and: "The outgoing that takes place in the Intellectual Principle is a descent to its own downward ultimate...." (IV, 8, 7); and: "the law is 'some life after the Primal Life, a second where there is a first'; *all linked in one unbroken chain*; all eternal; divergent types being engendered only in the sense of being secondary" (II, 9, 3). "It is of the essence of things that each gives of its being to another...." (ibid.)

> "For the Intellectual could not be the last of things, but must have a double act, one within itself and one outgoing; there must, then, be something later than the Divine; for only the thing with which all power ends fails to pass downwards something of itself." (II, 9, 8)

> "And since the higher exists, there must be the lower as well. The Universe is a thing of variety, and how could there be an inferior

without a superior, or a superior without an inferior?" (III, 3, 7). "We ought to understand both that the Reason-Principle must extend to every possible existent and, at the same time, that every greater must include lesser things. . . ." (III, 2, 14)

This is only a small selection of texts expressing this principle, and should there be any doubt as to how much it pervades Neoplatonic metaphysics, let us note that it plays a similar role in the writings of Proclus. In propositions 25–30 of the *Elements of Theology,* he develops the idea that the Good is the cause of all things, and that beings participate to many different degrees in the Good. From this it follows that all beings have a productive causal power in proportion to their proximity to the Good, and, implicitly, the highest beings have not only the greatest causality, but also the same *kind* of causality as that of the Good, that of instantiation. Consequently the only things with no causal power are those which are most remote from the Good. For reasons of space, we can quote only the headings of these texts, but they make it clear enough what principle is involved:

> Whatever is complete proceeds to generate those things which it is capable of producing, imitating in turn the one originative principle of the universe. (25)

> Every productive cause produces the next and all subsequent principles while itself remaining steadfast. (26)

> Every producing cause is productive of secondary existences because of its completeness and superfluity of potency. (27)

> Every productive cause brings into existence things like to itself before the unlike. (28)

The texts under these headings show implicitly how the Principle of Plenitude is fundamental to the *eidos*-instance relation. It is true that Lovejoy observes the presence of this conception in Plotinus,[43] but he only does so in connection with the ideas of cosmic necessity and of the grounds for optimism, not with regard to its deeper theoretical meaning in relation to the Forms.

Subject to this principle, then, the descending orders of universality necessarily extend downward through all possible degrees to the point where no further descent is possible. As something's position in this hierarchy is linked to the number of instances that can be caused by it, this lower limit of universality would consist in a Form which has only one instance, and which *can* have only one, corresponding to its position at the opposite extreme from the Form of Being, which is necessarily instanced in all things. Such a possibility as this was also recognized by the Scholastics, whether independently of Platonic influence or not, as alluded to by Leibniz:

> What St. Thomas assures us on this point of angels or intelligences is true of all substances [*quod ibi omne individuum sit species infima*] . . . "That with them, every individual is a lowest species," i.e. every individual constitutes a species, the lowest species [next above individual], each having only one member.[44]

This idea of a species which has only one member is easily translatable into Platonic terms as the final, limiting class of Forms referred to above, that of the Form with only one instance. In regard to the place of the Principle of Plenitude and the theory of Forms in Platonism, the Form of the individual can thus be seen to be a strictly rigorous conclusion on the grounds of this philosophical system, though apparently Plotinus did not see this very clearly.

In regard to personal identity, the above conclusion means that the unique individual person is necessitated by the universals. So far from being irreconcilable opposites, universal Forms and individuals are equally parts of the same continuum, such that there is no need for either to be treated as unreal if one's standpoint is based on the other. The exclusive positions taken, for example, by Hegel and Kierkegaard on this subject therefore result from a lack of understanding of this principle. We also have the solution to the Platonic dichotomy referred to by Lovejoy:

> Plato had in his philosophy two classes of super-sensible and permanent beings which were in other respects quite different in nature . . . "Ideas" and "Souls," . . . and since the former were universals or essences and the latter were individuals, they could not easily be reduced to unity.[45]

Not merely soul as such, but specifically individual ones, result from souls being thus a special case of Forms, this also supporting what was said previously, where soul was implicitly treated as functioning as a Form in relation to the body. The individual Form also implies free will, because the total system cannot give rise to specific unique beings without allowing at least part of their activity to result directly from their individual natures; otherwise it would be all the same as if it did not give rise to them. But to act in accordance with a specific individual nature, and not merely in accordance with one's cosmic condition, is what is essential for free will.

This conclusion contradicts the idea that the Principle of Plenitude must mean universal determinism. In reality, it is no more strange that a realm of freedom should result from a system of determination than that an individual being should result from a system of universals, these occurrences constituting the same phenomenon considered from different points of view. The effect of this is to confirm values essential to both Platonism and Christianity, without need for compromise. There is no need to choose between the ontologistic and universalistic position of the one and the personalistic and voluntaristic position of the other.

The theory of the individual Form implies that personal identity has a principial origin *per se,* and so is not simply an accident of material or eidetic combinations. Moreover, the creation of unique individuals does not have to be assigned to a more-or-less arbitrary act of the Creator, while at the same time this corresponds to the conception of a Creator who confers real being on the beings He creates, and not just an illusion of it. Many have acted on the assumption that the Neoplatonic and Christian principles are compatible, but I do not think that the essential reason for this has been brought to light by any of the main representatives of either tradition.

If there should still seem to be a question of a contradiction in the idea of an individual Form, one should consider the attribute of infinity proper to the Forms. Each of them manifests this by the infinite number of instantiations to which it can give rise, and it follows that this property cannot be lacking to the soul, if it is rightly included among the Forms. That it does possess infinity has already been argued from other considerations, but the fact remains that it must be manifested in a fundamentally different manner to that of

Forms in general, if it is capable of only one instantiation. The answer lies in its capacity for knowledge, in which it effectively "becomes" the things it knows by participation in the relevant Forms. This capacity is realized in the soul as a microcosm of the whole system of Forms as images in its own substance. This means an internalized or self-concentrated infinity which corresponds effectively with the infinite power of forming instantiations which each of the universal Forms possesses. In Neoplatonic terms, the nature of the Forms in their absolute state is said to be "noetic," while in their manifestation in the soul their state is termed "noeric." This latter state is still pre-instantial, but its contents are effects in relation to the noetic Forms, and formal causes in relation to material instantiations.

Form, Individual, and Person

Plotinus's tentative acceptance of the Form of the individual certainly does not mean that he was inclined to conceive of Forms for all individual things. In particular, he denies that there are Forms of parts of things, for instance; and where natural forces are concerned, he asserts that all separate fires, for example, are solely instances of the Idea of Fire.[46] Nevertheless, individual Forms would be in question wherever there are real individuals or individualities, and so would add immensely to the range of content of the realm of Forms.

While this shows that Plotinus attached a high value to personality, it is clear that he did not simply equate the individual Form with the higher self as well, for he also says that the intellect transcends the highest part of the individual. He characteristically speaks of a part of the soul which is always joined to the intelligible world such that it never descends to operate *per se* on the physical level; and this clearly lies outside the bounds of what is specifically individual.

The Plotinian higher self therefore has the twofold function of being Formal cause of the individual while also being a world of supra-individual possibilities to which the person has access. This is what Armstrong calls "the extraordinary capacity which Plotinian man possesses for getting out of himself, traveling beyond his own horizons."[47] This has clear consequences for the ideal of self-transcendence: rather than a discarding of the self, it must be an expansion of the self into its higher levels. What the person is, then, is held to be the soul, which mediates between "the lower embodied self, and the Intellect." Passages which seem rather to equate the self with the Intellect should be taken to mean that the soul in one of its phases can relate directly to Intellect and function in concert with it. In that way, we "are" the higher reality, and "being in accord with Intellect" means just this integration of soul with it.

The function of self-transcendence based on this, the ability to "snatch oneself up into the higher world," depends on a conscious merging of the empirical self with his individual Form, by a combination of mental concentration and ascetic practices. It is implied that the reach of self-transcendence goes even further than this, because Intellect has its own inherent act of self-transcendence owing to the interconnectedness of the Soul, the *Nous,* and the One. Apart from its intellection, its notion extends conversively to the pure unity of the One, just as the human soul in its own way can convert its own act to that of the Intellect. From this connection with the highest unity, it draws to itself the original substance of the Forms which are the subject of the intellective act which is peculiar to itself.

Thus, besides the function of "grasping intellectively its own content,"[48] it has another, that of "advancing, and receiving whereby to know its own transcendent."[49] In this same passage, Plotinus illustrates the same point by saying that the universal Intellect (*Nous*) can be "in love," and be drunken with nectar, because "to be drunken is better for it than to be too staid for these revels."[50] Such non-rational possibilities must exist if all levels of being are to be connected and relate to one another in a conversive manner.

The significance of what is said here of the universal Intellect or Second Hypostasis is that it comprises the archetype of the soul's relation to what transcends its own level. Just as Intellect does not cease to have its own specific nature despite the non-intellective way in which it is related to the First Hypostasis, so the ensouled human personality has essentially the same nature whether its action is conversive toward material realities, or toward the Intellect, or toward the one even higher than that. Even then, as Armstrong puts it, our identity of self persists, "and all its lower powers and activities remain in being, ready for use when required" (ibid., XX, 59).

This contrasts with some interpretations of Plotinus, like that of W.R. Inge, which would make the personality of man to be just a complex of limitations which happens to have an urge to transcend itself, and in transcending itself ceases to be a person because no longer limited. There are in fact some passages in Plotinus which would seem to suggest this, although if taken literally they would refute what has been offered as proof of the immortality of the soul.

Such contrary statements need to be explained, however, where for example it is asserted that "there is the higher, knowing himself by the Intellectual Principle with which he becomes identical...,"[51] and that "a man becomes Intellectual-Principle when, ignoring all other phases of his being, he sees through that only and sees only that, and so knows himself...."[52]

It could be that the becoming or reversion involved here is not meant to be understood in a serial or temporal manner. According to A.C. Lloyd,

> It is certain that, although they are distinct, remaining, proceeding, and reverting cannot be separated. Because they are a timeless movement, this is represented as a circular movement of the universe and its contents. This was found objectionable only when reversion was taken to mean return instead of inclination to a cause, and identification instead of continuity with it. Because it is in time, a particular soul can undergo the change which return and ascent entail, and these will doubtless contain in microcosm the cosmic changeless process.[53]

Thus, whether they involve a human soul or one of the highest Hypostases, becoming and reversion imply an assimilation to another nature which depends on the retention of an entity's own self-nature, and which would cease with the loss of that nature.

How Far the Self is Empirical

A.H. Armstrong has pointed out that it is a difficulty for the theory of the individual Form that Plotinus is willing to admit that much or most of our personality derives from heredity and our environment, such that our personality has an external derivation as well as an internal: "Marriages, similarly, are brought about either by choice or by chance interplay of circumstance. And births are determined by marriages: the child is moulded true to type when all goes well; otherwise it is marred by some inner detriment. . . ."[54]

Can the personality really be determined by a Form if it can be seen to be determined by manifest physical causes? For common sense, probably not; but it is possible to show that this objection is like asking how a picture can be caused by an idea in the mind of an artist if it results from a series of brush strokes. It appears to some minds that most of the empirical self cannot be truly personal because it is the outcome of the influences of an impersonal kind, including natural laws.

But Plotinus does not intend by this to confine the personal to our acts of will, or to retreat into mysticism; the problem here results from a failure to use the full range of ideas he offers us. He would not have accepted this supposed antithesis between the eidetic principle of the individual and his conditioning by natural forces. In this respect, we shall see that he clearly anticipates Kant's account of free will, whereby each person before birth has a total overview of his conditions of life, to which he assents. These conditions of life are determined by natural forces, but there is no incompatibility between their contents and the will of the individual because of the prenatal choice of the former. (This also recalls Plato's myth in *Republic* X, where souls gather to choose their lots before their birth.)

In this way, the will can be free in a world subject to physical determinism. This conception can be seen to be derived from Leibniz's pre-established harmony, being as much of it as Kant saw fit to retain, though both these conceptions are weakened in comparison with that of Plotinus in that they require a harmonization outside the function of *eidos* and instantiation. Thus although there is a common-sense truism that "nobody asks to be born," it would appear from the principles of Plotinus and Kant that there is a sense in which they in fact do ask, no doubt with numerous consequences for personal responsibility.

There is no lack of passages where Plotinus explains how the inner nature of each soul leads it to the conditions which most fully express that nature, whether from before birth or during life, like migrating to like by something like magnetism: "the souls are, in a fair sense, members of this Reason-Principle and it has not adapted them to the creation by perverting them, but has set them in the place to which their quality entitles them."[55]

As "members of this Reason-Principle," souls will not encounter anything in the instantial world which would be inimical to the archetypal reality from which both they and it derive. Plotinus pursues the same idea elsewhere: "The soul's quality exists before any bodily life; it has exactly what it chose to have . . . therefore neither the good man nor the bad is the product of this life . . . the real determination lies with the souls, who adapt the allotted conditions to their own particular quality."[56]

This transition of souls to conditions which match their inner qualities is recognized by R.T. Wallis as "the Stoic doctrine of cosmic sympathy,"[57] which Plotinus accepted and developed. This, he says, is all part of the idea of the world as a living organism, where every change in one part gives rise to a corresponding change in some other part: "there is a pre-established harmony linking the destinies of all souls. From this follows Plotinus' view of divine justice . . . each individual tends to his appropriate place, leaving the individual's free will to take care of the rest."[58]

The operation of this law is effectively an automatic result of the *eidos*-instance relation, together with the organic wholeness of the world. It is also a theoretical basis for the efficacy of magic and even intercessory prayer, as Plotinus understands it. In Plotinian terms, both could be successful in an impersonal way, according as a change in any one part of the world entails a corresponding change in another. This principle also explains the "return" of the soul to the Intellect and the One, from another point of view. A change first takes place in the qualitative nature of the soul, and this is what puts it into a closer relation with the divine, there being something like a state of resonance between them. The effect of this will be, as J.M. Rist says, that "When any individual soul returns and is joined in communion with its source, it must be presumed to share in its source's creativity and causal energy. In other words, each soul will become responsible for the creation and maintenance of all things."[59]

As this conception clearly minimizes the amount of real, as opposed to apparent, interaction between the soul and its world, it would, as Wallis indicates, turn out to be the pre-established harmony as taught by Leibniz, if taken to an extreme. However, Plotinus does not go as far as does Leibniz, because he grants that the soul can interact on its own account as well. He compares this with the way in which an actor chooses to play his role: "In dramas of human art, the poet provides the words, but the actors provide their own quality, good or bad, for they have more to do than merely repeat the author's words."[60]

Thus the entrance of the soul is compared to an actor taking a part in a play which he can make or spoil. This margin of self-directed action is important, not merely for free will, but because of its function in shaping future developments for the soul, which will in turn determine the next set of conditions under which it is to exist, whether this be elsewhere or in the same place. A pure doctrine of pre-established harmony would not allow this, as it would exclude the action of the will. No changes could in this case occur in the soul except in concert with changes to its environment, and as a result, the latter would predetermine the soul's transition to its next set of conditions.

A looser version of this idea, which is in question here, can be seen to result from the way in which eidetic realities form certain combinations in their principial state, such that they could not be veridically instanced unless their instances exhibited corresponding relations and affinities: "All things must be enchained; and the sympathy and correspondence obtaining in any one closely knit organism must exist, first, and most intensely, in the All."[61]

The fact that many of our personal qualities are apparently derived from those of the towns and countries where we grew up, and from the racial qualities of our parents, is thus in some respects a deceptive appearance. Instead of those qualities having been stamped upon the soul by outside agencies, as common sense would see it, it is rather the soul which has brought itself into relation with the qualities which correspond most closely to its intrinsic nature. It has sought them, and not *vice-versa*. The implication is that our situation merely reflects our essential tendency, and where it does not, our removal from it will follow by necessity. This contrasts with conventional beliefs about the injustices of life; but, curiously enough, the opposite position of pure empiricism leads to a similar moral result in this regard. If there were no real self, and persons were simply products of their environment and their heredity, there would be no self-nature to be the subject of any injustice arising from the conditions of life; the victim of circumstances and the circumstances themselves would not really differ.

The natural forces which appear to shape the personality are, on the basis of the real self, simply the means whereby the instantiation of the individual Form is effected. It should be apparent, therefore, that if Plotinus admits the effect of material forces, it is because he does not think he is conceding anything against his metaphysic. This point is missed by naturalistic thinkers, for whom the lack of any apparent solution to this question is simply seen as an occasion for mysticism.

Plotinus and Monism

Finally, there is the question as to whether the ideas expressed here are true to Plotinus's own intentions, which would not be the case if his real position were one of Monism, as is claimed by an Orientalizing school of thought equating human identity with that of the divine. Rist instances E. Bréhier among scholars who have maintained that the *Enneads* express a Monistic doctrine like that of the *Advaita* Vedanta. It is inevitable that a mystically inclined philosophy with profound conceptions of self-transcendence, such as that of Plotinus, should be considered in this way in a culture where popular thought is widely influenced by pantheism.

However, it is admitted even by one of those most committed to the Monistic view that direct expressions of identity with Brahman have "no such conspicuous counterpart in the *Enneads,* in which the sentiment of the transcendence of the One appears more emphatically."[62] The Plotinian idea of union with the One has already been shown to mean union in the literal sense of the word, that is, as obtaining between really different beings.

If a more conclusive answer should be required, it can be found in the terminology used. O'Daly, who reaches a conclusion similar to that of Rist on this subject, quotes a text from Plotinus which seems to say as directly as possible what the Monistic pantheists maintain: "but our concern is not merely to be sinless, but to be God."[63]

Nevertheless, O'Daly proceeds rather more laboriously than is necessary to show that this is not literally what is intended. The crux of the issue here, and in other texts like it, is the translation of the word *theos* as "God." In certain ancient Greek sources, such as Hesiod, God is referred to as Zeus, while in Plato God is named as "*theos*" about as often as "Zeus." But by Plotinus's time Zeus was the name in popular use, while the One (*to hen*) was used by the learned, with *theos* having only a rather unspecific role.

Despite the precedent in Plato, the practice of referring to the Supreme Being by the impersonal word "God" was, from the first century AD onward a characteristically Christian practice, arising from the need to avoid the Hebrew Yahweh and the Hellenistic Zeus and so escape identification with either tradition, so that the new religion could discover its own identity. There is no way a Neoplatonist philosopher of late antiquity like Plotinus would refer to the Supreme Being in this manner, and to think otherwise is to fall into an anachronism. In nearly all cases, a *theos* simply meant "an immortal," and there is no doubt that this is how Plotinus understands it, in view of his constant references to the One and the *Nous* where we would say "God."

In classical antiquity generally, it appears that there are no examples of claims on behalf of individuals of identity with the One, the *Nous,* or Zeus, or even with the World Soul. The absence of Monistic-pantheistic meaning from the *Enneads* can therefore be taken as certain, and it is also very unlikely that this notion would have escaped the notice of Plotinus, whether he would have endorsed it or not, if it had been current in the West at all. This is an objection to attempts to claim universality for Monism, which should be significant for comparative religion.

Notes

1 Wallis, *Neoplatonism*, 128.
2 *Enn.* IV, 7, 1.
3 *Alcib.* I, 130 a–b.
4 *Nichomachean Ethics*, X, 1178a.
5 *Enn.* IV, 7, 3.
6 F. E. Winkler, *Man: the Bridge Between Two Worlds*, 97.
7 *Summa Contra Gentiles*, II, 55, 7.
8 *Enn.* IV, 7, 6.
9 Chapter 7, I.
10 *Enn.* IV, 7, 7.
11 Ibid., IV, 1, 2.
12 Chapter 6, II.
13 *Enn.* IV, 7, 12.
14 *Enn.* IV, 7, 8, 10.
15 *The Philosophy of Plotinus*, Vol. 1, 137–138.
16 *The Range of Reason*, 12.
17 *Plotinus' Philosophy of the Self*
18 Ibid. 41.
19 Ibid., 22.
20 Ibid., 24.
21 Ibid., 25.
22 See 83–87.
23 Ibid., 27.
24 *Enn.* IV, 6, 3.
25 *Enn.* VI, 6, 15.
26 *Enn.* VI, 7, 6.
27 *Plotinus' Philosophy of the Self*, 33.
28 Ibid., 35.
29 J. M. Rist, *Plotinus: The Road to Reality*, 84.
30 Ibid.
31 *Enn.* VI, 7, 6.
32 *Enn.* V, 6, 1.
33 O'Daly, *Plotinus' Philosophy of the Self*, 64.
34 Ibid., 64.
35 *Enn.* V, 3, 3.
36 *Plotinian and Christian Studies*, Ch. XX.
37 *Enn.* V, 7, 1.
38 *Plotinian and Christian Studies*, 52.
39 Ibid., 54.
40 *Enn.* V, 9, 13.
41 *Plotinian and Christian Studies*, 55.
42 The Principle of Plenitude applies on the same basis as the ontological proof of God.
43 *The Great Chain of Being*, 63–6.
44 Leibniz, *Discourse on Metaphysics*, IX.
45 *The Great Chain of Being*, 48.
46 *Enn.* VI, 5, 8.
47 *Plotinian and Christian Studies*, 58.
48 *Enn.* VI, 7, 35.
49–50 Ibid.
51 *Enn.* V, 3–4.
52 Ibid.
53 A. C. Lloyd, *The Anatomy of Platonism*, 130.
54 A. H. Armstrong, *Plotinian and Christian Studies*, XX, 58.
55 *Enn.* III, 2, 12.
56 *Enn.* III, 4, 5.
57 *Neoplatonism*, 70.
58 Ibid.
59 *Plotinus: The Road to Reality*, 163.
60 *Enn.* III, 2, 17.
61 *Enn.* II, 3, 7.
62 *Plotinus: The Road to Reality*, 229.
63 *Enn.* I, 2, 6.

3

Soul and Identity in St. Augustine

The Relevance of Augustine's Idea of Identity

There are good reasons for applying Augustine's thought to this stage of the argument, one of which lies in the manner in which Christian doctrine arose against the background of Greek philosophy. We have seen how the individual Form is the final outcome of the universal Forms, and from this point of view it is highly appropriate that the historical emergence of a doctrine centered on the salvation of individual persons should issue from a culture based on universal values, as though the temporal order were following that of *a priori* principles.

Be that as it may, there need be no doubt that the success of Christianity was to some extent owing to the fact that its idea of the significance of the individual was in reality the logical outcome of what had been thought hitherto. All earlier thought had inadvertently worked on the assumption that knowledge grew in a void, as though it were effected by the universal Forms themselves. It did not allow for the fact that the universal aesthetic, moral, and intellectual values could prove something about the persons in whom and through whom they were realized and made known. The tensions resulting from this inconsistency created a vacuum which Christianity was able to fill, for the reasons just given.

It happens that St. Augustine is practically a personification of this philosophical change, so that the development he represents is also a necessary development in the idea of personal identity which is being sought here. To begin with, Augustine had studied the *Enneads* and was lastingly influenced by them, and consequently saw the spirituality and immortality of the soul as an essential element in personal identity. Besides this, Augustine's thought took in the full impact of an age of philosophical skepticism, to which he provided counter-arguments which are, it is believed, wholly original.

Not unconnected with this is the fact that he is also the first major thinker for whom thinking as an individual person was a real intellectual issue, because of both his religion and his philosophy. For this reason, there is a sense in which he has been rightly called the first "modern" thinker. His own development in this direction on the basis of his Neoplatonism means that his philosophical thought has a central place in the topic we are treating, and will be found to add a new element of rigor to the Platonic principles we have already discussed.

Exemption from Magnitude

To begin with, we shall consider the aspect of Augustine's thought which clearly follows that of Plotinus, particularly in *The Greatness of the Soul* and *The Trinity,* before proceeding to other ideas which do not seem to depend so much on earlier influences. In the former work, there are some questions[1] which Augustine passes over too briefly, for instance that of the essential nature of the soul, in regard to both where it must reside and what it should be composed of. That it comes from God is really made a starting point and not argued for directly, and the question of an analogy between the creative powers of God and those of man is considered only so far as the one is said to create everlasting things while the other creates temporal things.

He deals at greater length, however, with the question as to what kind of magnitude the soul may have, beginning with the negative answer that one reaches it by the negation of all corporeal quantities like those of extension, solidity and mass. A comparison is made between the soul and a value like that of Justice,[2] which like the soul has no material properties but without that lessening its reality. The soul, therefore, need not be counted as nothing simply because it is immaterial. But this point is countered by a comparison between the soul and the air, which likewise does not have quantitative properties like length and breadth, while for all that being still just a material thing which can be physically perceived. This shows that the negative definition used first is by itself ineffective for its purpose.

The argument then turns back to the question of whether the soul resides in the body or not. One possible answer, that it resides *only* in the body, is rejected because its consciousness extends into far larger regions of space. It retains images of distant cities and of the lands in between them, such that the soul has images as well as perceptions of things whose size is far greater than that of the body. Its image-making activity is effectively as large in scope as the world itself, in which it can be said to reside in as real a sense as it can be said to reside in the body. Thus, despite having no spatial dimensions of its own, it comprehends everything which exists in those dimensions. The fact that the soul in some special sense occupies the small space of the body has no effect on the size of the images it is able to form.

Does this conflict with the idea that only like can know like? It might seem that the soul would have to be spatial in order to know space, but for the fact that it makes no difference to this knowledge whether its object occupies the vastest or the tiniest portion of space. If soul had spatial magnitude of its own, it would not be able to respond to objects which were significantly bigger or smaller than itself. It is free to represent spatial magnitudes through being free from spatial determinations itself.

But images account for only one part of the soul's activity. This is shown by the example of thinking about length without breadth. At first it appears that we cannot do this,[3] because even the thinnest visible line must still have some thickness; but the fallacy here is that we are speaking only of an image of length, and not of the conception of it. In fact we can conceive pure length, of course, precisely because the scope of thought extends beyond that of imagination. Imagination is confined to sensory things, and this means that thought, and by implication the soul, is something quite different from the material things which are inseparable from extension.

This leads to a discussion of the role of lines and points in geometrical figures, so as to provide further examples of the ways in which our minds can function with the unextended. Much is made of the essential role of the geometrical point in the construction of figures, a point being by definition without extension. From this it is concluded that the soul sees with an incorporeal eye by which we perceive the questions and solutions of geometry, just as Plato says of the eye of the soul.[4]

However, the thought of later antiquity did not consider the question of whether we might only be using the words "point," "line," and "extension" in accordance with a systematic set of definitions which would apply regardless of whether such things existed in the outside world. Modern philosophy inclines to this approach, in fact, and it would rather accept that all our perception is of material extensions while thought, which appears to relate to things of a more subtle nature, is only a form of discourse which by convention expresses objects and relations which are not sensorially perceived without this implying that they have any substantive existence of their own. If Augustine had known of this objection, how would he have replied to it? On the basis of what he says in these chapters with geometrical examples (namely 5 through 12), he would most likely have admitted that the unextended points and lines belong to a specialized subject which is bound to have a formalized language, but that, useful as it may be, it was not the only source of relevant examples. One could still draw similar ones from things of a more general nature, and which are simple enough to preexist all technical definitions.

For example, the perception of a single physical object like a rock comprises numerous elements which in their own way are just as subtle as the lines and points of geometry, and in such cases we do in fact "just see" them with as much right as we see the material bulk itself. In the extended object we distinguish parts that are to the left and to the right, above and below, nearer and farther, greater and smaller, along with aspects of equality and proportion. Thus we necessarily perceive a set of relations in this object, without which there could not be any object, or pure thinghood.

None of these things is anything like an extended object, and the removal of them, if it were possible, would merely dissolve the object, or at very least render it unrecognizable. Consequently, the objection leveled at the geometrical examples is really only applicable to a special subject where intangibles are completely abstracted from its materials, and its validity even there is made doubtful by these more nearly primordial cases of intuited non-extensibles. Besides, the mathematician's unextended points and lines must have some kind of objective reality, or mathematics would have no practical applications.

Consequently, it is not unreasonable to draw examples from geometry for the present purpose, because this is the best-known field in which things beyond the range of sensation and imagination are deliberately set forth or disengaged from the usual mixture of sense-experience. For some such reasons as the above, then, Augustine would claim that he was justified in teaching that unextended, immaterial things objectively exist, and that our cognition of them implies that our minds possess the same combination of properties. As we have bodies about which the soul's activity is distributed, we know extended material things, and as we have extension-less immaterial minds, we know the extension-less immaterial elements which are in any case essential to bodies: "But if, by some sort of remarkable affinity of realities, bodily things are seen with bodily eyes, it must be that the soul by means of which we see these incorporeal things is not a body, nor like a body."[5]

As such, the soul is said to be not resolvable into anything simpler, and is compared in this respect with the elements called fire, air, water, and earth. If such things as these are irreducible, it is not surprising that the soul should be so as well, granted that these elements are the igneous, gaseous, liquid and solid states of matter. The soul is not material, because it is not composed of anything in these states; it is rather "a special substance, endowed with reason, adapted to rule the body"[6]—a conception which derives from Plato, and which was taken over with little or no change by Descartes.

The soul's immateriality is not the same thing as its unextendedness, but to equate the two could perhaps be justified on the grounds that material things are essentially extended, and that the arguments for the soul's being unextended must therefore serve for its immateriality in an implicit sense. The kind of argument used here is similar to the one used in Chapter 2, based on the idea that like knows like.

How the soul could in fact be material without extension is far from clear, but immateriality alone is not enough, since this includes many things which comprise far less than what we understand by soul, as with the lines and points of geometry.

Growth Without Extension

Regarding extension, Augustine further argues that the geometrical line should be taken as superior to plane extension because of its indivisibility along its length, while the soul should be regarded as superior to the line. The latter superiority would imply that the soul has no extension at all, of course, although the superiority supposed here is ill-defined, and there is more than a little circularity in the reasoning. This is because "indivisible" and "superior" are not adequately distinguished, such that the attribution of superiority really only restates what had already been said as to relative degrees of indivisibility.

The question of the soul's independence from the body is approached through the evident lack of relation between bodily extension and psychical activity. The facts that creatures physically much bigger than man have nothing like his intelligence and that there is no tendency for physically bigger men to be more intelligent than smaller ones show that the soul is not likely to consist in anything material, or in anything that could vary with the body's bulk.

However, the soul can be said to grow with age, metaphorically speaking, just as the body can be said to do. (What is involved in the soul's growth will be examined in more detail in Chapter 7.) Both the soul and body of a child can thus be said to grow together, and the question this raises is whether the development of the soul with time means that it does depend on the body after all. The answer to this can only be found after one has defined what could be called "growth" in the soul.

It is allowed that the soul can be said to grow when it learns and to diminish when it forgets, though in a strictly metaphorical sense. Its growth more fully understood takes the form of "a greater potency to act when it is trained than when it is untrained."[7] Bodily growth is then divided between that which is necessary for its maturation and conservation, and that which is either unnecessary or harmful to it, like tumors or extra fingers, and possibly superfluous weight. The corresponding kinds of growth in the soul are knowledge of what is necessary for leading a good and happy life, and knowledge that can only satisfy curiosity.

The fact that body and soul can in some sense be said to grow together, at least in the first part of life, might argue that the soul's kind of growth should be for purposes just as limited and transient as those of the body: "Why, if it is eternal, has it not brought art along with it?"[8] Augustine answers this objection with the Platonic claim that it has in reality brought all of the arts along with itself, and that what we call learning is really "remembering and recalling." It was on account of this passage that Augustine later denied that he held any belief in the preexistence of souls, such that they could do good or evil before birth.

However, if learning really is a process of recollection, it still takes place in tandem with bodily development, at least for the early part of life. That there is in fact no true joint development is argued on the grounds that the increasing strength of the body is in reality that of the soul. Bodies without souls have no strength at all. But this leads to the new difficulty that the decline of physical strength with age should not be attributable to the body, but must rather imply a decline of the soul.

The alternatives are that the body gains and loses strength independently of the soul, in which case the soul's strength may be unaffected, but at the price of a dualism of powers in the same person, which seems to have no foundation in experience; or that all strength, bodily as well as psychical, is ultimately that of the soul only. This avoids twin powers and twin growths of each, but would make the life of the soul a finite temporal cycle.

The answer is to find a way of denying that the soul really grows in strength with the body. There are many different forms of physical strength, and their significance depends on the way in which they originate. Examples are given of greater stamina occurring at an earlier age because of regular exercise taken then, but not in later life. There is, in any case, a great difference between strength and stamina, and it is highly unlikely that the same individual should excel in both. These qualities do indeed come into being with the passage of time, but only because of the appropriate exercise. The mere passage of time is not responsible for any such development.[9]

Physical strength, whether due to body or soul, is not proportioned to bodily size any more than is intelligence. It therefore does not result intrinsically from natural physical growth, although it may do so accidentally. The comparison Augustine draws in this connection is that of an archer shooting first small, light reeds, and then real arrows weighted with iron, applying the same effort to both. The fact that the latter go a long way while the former go only a little way is not due to the agent, but to the instrument used; and likewise the changes in man's physical strength do not imply any change in the strength of the soul, but only in the composition of its bodily instrument. At the same time, there is nothing to prevent the decline in physical strength from being accompanied by a growth of the soul, as with increases in knowledge and skill.

Here,[10] Augustine maintains the body-soul dualism along these lines: all strength is from the soul, which is not diminished in itself with time, and can in a sense grow; but the part of its strength employed by the body does increase and decrease, though this is due only to corresponding changes in the body's aptitude for receiving it. This is another application of Aristotle's reasoning concerning loss of the body's powers. On this basis, one can defend the view that the decline in strength with age points toward the soul's independence from the body, rather than its dependence on the body.

Sensation as Psychical Activity

The next subject to be discussed is sensation, particularly sight, and how knowledge is to be distinguished from it.[11] Sensation is tentatively defined as the soul's "not being unaware of the body's experience."[12]

A distinction is noted between what the eyes perceive directly and what is sensed indirectly by means of them. Thus they do not actually see pain, but they undeniably perceive what signifies it. In this case, it is doubtful whether the body can be said to be the source of such indirect sensation, since it depends on the mind's construction.

Thus we do not see everything which is sensed by means of the eyes, but Augustine also puts forward the converse of this as true, that everything so sensed is also seen. There is still a need for a definition of "sensed," which is taken to mean the same as "acted upon," in which case sight will belong among the things by which we are acted upon. In the case of the eyes being acted upon, this involves action at a distance, because of the space between the eyes and what is seen, such that the eyes are said to have sensation where they are not themselves present. This is linked to the theory, common in antiquity, that sight radiates outward from the eyes, lighting up what is seen. It is hard to tell whether this is meant literally or is rather a graphic way of expressing the mental act of attention that must be applied to the optical sensations if the latter are to form perceptions. Probably it was a mixture of both, as the need to separate the literal from the symbolical was not felt very strongly in antiquity, as also where the elements were identified as earth, water, air and fire. Augustine does not here consider the physical aspect of sight, rather treating it wholly as an activity of the soul.

However, the definition of sensation as an effect on the body of which we are not unaware is, as it stands, too easily disposed of,[13] on the grounds that the body undergoes changes like those of growth or aging, or the growth of hair and fingernails—all of which we infer to be taking place, though we never directly perceive them happening. The nature of definition itself now has to be examined.

Definitions fail in practice when they either take in too much or too little to adequately represent their subject. This point is illustrated by the definition of man as a "mortal animal," which is true of all men, but is true of innumerable other creatures as well. If the definition is qualified too much, say, to "mortal, rational, grammarian animal," it is true that it is adequate for all the human beings it applies to, but it is still only thus adequate for a minority among them. However, if it is restricted to "mortal rational animal," it is neither too much nor too little, as is shown by its being reversible, which the other cases are not.

These distinctions reflect on the definition of sensation as an effect on the body which we are not unaware of, because, like the definition of man as "mortal animal," it takes in too much. It is also like the latter in that it is not reversible, as it should be if it were valid. Effects on the body which do not escape attention clearly cannot be simply equated with the category of sensations, since the former include things known by inference. This possibility of inference arises because some actions concerning the body are known to us, not through themselves, but through something other than them, as for example where the appearance of the hair or fingernails at different times shows us that growth has taken place in the meantime.

This allows us to tighten up the definition, such that sensation can be said to be a bodily process which *of itself* engages the soul's awareness, or at least does not escape it. There now only remains the possibility that this more restricted form of the definition might be too restricted, and so fail in the manner of "mortal, rational, grammarian animal." What if some sensations were not bodily effects known through themselves? Knowledge is involved in them, and knowledge is said to result from reason, presumably because without the verdict of reason it could only remain mere opinion. But reason is not possessed by non-human animals, and so we must conclude that they do not have knowledge either.[14]

This must lead to a contradiction if we are to allow that awareness of things also means knowledge, because animals undoubtedly have awareness of physical changes and sensation. Odysseus's dog must have had knowledge, it would seem, in order to recognize his master after the latter's absence of twenty years. Infants are also obviously capable of recognition, long before the age of reason.

For this reason, we are obliged to choose between saying that knowledge comes from the application of reason, or that it comes as if ready-made in sensory experience. The latter alternative would seem to be the more likely, as reason requires some known datum of experience as its point of departure,[15] although this is not a conclusion which Augustine will wish to admit. When reason is considered more closely, it appears that there is a faculty, reason, which is present all the time, while its activity, reasoning, is only present intermittently. Reasoning is only a searching for truth which, when found, stands in the light of reason. Reason is to reasoning as vision is to looking.

However, in some of Augustine's other works this faculty of rational knowledge involves knowing *that* one knows something, which would in itself be grounds for denying it to animals. In the present instance, the often superior sensory faculties of animals are thought not to involve knowledge after all, because their behavior can be explained by an acuteness of sense combined with force of habit, that is, of habits of reacting in the same ways to the same stimuli. They have no means of making themselves independent of the body for any purpose.

For this reason, it is concluded that the faculty of sensation in human experience should not be relied upon any more than is necessary, and that the soul should rather "retire into itself, away from the senses. . . . This is what it means to become a new man by putting off the old"; and "Sacred Scripture contains no greater truth, none more profound."[16]

This passage clearly parallels one which we have already quoted from the *Phaedo*: "But when returning into herself, she reflects, then she passes into the other world, the region of purity and eternity, and immortality and unchangeableness. . ." (79d).

The difficulty of realizing this potentiality is extreme, while the activity involved seems more like inaction than anything else, and the inapplicability of this to the animals should speak for itself. A continual act of will is necessary to shift the center of attention from the realm of sense to that of mind, and the more this is done, the more one will be able to distinguish knowing from opinion based on sensation.

The point at issue here is that of whether it was right to identify sensation with awareness, or rather with not-being-unaware. If awareness is identical to knowledge, animals would have to be credited with knowledge, and those rational and contemplative qualities unique to man which have just been referred to. The answer we are given is that the ambivalence of the negative expression of awareness enables it to be common to both sensation and knowledge. At least some things of which one is not unaware are known, and some others are matters of sensation. Awareness may arise from the functioning of right reason, or it may arise from something that affects the body, but in man it contains a component which is not reducible to sensation alone, this being what depends on the rational soul. The dilemma involved here is Platonic and not Plotinian, and can be resolved in the light of what was said in our previous chapter concerning the relation between sensation and intellectual intuition. When we speak of sensation we can be referring either to the physical contents of sensation or to the ideas which those contents invoke. Both are always present, but in varying proportions. While sensation is a source only of opinion in respect of its content, it can be the raw material of knowledge when treated in contemplation.

Whether the Soul Can Be Divisible

However, it was thought to begin with that the soul must be coextensive with the body because its sensation was diffused throughout, from inside it to its extremities. This belief was shown to be contradicted by the example of eyesight, which functions where the eyes themselves are not in the same place as the objects seen. There is no necessity for the soul to be localized wherever sensation occurs, since the soul is taken to be the power behind the eyesight, and not vice-versa. The soul is not something diffused throughout the body like the blood, even though a certain class of its sensations is so distributed. A rather unnecessary chapter is added to show that vivisection cannot prove that souls are divided when bodies are.

The soul is accordingly held to be unextended and indivisible, and a different kind of example is given to illustrate what this means in practice. A word such as "sun" and the thing it denotes are considered. The meaning of the word has to be understood before one uses it, and the thing it means in our understanding is devoid of the spatial bulk of the original. The relationship between the (spoken) word and its meaning is then compared to that between body and soul.[17] Like the body, the word is divisible into its elements, the letters, while the conception it stands for is not. The breaking-down of the word into its letters and the resulting loss of meaning is then compared to the departure of the soul from the body when the latter perishes. On this basis, the soul is not in itself harmed by what happens to the body.

If the soul can remain undivided despite the demise of the body, it would follow that the various segments of the body must also be able to live in their various ways without this implying any division of the soul corresponding to them. This possibility is illustrated in a way similar to the previous example, this time by means of compound words, though the relevance of the comparison in this case is not so clear. The discussion here is an attempt to cover the same ground treated by Plotinus in *Ennead* IV, 7, which treats of the meaning of the soul's presence to all parts of the body. Unfortunately, Augustine's treatment of this issue suffices only to show that what he claims for the soul is not self-contradictory, and in fact corresponds to an actual pattern of possibilities. No attempt is made here to proceed from the not-necessarily-false to the positively true.

Self-Knowledge as Index of Spirituality

A more advanced argument for the soul's immateriality and spirituality is given in *The Trinity*. Here, Augustine turns to the objective self-knowledge which we can be shown to possess, namely, that we know that we are, that we live, and that we know. From these considerations, he lays it down as a principle that *"every mind knows and is certain concerning itself."*[18] He shows that the soul or self comprises a set of related certainties: "All know, however, that they understand and live; they refer what they understand to the understanding, but refer being and life to themselves. And no one doubts that no one understands who does not live, and that no one is who is not."[19] Materialistic accounts of the soul require that all these facets of self-consciousness should inhere in a material substance, consisting of one physical element or other, or a combination of various ones. Whether positing soul as a body or a "harmony of the body," the materialistic position would be much the same, but this choice of possible expressions reveals its greatest problem. The uncertainty about the particular nature of the soul's supposed material basis conflicts with the mind's certainty about itself. In view of this certainty, the uncertainty as to whether soul is "air, or fire, or a body, or anything of a body"[20] entitles us to conclude that it is none of these things.

The soul, moreover, is said to be "certain that it alone is the only thing of which it is certain," as is also supported by the idea that all its thoughts of material things are mediated through representations in the fantasy, whereas its knowledge of itself requires no such mediation. (The inability to imagine the soul would therefore argue for its being better known, not worse known, than external things.)

All the different material accounts of the soul can be supposed more or less equally plausible, which could not be the case if it actually were one of them. It is interesting to note that this reasoning based on certainty about self had to wait twelve centuries before being taken into the mainstream of philosophy by Descartes, whose extent of originality in the *Cogito* argument is far lesser than has been supposed.

Before looking more closely at the Augustinian forms of the *Cogito* argument, it should be observed that these involve the connection of knowledge and self-motion discussed in Chapter 1 of this book. Self-knowledge, like self-motion, involves an act which reverts upon itself, or relates the being as a whole to that same being as a whole. The latter is not possible for material things, whose parts are by definition mutually exclusive, whence the relevance of both self-knowledge and self-motion in regard to the immortality of the soul. The connections between these ideas were particularly evident to Proclus, who expressed them as follows:

> All that is capable of reverting upon itself is incorporeal. For it is not in the nature of any body to revert upon itself. That which reverts upon anything is conjoined with that upon which it reverts: hence it is evident that every part of a body reverted upon itself must be conjoined with every other part since self-reversion is precisely the case in which the reverted subject and that upon which it has reverted become identical. But this is impossible for a body, and universally for any divisible substance: for the whole of a divisible substance cannot be conjoined with the whole of itself, because of the separation of its parts, which occupy different positions in space. It is not in the nature, then, of any body to revert upon itself so that the whole is reverted upon the whole. Thus if there is anything which is capable of reverting upon itself, it is incorporeal and without part.[21]

A further consequence is expressed in the next proposition:

for that which reverts upon itself, being other than body, has an activity independent of the body and not conducted through it or with its cooperation, since neither the activity itself nor the end to which it is directed requires the body. Accordingly, that which reverts upon itself must be entirely separable from bodies.[22]

The relation to self-motion follows from this:

Everything originally self-moving is capable of reversion upon itself. For if it moves itself, its motive activity is directed upon itself, and mover and moved exist simultaneously as one thing. For either it moves with one part of itself and is moved in another; or the whole moves and is moved; or the whole originates motion which occurs in a part, or vice-versa. But if the mover be one part and the moved another, in itself the whole will not be self-moved, since it will be composed of parts which are not self-moved: it will have the appearance of a self-mover, but will not be such in essence. . . .[23]

Self-knowledge can thus be seen to be the essential member of the closely-knit group consisting of knowledge, self-knowledge, self-motion, and transcendence of the body. In view of its central importance for our subject, we will treat at some length its place in Augustine's work, which indicates that he was the first philosopher to realize its importance.

Sources of the Cogito Argument in St. Augustine

Augustine's claim to have anticipated Descartes' *Cogito* argument as a refutation of skepticism has been observed by, for one, R. Sorabji, though Augustine's form of the argument typically does not go directly from thought to existence, as it includes an extra stage: thus, the "I think" leads to a mediating "I live," which joins thought and existence.

This kind of argument appears in at least seven places in Augustine's writings, which is a good indication of the importance he attached to it. It serves him for the refutation of skeptics and for a proof of the immateriality and immortality of the soul at the same time, besides its function as a foundation of knowledge whereby he could establish the existence of God. Of the version found at *The Trinity* XV, 12, 21, Sorabji says:

> he appears to see it as absolutely central to the refutation of scepticism. He seems to have realized its importance without the advantage of taking Descartes' intermediate step of doubting the existence of the entire external world. Descartes himself offered a different reply, when it was suggested to him that Augustine anticipated the *Cogito* argument. He maintained that Augustine had not put it to the same use. But this reply is only partly justified. For Augustine bases on one version of the *Cogito* a proof that the substance of the mind is not anything material, and he uses another version as a step in his argument for God's existence.[24]

Sorabji here also notes that A.C. Lloyd has sought examples of Augustine's *Cogito* in earlier Greek philosophy, but the results do not look at all decisive, as they seem to depend on a reconstructed passage from a very obscure source. It is probably justifiable to credit Augustine with being its originator, therefore. It appears in one of his earlier works[25] expressly in connection with the need to know oneself:

> You who wish to know yourself, do you know that you exist? A: I do. R: How do you know? A: That I do not know. R: Do you perceive yourself to be simple or uncompounded? A: I do not know. R: You know that you have motion? A: No, I don't. R: You know that you think? A: I do. R: Then it is true that you think. A: It is true. R: Do you know that you are immortal? A: No. R: Of all those things which you say you do not know, which would you prefer to know? A: Whether I am immortal. R: So you love to live? A: I admit I do. R: Will it satisfy you to learn that you are immortal? A: It will be a great matter, but not sufficient.... R: So you love life not for the sake of living but for the sake of knowing? A: I accept that conclusion. R: No one is happy unless he has life, and no one lives who does not exist. You want to be, to live, and to know, but to be in order to live, and to live in order to know. You know that you exist and live and have intelligence.[26]

First of all, this instance of the argument shows that the questioner can know that he wants to continue in being, and that he can think of this. His lack of knowledge does not prevent him from knowing his desire for knowledge, or from knowing that immortality should bring the fullness of it. One knows at very least the desire "to be, to live, and to know"; and to know this one does not need to think away the reality of everything else. It is rather a question of distinguishing what can be fully known from what is only doubtful.

The next passage is more Cartesian in tendency because it emphasizes the relation between doubt and certainty. Doubt itself implies that we are in fact certain about something:

> [At] least make up your mind whether you have any doubt about your doubts. If it is certain that you do indeed have doubts, inquire whence comes that certainty. It will never occur to you to imagine that it comes from the light of the sun, but rather from that "true light which lighteth every man that cometh into the world." It cannot be seen with these eyes, nor with the eyes which seem to see the phantasms of the brain, but with those eyes that can say to phantasms: You are not the thing I am seeking. Nor are you the standard by which I put you in your rightful place, disapproving of all that is base in you and approving all that is beautiful. . . . Everyone who knows that he has doubts knows with certainty that something is true, namely, that he doubts. He is certain, therefore, about a truth. Therefore everyone who doubts whether there be such a thing as *the* truth has at least a truth to set a limit to his doubt; and nothing can be true except truth be in it. Accordingly, no one ought to have doubts about the existence of *the* truth, even if doubts arise for him from every quarter. Wherever this is seen, there is light that transcends space and time and all phantasms that spring from spatial and temporal things. Could this be in the least destroyed, even if every reasoner should perish and grow old among inferior carnal things? Reasoning does not create truth but discovers it. Before it is discovered it abides in itself; and when it is discovered it renews us.[27]

What is said here is also relevant to a criticism by A. Kenny[28] of the Cartesian argument according to which it really only relates directly to an imaginary picture of the mind, made up from the contents of its inner dialogue, and not to the mind itself. The power of self-reflection involved here has expressly the property of discriminating against "phantasms of the brain," besides which the independence of self-knowledge from imagination is clearly stated in our next text. The implication is that we must have in us a standard of truth with which we constantly compare all our other forms of knowledge, by which some of them appear either doubtful or not true at all. Doubt is thus merely the sign that this standard is functioning correctly, and truth is innate in us. Were it otherwise, we should never have any inclination to doubt or skepticism about anything.

This is the basis of Augustine's distinction between the "inward man" and the "outward man,"[29] where the former comprises the paradigmatic reality by means of which defectiveness and doubtfulness are seen in other things. The renewal of the "inward man" by his discovery of truth is part of what is meant by his immortality, whereas there is no corresponding possibility for the "outward man," who is therefore corruptible.

The idea of a paradigmatic reality within us, forming the essential part of the self, is developed further with the next appearance of the argument. Here, it supports the idea that there is an image of the Trinity naturally in us. The members of this reflected Trinity in us are those of our *being*, our *knowledge*, and our *love of them both*:

> And we have in ourselves an image of that Holy Trinity which shall be perfected by reformation, and made very like it . . . for we both have a being, know it, and love both our being and knowledge. And in these three no false appearance can ever deceive us. For we do not discern them as things visible, by sense, as we see colors, hear sounds, scent smells. . . . In those three it is not so; *I know without any fantastical imagination* that I am myself, that this I know and love. I fear not the Academic arguments on these truths, that say: "What if you err?" If I err, I am. For he that has no being cannot err, and therefore mine error proves my being. Which being so, how can I err in believing in my being? For though I be the one that may err, yet doubtless in that I know my being I err not: and consequently, if I know that, I know my being: and loving these two, I adjoin this love as a third of equal esteem with the two. For I do not err in that I love, knowing the two things I love without error: if they were false, it were true that I loved false things. For how could I be justly checked for loving false things if it were false that I loved them? But seeing the things loved are true and sure, how can the love of them be other than true and sure?[30]

The manner in which we know these things in ourselves is superior to the way in which we know the things of sense, since the former do not admit of error or deception. In this text, it is love of being and knowledge which is spoken of, rather than life, because that emphasizes the interconnection between them all. Had Augustine been criticized on the question of interaction between mind and body, he would probably have denied that he was making any such simple dichotomy, on the grounds that he always included life, and its correlate, love, to mediate between them. Being, life or love, and knowledge together make in effect a compound *eidos* of everything in nature and in the intelligible world as well, and so are perfectly appropriate for showing that man is made in the divine image. As life proceeds from being, and knowledge from life, so knowledge completes the circle by grasping being. This argument is used in *The Free Choice of the Will*, where it is also a matter of proving God's existence, because for Augustine "knowing how we apprehend truth and knowing the existence of truth are one and the same." Here he does not begin with doubt but with one's own existence, which is taken to be self-evident this time, and as such the foundation of knowledge:

> Aug. Then since it is evident that you exist, and that this could not be so unless you were living, the fact that you are living is also evident. Do you understand that these two points are absolutely true? Ev. I understand that perfectly well. Aug. Then the third point is also evident, namely, that you understand. Ev. It is evident. Aug. Which of these three, in your opinion, is the most excellent? Ev. Understanding. Aug. Why do you think so? Ev. Because, while these are three in number, existence, life and understanding, and though the stone exists and the animal lives, yet I do not think that the stone lives or that the animal understands, whereas it is absolutely certain that whoever understands also exists and is living. That is why I have no hesitation in concluding that the one which contains all three is more excellent than that which is lacking in one or both of these. . . . Aug. We likewise maintain that the most excellent among the three is what man possesses together with the other two, namely, understanding, and that having this, he must also exist and live.[31]

This leads on to a consideration of the various faculties and the kinds of objects they enable us to know. Reason differs from sense-faculties in that it not only knows them *qua* faculties (while they know only their proper objects), but that it alone is able to know itself.[32] As knowledge and reason are identified with the highest part of our nature, their reality being attested by our very existence, anything of a still higher nature may be identified with God. Proclus treats this subject in much the same manner, where he states that intellect and reason know themselves along with all the other faculties, including[33] imagination and sense, but that neither imagination nor sense knows intellect or reason. For this reason, the latter cannot be said to know themselves either, whence they cannot be a source of self-knowledge. Proclus is not drawing on Augustine, though; rather it is a case of Augustine and Proclus each appealing to the principles of a tradition common to them both.

But although reason grasps unchanging realities, it does so through an activity which is in itself variable, since its use is far from constant, and this is what leads us to the idea of a being who employs intelligence without any lapse or variation, that is to say the divine mind.

In *The Trinity*[34] the point of departure is the fact that we live: "even he who is deceived lives," a reality for which no sense faculty is needed:

> It is an inner knowledge by which we know that we live, where not even the Academician can say: "Perhaps you are sleeping, and you do not know, and you see in dreams." For who does not know that things seen by those who are asleep are very similar to things seen by those who are awake? But he who is certain about the knowledge of his own life does not say of it: "I know that I am awake," but "I know that I live"; whether he, therefore, sleeps or whether he is awake, he lives. He cannot be deceived in his knowledge of this even by dreams, because to sleep and see in dreams is characteristic of one who lives. Nor can the Academician argue as follows against this knowledge: "Perhaps you are insane, and do not know it, because the things seen by the sane are very similar to those seen by the insane, but he who is insane lives"; nor does he make this retort to the Academicians: "I know that I am not

insane," but "I know that I live." He can never, therefore, be deceived nor lie who says that he knows and lives.[35]

What is thus certainly known can also be indefinitely multiplied:

For he who says: "I know that I live," says that he knows one thing; if he were then to say: "I know that I know that I live," then there are already two things, but that he knows these two is to know a third thing; and so he could add a fourth, and a fifth, and innumerable more. . . .[36]

This certainty of living is now taken to be the key to a process of self-generating *a priori* knowledge which is in principle without limit. The mind is characterized by an ability to know things through itself alone. The fact that we err shows not only that we know something that reveals this, but that we do not will to err. The word of our knowledge is "the word that belongs to no language, the true word about a true thing, having nothing from itself but everything from that knowledge from whence it was born."[37]

This could also be taken as an answer in anticipation to the conception of thought as merely an inner speech. If speech is to be about intelligible reality, and not merely about other speech in an infinite regress, we shall need to establish some such conception as this one. Speech, whether inner or outer, needs a causal center which is logically anterior to all verbal diversity and process, and this is found to be peculiar to the nature of the knowing self.

Finally, we find this argument used in connection with self-knowledge as it relates to the immaterial nature of the soul in *The Trinity*, (Bk. X, 13–16, Ch. 10), where it is laid down that the mind's self-knowledge is in a unique category, because mind is directly "present to itself," without the need for any kind of symbolic or physical communication, just as with the power of "reverting upon itself" in Proclus. The principle that "every mind knows and is certain concerning itself" is especially significant in regard to the immateriality of mind or soul. There are numerous different material explanations for mind, and so the mere fact that they are all more or less dubious means that they should be considered untrue, in the light of the above principle. We cannot be in a state of doubt about something which is *per se* certain:

Moreover, they know that they will, and likewise know that no one can will, who is not and does not live; and similarly, they refer the will to something which they will with that will. They also know that they remember, and they know at the same time that no one would remember unless he both was and lived; but we also refer the memory itself to something which we remember with the memory. In two of the three, therefore, in the memory and the understanding, the knowledge and science of many things are contained.... But since we are investigating the nature of the mind, let us not take into consideration any knowledge that is obtained from without through the senses of the body, and consider more attentively the principle which we have laid down: that every mind knows and is certain concerning itself. For men have doubted whether the power to live, to remember, to understand, to will, to think, to know, and to judge is due to air, to fire, or to the brain, or to the blood, or to atoms, or to a fifth body—I do not know what it is—but it differs from the four customary elements; on the other hand, who would doubt that he lives, remembers, understands, wills, thinks, knows, judges? For even if he doubts, he understands that he doubts; if he doubts, he wishes to be certain; if he doubts, he thinks, if he doubts, he knows he does not know; if he doubts, he judges that he ought not to consent rashly. Whoever then doubts about anything ought never to doubt about all of these; for if they were not, he would be unable to doubt about anything at all.... [The knowing mind] is certain that it is none of those things of which it is uncertain, and certain that it alone is the only thing of which it is certain. (1.138)

Whether it reduces the mind to the body or to a "harmony of the body," the materialistic position would be essentially the same in regards to this certainty, which is equally incompatible with it in either form. The nature of personal identity is thus closely bound up with a capacity for knowledge which logically precedes all other kinds of knowledge. Not only is an immaterial kind of being indicated, but one which comprises the essential eidetic patterns of the things it knows empirically in the outside world. The self's liability to have doubts about itself and its knowledge has been shown to support a position at the opposite extreme from skepticism.

Soul and Identity in St. Augustine

Some Consequences of the Augustinian Cogito *Argument*

In these six texts we have the traditional basis for metaphysical certainty and *a priori* knowledge, besides an important key to knowledge of the self. Doubt itself, it appears, is only possible for us on the condition that there is an inherent knowledge in us which is beyond the reach of doubt. The fact that rational thought can give rise to any *a priori* knowledge at all is grounds for thinking that the limitations on our metaphysical knowledge are merely those of our own abilities, and not of this kind of knowledge itself.

The skeptic cannot say that he knows that he has no such certainty about the above argument, since it is knowing that he must exclude. However, he might say that he did not know that he did not know, but just thought it possible that he might not know. In this case, it might be argued again that he would have to *mean* that he knew that he possibly did not know the truth of the proof of being. But he could still just possibly know that maybe he did not know the truth of it; however many "possiblys" and "maybes" are inserted, it is not at all clear that there must be an "I know" at the end of them. Is there, then, a point anywhere at which the skeptic has to claim to know something? In fact there is, not at the end of the string of "maybes" but at the very beginning, because he must at least know or claim to understand what Augustine means by his proofs of being if he is to dispute them.

If, in fact, he knows or understands what the proof purports to establish, he knows something, and so his objection fails. But if he does *not* know what the argument means, he must forfeit the right to argue against it. "I don't think I understand what you are saying, but I beg to differ" is simply not a philosophical position, because philosophy presupposes that we at least know what we disagree about. In such a case of not-knowing, one could only suppose oneself to disagree with one's own personal impression of the proof, and not the proof itself.

There is also a significant lack of symmetry between knowing and not-knowing in this connection. If I know something, it means that others can know it as well. Yet if I do not know or am uncertain about the supposed proof, it could possibly mean that the proof is defective in itself and therefore must be so for others as well; but it equally well may be a sign of incapacity on my part. It gives no grounds for holding that the same subject must necessarily be equally obscure for other minds. In other words, disproof of a theorem requires that one should demonstrate an uncertainty in the proof itself, and not one which is peculiar to oneself. But that is just what the skeptic cannot do if he cannot claim actually to know the argument he opposes.

If it were possible to be subjectively in a state of complete uncertainty, it would follow that all arguments purporting to be certain would have to appear as uncertain. This is an indication of how a central epistemic state affects everything related to it. Conversely, a central certainty in the knower will be a foundation for any number of certainties in other things related to it.

A separate argument in regard to certainty concerns the relation of knowledge to action. If we dispute against certainty, we are at least taking action to the extent that we do so, though there is no such thing as action in any human sense of the word without knowledge, even if some knowledge may prove inadequate for its purpose. One must know oneself to be responsible for some part of an activity, however minimal, if it is to be distinguished from phenomena such as reflexes and somnambulism.

Conversely, the uncertainty professed by the skeptic is the essential characteristic of states of mind which reveal themselves in hesitation, passivity, and confusion. The consistent efforts made by the skeptical disputant therefore belie the uncertainty he claims for himself and others. Anyone who reflects on the effects of a real and not an assumed perplexity will see why this is so.

Knowledge of Eternal Truths

Augustine drew consequences for the knower in regard to the eternity of the truths he was able to know. But before making any attempt to deduce this, he first argued that truth itself necessarily must be eternal; if it could cease to be, it would still be true that it had ceased to be. Truth would still exist, even if the world ceased to exist, this being an aspect of the way in which values are logically antecedent to the whole realm of phenomena.[39] Even here one can see the outline of the *Cogito* argument's principle.

Further on, the question is raised as to what we mean by saying that truth is "in" the mind or soul.[40] If it is in it as a sailor is in a ship, our conclusions about the nature of truth would have no necessary implications for the soul. This kind of relation is not the one which Augustine attributes to mind and knowledge, however. One thing can be said to be in another in the manner of spatial location, like the sun in the East, or a fish in the sea, and in all such cases the things in question are clearly separable, and this is the case for which a disproof is offered insofar as it relates to the mind and its contents.

A second way in which one thing can be in another is exemplified by how heat resides in fire, whiteness in snow, and imminent forms in physical objects. Such things exist inseparably in their subjects, such that one could not remove the property without destroying the subject. The persistence of the subject, however, does not mean that its property (that which is in it) must persist likewise, because there are qualities which are not essential for the subject. Nevertheless, there are also cases where the subject would cease to be itself with the removal of a quality, as with fire and its heat.

Thus, where Augustine asks, "Who would allow or admit as a possibility that what exists in a subject could continue to exist when the subject has ceased to exist?," he is considering the case where things cannot exist *except* in a given subject. His intention here is to show that truths, however eternal, cannot exist except in minds which know them, although this brings in the problem that it apparently means that truths are in need of something other than their truth in order to be. If it is admitted that truth would still exist even if the world ceased to exist, that must involve the non-existence of all minds that know it. His idea that truth cannot exist except in a knowing subject would therefore seem to be in contradiction with this earlier position.

To make truth *per se* dependent on knowers would be to give up its objectivity, a thing which one can be sure Augustine does not intend to do. One could not claim that God was in any way dependent on those who knew or believed in Him, within any kind of

Christian perspective. Further on, Augustine asserts: "If a thing, A, existing in another thing, B, lasts for ever, B must last for ever,"[41] the example being that of scientific learning, which is eternal and, it is claimed, implies an eternal nature for the mind which knows it.

Here, one is faced with the question as to why something eternal may not be contained in something ephemeral, even if the manner of its containment is not like that of spatial location but that of modification by a quality. Given the latter condition, an eternal quality could presumably inform a transient substance. At this point, we are told that scientific learning exists in a subject, but not whether it can *only* exist in a subject, though it seems that the latter is intended. Part of the assertion seems to be that the subject is only able to know these scientific truths through being as eternal as they are. An objection is raised at this point, on the grounds that it is hard to see how a scholastic discipline can be in the mind eternally, besides which it cannot be said to be thus in minds generally because comparatively few people know such things.

This prompts a return to the earlier conclusion about truth, and how it could not perish even if the world did so.[42] This is reaffirmed as correct, with truth being understood in the Platonic sense of "that by which anything that is true is true." The corresponding idea of falsehood is then examined, and found to lie in a certain imitation of the true. If it fails to correspond to the real at all, it cannot properly even be called false. It would be false to call a stone silver, but to call it false silver would simply be without meaning.

Truth is also found to be distinguished from matter and from the void. It is to be found in thought and its objects, such as geometrical figures. The latter are contained in our minds, as truth is contained in them. This containment is held to exist "inseparably," because knowledge is taken to be a form of reminiscence. No matter how often we may forget a given piece of knowledge, it only requires the right stimuli for us to be able to convince ourselves of its existence again. Were it really not one with the soul, that would not be possible. Augustine uses examples of random questioning to elicit memory:

Suppose you have forgotten something and your friends want you to recall it to your memory. They will say, "Is it this?" "Is it that?" mentioning various things of a similar kind. You do not recall what you are seeking, but you know that it is none of the things mentioned . . . the discernment which refuses to accept a false suggestion is itself a kind of memory.[43]

Augustine later retracted this idea of knowledge as recollection and substituted the idea of divine illumination, whereby one is said to receive the light of the eternal reason where knowledge arises. However, he only issued this retraction because the Platonic idea of reminiscence was taken too literally as implying previous lives in which the knowledge was acquired. However, Augustine did not acknowledge or realize that the role of divine illumination in regard to knowledge is also a Platonic idea, only with the difference that Plato did not think that it sufficed without reminiscence as well.

In *Republic* VI (508d–509e) the Form of the Good has a function in regard to the knower and the known analogous to that of the sun in regard to eyesight and visible objects. The Good is understood to be an intelligible light in which the eye of the soul can see intelligibles, which is held to be necessary since the mind is never able to guarantee beforehand that it will perform a given function, however certain it is in retrospect. This is a way of explaining how the mind connects with its objects at all, which does not account for the element of certainty in them, which is rather the function of reminiscence. The Platonic reminiscence can in any case be separated from a literal belief in past lives, in a way which makes its function stronger, not weaker. This is how it appears in the form given it by Leibniz, as will be shown in the next chapter.[44]

The discussion in the *Soliloquies* is left incomplete, but the overall plan of the argument is fairly clear, despite many digressions. There are four main discernible claims: 1) that truth by its very nature is eternal; 2) that truth is inherent in intelligibles, which inhere in the soul as the physical form of an object informs that object; 3) that unlike some kinds of in-forming, the truth-form is not a merely accidental one, but essential to the knower; 4) that the essentiality of its relation to the knower can be discerned by the way in which knowledge arises as a kind of reminiscence. In this way, its presence in the knower can be seen to exist independently of the temporal accidents which bring it into operation in particular cases.

This line of reasoning follows naturally from the *Cogito* argument which appears earlier in the *Soliloquies* and in the other writings, where it was shown that we can know things from our very being. The reasoning by which Augustine deduces the eternity of the soul from that of the truths it knows follows naturally from the argument that if we know that we live we must know that we exist as well.

Something may be added to Augustine's argument concerning the question of whether minds are essentially temporal or not. Regular processes of change can produce stable appearances, as with the arc of a fountain. What if a wholly temporal mind could know eternal truths in a way comparable to this kind of effect? One answer is that while the mind also knows space and spatial relations, and can do geometry, thought itself is in no way a spatial entity. Similarly in regard to time, if we take it as simply the fourth dimension, it may be that the mind no more need be a temporal thing in order to comprehend time and temporal relations than it need be spatial in order to comprehend spatial things. The mere fact of this possibility is enough to make us reappraise the idea of mind's supposed temporality.

There is a difficulty here, however, inasmuch as spatial objects occupy just one clearly defined region in our thoughts, whereas time and temporality evidently enter into all of them. Just to contemplate an unchanging object is to know it in a series of moments. Is it not a fact that all thought takes the form of a temporal series? Granted that this is so, it still does not suffice to make mind wholly temporal, though it does show that mind is more closely related to time than it is to space. The fact that mind knows its activities to be a temporal series is in fact just what shows that it is fundamentally non-temporal, since only a consciousness outside that temporality could know the series as one thing, as *a* series. Conversely, if it were wholly temporal, the successive parts of the series would be oblivious of one another.

For this reason, the temporality attaching to all mental activities is far from meaning that thought is *per se* temporal. Such is the point made by Kant in the First Analogy, The Principle of the Permanence of Substance: "Only the permanent [substance] is subject to change; the mutable suffers no change, but rather *alternation*, that is, when certain determinations cease, others begin."[45]

While neither God nor truth have need of human minds in order to exist, human minds have need of them in order to be what they are; but this need could not exist unless minds were essentially supra-temporal. Given that *a priori* knowledge is innate in the mind, and that only like knows like, it would follow that the eternity of truth points toward a corresponding eternity in the knower.

Summary

Without arguing for any more attributes of the soul, it may be seen from the ones examined so far that, taken all together, they form the basis for a general conception which embraces them all. This conception is the principal crux of the subject, and it is one which demands a considerable modification to the common-sense idea of the soul-body relation. As will be seen, the popular conception of soul as being simply something within the body is so prevalent that it has even found its way into philosophical discussions of the soul. This misconception is enough to subvert arguments against the existence of the soul, which are affected by it.

Attention has already been drawn to the tendency of Platonism to invert the common-sense ranking of ideas and physical things in regard to their degree of reality. In addition to this, it is now possible to see why we must consider a second such inversion of priorities, this time in regard to the relation of body and soul. The properties adduced for the soul include those of being essentially self-motive; knowing truth by a non-physical causality; having infinity as an "all everywhere"; comprising an *a priori certainty* of its own existence; participating in the supra-temporal order.

All these things point to the conclusion that the soul cannot by any means exist in or be a part of the material world, because none of its aforementioned properties are those of natural phenomena. This points to the familiar and hopeless question as to where the soul might in fact be located, but the real meaning of the fact that it cannot be found on the physical level is that the body and the physical world are *in it*. The exact way in which they so exist is through the representations which the soul makes of them (and let us not forget that the whole of modern scientific theory from Copernicus onwards is based on the idea that the physical world itself differs profoundly from what it appears to be for the observer).

This does not mean parting ways with common-sense ideas altogether, for there is still a limited sense in which it is true that the soul is in the body, even though this claim has not the same scope as its converse. The relationship of soul and body both is and is not reciprocal. To illustrate this, it may be said that if London is in the United Kingdom, then the United Kingdom, or some part of it, must be in London. More generally, if a house exists in space, there must be space in the house. In these examples, it can easily be seen that while each member of the duality is in the other, this applies only very unequally. The analogy should not be taken too far, however, because the relation between a spatial object and a larger region of space, or space as a whole, is indissoluble, because the essential natures of the two are the same. That is not true of body and soul, however, and they are accordingly separable.

During natural life, the soul maintains a relation to the physical world and the body, or rather to their objective substance, which antecedes experience. Its connection with the body is experienced as the world-representation which contains the body, and can only be ended in death through a change in the body which makes it unable to continue to be an instantiation of its individual Form, the soul. What brings this about is a critical reduction in the body's powers of activity and sensitivity, because only by its physical activity can it correspond to the soul's activity. Self-motive activity is part of the soul's essence. Therefore, while activity can decline in the body, in the soul it cannot do so, and this is why a loss of active power by the body sets up strains between it and the soul which, if they go beyond a certain point, produce a conflict between body and soul strong enough to force them apart.

Augustine's writings, as quoted in this chapter, show by means of his *Cogito* argument how a new dimension can be added to our understanding of the soul. The deduction of a series of certain truths by the soul's own agency in relation to the intelligible Forms shows how the soul is not dependent on the material world as such. This discovery of non-material truths by the soul's own non-material agency gives us a realm of *a priori* knowledge which is neither trivial nor tautologous. Being capable of certainty, the soul has a standard of truth which can be related to knowledge where self-reflection is not relevant, as in natural science. Interior or *a priori* knowledge can be exact, whereas sense-based knowledge never is.

Being self-reflective and self-moved, the soul deploys powers which have no parallel on the sensory level, because its self-reflection and self-motion mean that the whole being acts as a whole on itself, whereas for material interactions only parts of things act on other parts. Thus there is a fundamental difference between body and soul which alleviates any problems about their being separable, no matter how deeply involved in the material world the soul may be. This independence of parts means that the soul is atomic in the literal sense of the word in relation to the world. Consequently it is not open to sublation into any other reality as is supposed in monistic or pantheistic thought. Because of this property, Leibniz calls the soul a "monad" or unitary substance, as will be explored more closely in Chapter 4.

Notes

[1] *The Greatness of the Soul*, Ch. 1.

[2] Ibid., Ch. 4.

[3] Ibid., Ch. 6.

[4] *Phaedo*, 99d–e.

[5] *The Greatness of the Soul*, Ch. 13.

[6] Ibid., 40.

[7] Ibid., Ch. 19.

[8] Ibid., Ch. 20.

[9] Ibid., Ch. 19.

[10] Ibid., Ch. 22.

[11] Ibid., Chs. 23–28.

[12] Ibid., Ch. 23, 63.

[13] Ibid., Ch. 24, 70.

[14] Ibid., Ch. 26.

[15] Ibid.

[16] Ibid., Ch. 28.

[17] Ibid., Ch. 32.

[18] *The Trinity*, Bk. X, Ch. 10.

[19] Ibid.

[20] Ibid., Ch. 10, 16.

[21] *Elements of Theology*, Prop. 15.

[22] Ibid., Prop. 16.

[23] Ibid., Prop. 17.

[24] *Time, Creation and the Continuum*, 289.

[25] *Soliloquies*, Bk. II, 1, 1.

[26] Ibid.

[27] *True Religion*, XXIX, 72–73.

[28] *The Metaphysics of Mind*.

[29] *True Religion*, XL, 74.

[30] *City of God*, Vol. 1, Bk. XI, Ch. XXVI.
[31] *The Free Choice of the Will*, Bk. II, Ch. 3.
[32] Ibid.
[33] In *Rep.* Bk. X, Section 277, 20–30 (Festugière tr.).
[34] *The Trinity*, XV, 12, 21.
[35-37] Ibid.
[38] *The Trinity*, Bk. X, Ch. 10, 13–15.

[39] *Soliloquies*, Bk. II, ii.
[40] Ibid., Bk. II, xii, 22.
[41] Ibid., Bk. II, 24.
[42] Ibid., Bk. II, 28.
[43] Ibid., Bk. II, 34.
[44] Chapter 4, 134–37.
[45] *Critique of Pure Reason*, Transcendental Analytic, Bk. II, Ch. II, Sec. iii, 3b.

4

Substance, Individuation, and Plenitude

Personal Identity According to Leibniz

"T he metaphysics of the unique individual" would be a good
way of characterizing Leibniz's philosophy. But besides this,
it is appropriate for us to discuss here for several reasons.
Firstly, his system is steeped in Neoplatonic principles, as I shall try
to show later, so that it can serve to reveal more of the scope of the
ideas introduced in the previous chapters. Secondly, this relation to
the Neoplatonists appears particularly in the fact that Leibniz's system is, more than any other, dependent on the Principle of Plenitude, which is also an essential part of the present theory. This
appears in the fact that his world is a sum of monads which constitute every possible gradation of being from God down to the edge
of non-existence.

The third and most important reason arises from a key factor in
the credibility of this kind of philosophy. The main obstacle to the
acceptance of what is argued for here is not so much philosophical
as psychological. Common sense is dominated by a picture of the
Real World as consisting essentially of space with objects moving
about in it, to which minds or souls could relate only as ghostly
attendants, if they are there at all.

Of course, one knows by reason that the Real World is actually
the combination of the spatial-material world with the conscious
minds that know it; but that is not something which engages the
imagination. Leibniz's philosophy, on the other hand, sees the Real
World as consisting in souls or monads. Far from being peripheral
entities, these are the very core of reality, while the world of space

and matter becomes the medium in which the spiritual beings orga-
nize their perceptions. Thus he shows us a way in which the perspective of materialistic common sense can be turned inside-out
without doing violence to the facts.

The common-sense belief in the world as being purely and simply space, with physical objects in it, is an illusion which invites
comparison with the way in which members of the animal kingdom
acquire their identities. Typically, each animal and bird identifies
itself with the first thing it sees after it is born or hatched, which is
normally an adult member of its own species. This form of self-
identification is so automatic that for some species even an inanimate object can be substituted, with the result that the newborn
creature relates to the object as to a parent. In an experiment conducted by Konrad Lorenz, a duckling was led to identify in this way
with a tin can. The human parallel for this confusion appears in the
way in which human minds become so absorbed in their perceptions of the outside world that they become blind to their interior
agency which makes such perceptions possible. One's identity as
knower can be stifled by the volume of the content of the known,
just as the perception of the tin can blinded the duckling to its identity as a duck. It is all very well for practical common sense to be
permeated with such a confusion, but it cannot have any place in
philosophy except as an object of study. It is noteworthy that analytical philosophy, though it may subject everything else to critical
analysis, has accepted this confusion of popular thinking without a
murmur.

An Answer to Locke: Innate Ideas

The perceiver's awareness of his own agency *qua* perceiver is the
necessary though not sufficient precondition for an understanding
of arguments for innate ideas or Forms, which are part of Leibniz's
philosophy. Accordingly, the Introduction to Leibniz's *New Essays*
explains the criticism and counter-argument which is to be applied
to Locke's *Essay Concerning Human Understanding* by way of
affirming the rationalist as opposed to the empiricist perspective.
For this purpose, Leibniz defends the conception of innate ideas,

which he maintains constitute an essential difference between man and the animals. Animals' thought never goes beyond the connection of related sensations. Man has the principles to judge whether such sensations or impressions should be accepted or not, when they are trustworthy and when not. Locke has to admit that some ideas do not come from sensation, but from "reflection," and Leibniz regards these as a bridge to his own philosophy.

Reflection is a state of attention to what is within us, since the self at very least is innate to itself, besides having numerous conceptions which are not reducible to sensation, such as being, unity, substance, duration, change and activity. The argument Leibniz directs particularly against Locke's conception of the soul as *tabula rasa*, and the idea that everything inscribed upon it comes by sense-perception, is that, if this were true, ideas would be in us as contingently as a statue of Hercules can be found in a block of marble because a sculptor chooses to carve it that way.

If all our knowledge arose in this accidental manner, it would all depend on experience, and as no two persons ever have the same experiences (unique place-time combinations), it would be very hard to see how any two persons could ever reach the truth or agree about anything. Mediation between disputants would be pointless, as the experiences of the mediator would be just as irrelevant to those of the disputants as those of the latter to one another. This defines the position held by Protagoras, argued against by Plato in the *Theaetetus*, that the experiences of each individual are always "true" for him, and that no truth need be common.

In reality, we have to be able to distill from our different experiences certain ideas which transcend the limitations of our individualities. If we have innate ideas, we would have something by which to arrange our experiences in ways which may be adequate to a universal standard. In this connection, the innate ideas are compared to veins in the marble block which delineate the form of Hercules, and guide the activity of the sculptor. Work is still necessary to arrive at the truth, yet now it is no longer in a featureless void, but is guided by pre-existent Forms.

For Plato, this point leads naturally to the idea that all knowledge is reminiscence (*anamnêsis*), particular experiences serving to awaken the innate truths dormant in us: "Such an one, as soon as he beholds the beauty of this world, is reminded of true beauty.... Few indeed are left that can still remember much: but when these discern some likeness of the things yonder, they are amazed...."[1]; and similarly:

> Either then he has at some time acquired the knowledge which he now has, or he has always possessed it. If he always possessed it, he must always have known; if on the other hand he acquired it at some previous time, it cannot have been in this life, unless somebody has taught him geometry.[2]

Leibniz shows that the myth of recollection as it stands is inadequate for its purpose if it is taken literally. The literal sense can imply two possibilities, one of which is that our acquisition of knowledge in the previous life was just as contingent and empirical as it would be in this life. In this case, the fact that it occurred in a previous life makes no logical difference, because if the origin is empirical at any time, however remote, it may just as well have arisen empirically in the last five minutes, as far as intrinsic certainty is concerned. This would defeat the objective of the idea behind recollection, which is to show that knowledge has a foundation in us which goes beyond the accidents of our worldly experiences. In reality, the "previous life" is merely a symbol of this transcendence.

The second possibility which Leibniz indicates is that the knowledge we are alleged to have gained in a previous life was innate then as well as now. In that case, that innateness could only have been due to another life previous to that one (if "previous lives" were the decisive factor), and so on, in a vicious infinite regress, such that the all-important acquisition of necessary truths remains permanently unreachable beyond the end of it. This shows that what matters is not a previous life, or any number thereof, but something peculiar to the soul itself. This would be the actual reality indicated by the mythical stories, that of a system of ideas present in the soul in a manner consubstantial and coeval with it. As R. Latta puts it, "He [Leibniz] accepts the Platonic doctrine in so far as it implies that knowledge of the eternally true comes to the soul not through external sense, but by development from its own inner being."[3]

This conclusion seems to prompt Leibniz's own question: "Why, then, should we not also be able to provide ourselves with some sort of thought out of our own inner being when we deliberately try to penetrate its depths?"[4]

This question is one which has already been raised and answered in the affirmative by Augustine in a text quoted in the previous chapter: "For he who says: 'I know that I live' says that he knows one thing; if he were then to say: 'I know that I know that I live,' there are already two things ... and so he can add a fourth and a fifth and innumerable more. . . ."[5]

More generally, the use of "previous lives" to explain the way in which a person lives now is ineffectual because it is too much like answering a question such as "Why are you ambitious?" with "Because I was so last year, and the year before that." The time-span over which a quality is manifested explains nothing, and cannot make it more or less innate. The presence of innate ideas in us, or eternal truths as they are also called, has an important connection with personal identity, as I shall try to show, because they manifest the world of the spirit in us.

Eternal Truths and Identity

The *Monadology* contains the idea that it is the knowledge of necessary and eternal truths which raises consciousness to the level of self-consciousness. This is because the recognition of such truths and the awareness of self both seem to require the same act of reflection. When a truth is understood to be absolute and eternal, it must pertain as much to the powers of the knower as to its direct object. This is the conception implicit in Leibniz, and which was later to be developed on so large a scale by Kant. For this reason, we learn something of our own nature as knowers from what is *prima facie* known about other things; for example, in geometry truths about triangles contain necessity and immutability, and also exactitude and universality, which attributes must also have their place in the constitution of the knower, as like relates to like. However, Kant parts ways with Platonism when he rejects the role of the universals in the objective world.

Could we have self-awareness if we did not know eternal truths? Animals presumably do not know such things, as their awareness is confined to the ever-varying and multiple, which does not contain any standard or point of reference like a universal Form or a self. Two different realities are combined in this reasoning, these being the self, as the most singular and unique reality, and eternal truths, which constitute the most universal. Thus by a different route we arrive again at the union of individual and universal which we have already deduced in the theory of the individual Form in Chapter 2.

The traditional idea of circular motion applied to the soul also has a connection with this idea. There is a kind of circular pattern in the way human thought keeps reverting to certain invariants such as the law of non-contradiction. Given this pattern of reversion, it is possible that human thought should give rise to the idea of self as the locus in relation to which it takes place, especially in view of the kinship between the eternal truths and the knower.

This relation of the universal to the individual depends also on what could be called a "second-order" consciousness which is the knower of the "first-order" consciousness, which is not in principle any different in the animals. The latter cannot revert upon any of its previous acts except by chance, which is extremely improbable. There is always a necessity for this "second-order" consciousness to survey the results of previous conscious acts, so as to direct a return to certain of them. This implies the function of intellect on a level above that of reason, because it surveys in advance what reason advances toward with connected steps, which reason is not able to direct in the first place.

By relating selfhood to eternal truths, Leibniz is also on Platonic ground, as will become apparent when we consider how much commonality there is between what is said in the *Monadology* and the passage from the *Phaedo*, already quoted at greater length in Chapter 1: "But when it (the soul) investigates by itself, it passes into the realm of the pure and everlasting, and immortal and changeless ... the soul is in every possible way more like the invariable than the variable."[6]

If knowledge of the immutable implies something immutable in the knower (as already argued in Chapter 3), this must constitute a core of reality on which a sense of selfhood can reasonably be based. A region is defined by first- and second-order consciousness in which knowledge of the objective realities and knowledge of self overlap. Otherwise put, it could be said to involve a kind of self-knowledge directed to the component of selfhood which is common to all conscious beings, and not to one's individual attributes. As Leibniz expresses it,

> It is through the knowledge of necessary truths, and through their abstract expression, that we rise to *acts of reflection,* which make us think of what is called I, and observe that this or that is within us: and thus, thinking of ourselves, we think of a being, of substance ... of the immaterial, and of God Himself. . . .[7]

The ability to form the idea of being in general is evidently one with our ability to conceive our selves as beings. A more relative principle, like the law of motion—"for every action there is an equal and opposite reaction"—requires a kind of experience which attains to the common elements among the multiple and the mutable, as much as in relation to the most universal principles. This same ability can as easily reach the conception of a single self persisting through all its changes as it can the idea of the law of action and reaction through all its perceptions of particular actions and reactions. This self is not a universal, although it is a Form, and accordingly it has properties in common with the universal Forms: firstly immateriality, secondly an intelligibility under the Form of Being, and thirdly the property of being a common principle among an indefinite series of physical appearances, like the center of a circle in relation to the points on the circumference.

This twofold aspect is neither more nor less than what we should expect to find in a being whose essence is an individual Form. It effectively is universal inasmuch as it comprises its own synthesis of the eternal truths it finds reflected in the outside world, but it is also singular in that it is a unique substance, as discrete in its own way as a material thing. This duality is worth comparing with that of the center of the personality, which is both consciousness and will, these being respectively universal and individual.

Eternal Truths and God

While eternal truths are found to be co-natural with the self and its world, they cannot be said to depend on it. What, then, do they depend on? Were they *per se* dependent on us, there would be no distinction between them and our subjective mentation based on emotion and imagination, whereas in fact their self-subsistence is not in doubt, however irregular our awareness of objective truth may be. The permanent being of truth has nothing to do with the duration of our personal awareness of it. This intrinsic reality of all truths, independent of us, is said by Leibniz to reside in God:

> For if there is a reality in essences or possibilities, or rather in eternal truths, this reality must needs be founded in something existing and actual, and consequently in the existence of the necessary Being, in whom essence involves existence, or in whom to be possible is to be actual.[8]

An argument for the existence of God is thus linked with an argument for the reality of the self, both being based on the eternal truths or ideas. But in what sense do the eternal truths need to exist "in" anything? Does not their intrinsic nature imply that they themselves are in no need of any kind of support? One part of the answer seems to lie in their common attribute of eternal reality. That they all have this quality would mean that each one of them participates in the divine attribute to which it corresponds. In this case, the different eternal truths evidently do not require individual ways of being eternal.

Another part of the answer lies in their mutual consistency, and in the way in which their instantiations combine to form a single coherent world. This could not be the case unless the eternal truths or Forms were relative to some higher unity with an overview of them all. There is an *a priori* harmony among the non-sensuous universals, as exemplified by Kant's Categories—for instance cause, substance, unity, being, equality—while there is a *de facto* harmony among the instances of the sensuous universals, where they appear as natural phenomena and species. This harmony or coherence is attributed by Leibniz to the creative action of God: "If there were no choice of God, possibilities would simply counteract one another."[9]

In Platonic terms, God must determine which Forms are to be instantiated, failing which the unity of the world could not be preserved. However, this dependence of truths upon God is not conceived in the manner of Descartes, who made their truth-content dependent on the divine will. For Leibniz, the absoluteness of truths is a participation in that of the divine nature, and is in no way a product of will. Here, he is close to the Platonic position that the divine will does not determine truth because the will is only an expression of the divine Power, which itself comes third in order among the primary attributes, namely, Goodness, Wisdom, Power. The eternal truths pertain to Wisdom, which logically and ontologically precedes the Power manifest in the will. (One may conceive of an intelligence without will, but a will without intelligence would be an absurdity.)

Leibniz also describes the controlling relation of the Divine will to the Forms, not in their intrinsic natures but in their manifestation, as follows: "Now there is none but God (from whom all individuals emanate continually...) to be the cause of this correspondence of their phenomena, and to make what is private to one public to all."[10] In this way, the externally manifest truths are effectively contained within a higher unity.

The order of necessary truths or instantiating Forms leads thus to *two* unities, the one being that of the self, and the other being that of God. Where truths are perceived to be necessary and eternal, one sees them as inherent in the knower himself, so making the conception of self practically inevitable by the reflection involved. At the same time, all such truths combine to form a single universe, owing to a unity which in some sense governs them, this being the divine unity. (These observations should be related to what I have said in Chapter 14 of *The Order of the Ages*.)

Self as Unique Monad

An examination of the exact nature of the self deduced above is pursued elsewhere in the *Monadology*, where Leibniz summarizes his doctrine on this subject. He uses the term "monad" rather than "soul" because he wanted to make it of more general application as a unitary psychic substance which could pertain not merely to rational beings but to animals and plants as well, and even to things we would not consider conscious at all. Monads would range in content and powers from God down to the confines of non-existence.

Leibniz specifies that the monad is a "simple substance," on the grounds that this follows directly from the fact that there are compounds.[11] Possibly he claims too much on this basis, because although compounds do presuppose elements, it does not follow that the latter will be of a kind suited to personal identity. This elemental simplicity is for him an absolute presupposition, and it has a function similar to that which the idea of the soul's "reversion upon itself" has for Proclus. In either case, it is a question of a principle capable of defining an immaterial substance so as to distinguish it from the material kind.

Both material and immaterial substances exhibit complexity and diversity, but the difference between them can be seen from the fact that in material substances each distinguishable part has no immediate contact with the others, except those which are most proximate to it. Conversely, in the spiritual substance, the continuity and mobility of consciousness ensures that each of its parts can enter into direct relation with every other part. This is what is implied by the whole substance "reverting upon itself."

The monadic selves are said to be "the real atoms of nature."[12] As such, they are not capable of dissolution, but can only begin by creation and end by annihilation. This simplicity gives rise to the problem of how such substances could interact with one another; and instead of attempting to say how, Leibniz simply asserts that they cannot do so.[13] Simplicity does not mean emptiness, however, as the qualitative differences between monads is part of their reason for existing. For two to be the same would defeat the purpose implicit in the reflection of the universe from all possible points of view in all different beings, which is the function of the monads. Each substance must realize in itself some different and distinctive possibility, no matter what else it has in common with others: "But if the number of monads is infinite, and if every monad differs in quality from every other, then the monads must be such that they might be considered as a series, each term or member of which differs from the next by an infinitely small degree of quality."[14] The idea of identical separate beings is not self-contradictory in itself, but it could be so if we were to proceed from a conception of existence as manifestation of unmanifest principles.

This involves the Principle of Plenitude, which Leibniz implicitly appeals to in his idea of the uniqueness of all substances together with their continuous gradation from the most to the least universal. To maintain that the world is created is to maintain that it is caused by an infinite being, but infinity cannot be manifested *qua* infinity because a second infinite (i.e., the manifestation of the first) would be contradictory. Consequently, the infinite must be manifest in some form which is compatible with finitude and multiplicity. The latter two are opposed by nature to the infinite, but they can be made to manifest it in a derivative manner by a serial infinity of individual beings, each manifesting something different.

The principle of non-repetition of possibilities which the infinite implies is best known as the Identity of Indiscernibles. According to Leibniz, this means that if two beings really were the same in all respects, they would in reality be only one. Although he does not present it as such, this is deeply Platonic, for the idea of instantiation implies that the instanced beings always fall short of the perfection of their Forms. Consequently, for two beings to be identical they would both need to have a degree of precision which only the Forms could have:

> This thing which I can see has a tendency to be like something else, but it falls short and cannot really be like it, only a poor imitation. Don't you agree with me that anyone who receives that impression must in fact have previous knowledge of that thing which he says that the other resembles, but inadequately?[15]

According to R.E. Cushman,

> it is this "falling short" or deficiency (*endeia*) of the particular, in contrast with the already known "absolute," which alerts the mind to the independent reality of the Form, as well as to the difference between the particular thing and the (*autê hê ousia*) in which it participates.[16]

If two entities fell short of the same Form in exactly the same ways, it would contradict the principle that it is by their imprecision that instanced things fall short of their Forms. The exact reason why all manifest beings must have imperfections which would preclude relations such as true identity has also been conceived in a way which shows how Platonism can be combined with an atomic theory of matter, in the writings of Giordano Bruno:

> For the want of perfect figures, we could not hope to find in the tangible universe two imperfect figures equal to one another. Even this equality is a kind of perfection no example of which is offered by the *ens mobile* . . . the irremediable imperfection of the tangible universe results from two causes, namely the discontinuity and the mobility of its elements. Broken up and in motion, it presents itself to our experience as partial and unstable objects that never fully correspond to the idea they evoke.[17]

The mutual exclusiveness of material things is also a factor here. Such beings are formed through a unique set of place-time locations, where each one of the latter is unique as well, and this implies correspondingly unique processes of formation for all things in nature. That alone is enough to exclude physical manifestation of perfect equality between two objects. Moreover, there is no question of there being two identical Forms, since they are by definition exempt from matter, so there is nothing that could multiply them *qua* Forms.

The Principle of Individuation

Leibniz often speaks as though the principle of Continuity prevailed without exception, but this cannot be the whole truth. The natural order requires relations between opposites, which depend on discontinuities. Consequently, the full continuum of beings cannot be manifest all at once. The element of discontinuity in nature appears in the way in which living species reproduce themselves, whether it is of unicellular organisms propagating by the division of cells into two or of higher forms of life from the fusion of two different cells, and likewise for countless chemical, electrical and magnetic phenomena. What more obvious discontinuity could there be than a new organism resulting from the fusion of two others? The union in practice between continuity and discontinuity can be seen in the emergence of new individuals, whether by organic growth or by crystallization—that is, discrete beings resulting from continuous processes.

The question, then, is how continuity and discontinuity can subsist together logically. It has been argued against the Principle of Plenitude that man, for example, should differ only infinitesimally from the animal species most closely related to him,[18] and likewise for the other species among themselves. This idea can be shown to be the result of a naive conception of continuity, which unwittingly identifies continuity with just one subdivision thereof, that of geometrical lines and surfaces. But what constitutes continuity in the general case is not a gradation of infinitesimals, but a progression in which each member is arrived at by a process equal to the one by which the previous member was arrived at. Thus 100, 200, 300, 400, etc., form a continuum, whereas 1, 4, 5, 9, 11, etc., do not; and these examples also show how the sizes of the intervals involved do not affect the issue.

Continuity among beings could be defined, therefore, in terms of a balance between sameness and difference, because difference alone would banish intelligible order from the world, while sameness alone would do effectively the same, by excluding any real *relata*. Moreover, a demand for continuity in everything would contradict Leibniz's purpose in proving the immortality of the soul, as will appear presently. It is true that Leibniz maintains "the idea of an infinite series of elements, each differing from its neighbor to an infinitely small extent."[19] To reconcile this with necessary discontinuities, beings would have to be distributed such that the most minimally differing ones were never in any near relation. If ten, say, were the minimal difference allowed between numbers, the numbers from one to a hundred could be put in ten sets: for instance, 1, 11, 21, …, 91; 2, 12, 22, …, 92; 3, 13, 23, 33, …, 93; and so on.

Leibniz denies the kind of continuity which would merge all identities into one on the grounds that no soul is ever disembodied, no matter how much any given body may change its composition: "God alone is completely without body."[20] Monads are therefore never without at least a material basis of individuation, and in this regard he is expressing a form of the idea that every soul has an ethereal body from which it is never separated. This "subtle body" appears in Plotinus as following from the principle that man is an epitome of all levels of being, and its presence and inseparability from the soul is explained in detail by Proclus.[21] Embodiment is also conceived as the means whereby souls or monads remain in relation to one another, though it is also the source of the passivity or confused perception which makes them inferior to God. Elsewhere, Leibniz asserts this subtle embodiment in a more Proclean manner in relating it to the subtle or ethereal bodies which theology attributes to the angels.[22]

However, we are also given a deeper and more intrinsic reason for the individuality of the soul, which, whether consciously for Leibniz or not, is a development of the Platonic conception of soul as the self-motive principle, which we examined in Chapter 1. This is a particularly important conception, because it is a point at which theory merges with direct experience. It is used to refute "some erring quietists, who imagine an absorption of the soul and its reunion with the ocean of divinity. . . ."[23]—an idea which had been made current in the seventeenth century by Molinos, from whom it was taken up by Fénélon and Madame Guyon.

Leibniz maintains that what the Quietists teach is impossible because no substance can be without an activity of its own. If the soul is *per se* a center of activity, it could not become fused with some greater entity without a cessation of this activity, which on the principles of both Plato and Leibniz would necessarily mean the cessation of its very existence. Leibniz does not narrowly conceive psychical activity as "motion" alone, as Plato does, but more generally as a dynamism which is expressive of the individual nature concerned, this being manifest in the continuous flow of volition. It is true that we are usually only conscious of the will when we try to change or resist something, but at other times we are equally willing when we will "no change," or will to "continue."

The main argument for soul as essential self-motion has already been given in Chapter 1, and so only certain details need be considered here. For example, it may be claimed that such-and-such saint came to know the will of God, and made his own will one and the same with it. Would this refute what has just been said? In reality, this kind of example concerns only the *content* of volition, and not the act itself. In this case, the volitive act of the saint remains as much his own as when the content of his willing was indifferent to, or opposed, to the will of God. In this way, there is a positive sense in which individuals can be subsumed into larger realities, such as when musicians learn to play in time together, so that their separate activities sound as one. Here again there is community of content, while the activity remains that of the individuals. Any literal absorption of individuals would remove their harmony along with them.

In the *Monadology*, Leibniz offers a third way to account for individuation, based on each monad's being a representation of the universe from a unique point of view, like "the same town, looked at from various sides,"[24] and secondly by the degree of distinctness or confusedness in its perceptions. The latter condition seems to carry the greater weight, because each monad is said to be capable of distinct perceptions only in regard to what is "nearest or greatest" in relation to it; "otherwise each monad would be a deity."[25]

This absence of qualitative distinction comes close to making monadic, and therefore personal, identity consist only in some kind of defect, individuals differing only in the degrees and combinations of their deficiencies. This was the conclusion drawn by Ortega y Gasset:

> for Leibniz "Perfection" is *quantitas realitatis.* Therefore there are no monads if there is not relative imperfection. This consists of confused perception, which is evil. From whence it results that without this intrinsic evil, ascribed to the root of whatever is— except God—there could not be anything.[26]

This applies to what is said in the *Monadology,* and in this context it looks as though Leibniz is making the mistake of equating the soul with its passive, reflective aspect. In so doing, he adopts the point of view of monistic philosophers like Spinoza, whom he was so concerned to argue against. On the basis of the above, the only alternative to Monism is to make the monads eternal, and thereby make evil eternal with them, which would amount to a Manichean dualism of monads and God.

However, this is only owing to an inconsistency: Leibniz also characterizes the essential elements of the monad as "perception" and "appetition,"[27] these being reflections of the divine knowledge and will. He states this position more fully in the "Principles of Nature and Grace": "each monad is a living mirror, *or a mirror endowed with inner activity,* representative of the universe."[28] The presence of this inner activity, inclusive of individual volition, is precisely what most differentiates each monad, then, just as the argument against Quietism in the *New Essays* shows.

These two accounts of individuation are not necessarily irreconcilable, because individuation can surely be determined by a combination of a specific nature, or Form, expressing itself in a flow of activity, together with a good deal that is mere limitation and therefore not truly essential.

A Criticism of Self-Individuation

P. F. Strawson, commenting on Leibniz's idea that the "complete notion" of an individual implies a description of the whole universe from a unique point of view, maintains that "no principle of individuation can be framed for consciousnesses as such, and hence that nothing can be a subject of predicates implying consciousness . . . unless it is a person."[29]

But Leibniz's individuals are not *per se* material, and so the question arises as to how they can be truly individuals *qua* spiritual. This is answered by taking the defining factor for each of them as its unique point of view in regard to the universe as a whole.

Strawson argues against this answer by means of a comparison with a chess board, where two corresponding squares on the same diagonal and equidistant from the corners have the same relations to the rest of the board. Their "points of view" thus fail to distinguish them—but only if one makes certain assumptions, the first of which is that direction makes no difference, as these squares have the same relations to the board only from opposite directions. That everything should appear the same from opposite directions would seem to be ruled out by the principle of the Identity of Indiscernibles, since this implies that all space is qualitatively determined, as opposed to the idea of "empty space," which is only an abstraction. But to take the example on its own level, these two squares may relate to the same number of other squares in the same manner, but not by any means to the *same* squares, as one can easily see when each one is named by its coordinates. Even if all the squares could be made indistinguishable to the eye, they remain so many different individuals; we know this to be the case, even if the observers believe they are both seeing the same things, and this, I think, defeats the point of the comparison.

We are reminded that "point of view" must in any case not be taken literally, as though there were a common space in which the monads reside like so many physical objects. According to Leibniz, space is internal to each monad, while the contents of their several spaces are closely similar, and differ no more than do the different points of view of beings in a single space.

They each possess a full representation of space as from a unique point of view, without being spatially related to one another. This is not as strange as it may seem, when we consider that, for most forms of dualistic philosophy, different minds all have their own representations of the same space, which are not themselves spatially related, any more than the perceptions they contain are spatially related to their objects.

However, this philosophy does assume a common spatial universe as the efficient cause of all its subjective representations. But for Leibniz, this function is carried out directly by God, without any natural instrument, rather as Berkeley's ideas do not have subsistent objects to cause them. (Logically, it may not be much stranger that God should be invoked for this purpose than that the unity of the physical world should be so. This is because this objective unity of the world never comes to us directly in our experiences of it, since the latter result from the mind's processing of the input from the objective world and reflecting on it, as the existence of God is evinced likewise.)

Strawson alleges in the same chapter that the idea of a world in each individual is dependent on an original idea of individuals in one world. There is no real conflict between this claim and Leibniz's, though, because in a temporal or biographical sense this order certainly prevails. The perspective of many individuals in one world is real enough up to a point, since it is simply the ego's perceived relationship to all the other egos around it. This is what self-aware-ness begins with, when one still assumes that the other egos are their self-subsistent originals, and not one's own processed repre-sentations of them.

He also maintains that individuation can only be real for "types or concepts," not of particulars, if it is to be unique. In this connec-tion it should be noted that the conception of identity as individual Form deduced from Plotinus's ideas constitutes a special field of unity between these otherwise conflicting realities, the particular and the universal. Several times, it is made clear that the focal point of this critique is the contention that individuation in Leibnizian terms can only be established at the price "of acknowledging that the individuals of the system are not particulars at all, but universals or types or concepts."[30]

But given that persons constitute the common ground between the individual and the universal, there need be no difficulty in admitting the uniqueness of each one without positing a special act of God as the cause of said uniqueness, which results rather from their inclusion among Forms. The supposed choice between real particular entities with no logical basis for their diversity, and non-particular entities or universals with logically necessary distinctions, is therefore transcended both by the theory of the individual Forms and the relation between eternal truths and personal identity dis-cussed earlier.

Even without the theory based on the Principle of Plenitude, one should not fall into the trap of discussing souls or monads as though they could be purely and simply particulars, if only because of their possession of intelligence. By virtue of this property they are in effect self-transcending particulars, whence the whole critique discussed in the above is based on a dichotomy which is applicable only to the commonest kinds of instances.

Whether Monads Can Interact

We have already pointed out that what Leibniz says about simplic-ity, uniqueness, and impassibility is linked to the principle of conti-nuity. This implies a continuous scale of beings, each realizing a possibility which differs only minutely from the next in order to it. This provides the basis for an answer to the problem as to how monads can affect one another if they have no direct interaction. Continuity implies a community of natures among those that are in juxtaposition. In Platonic terms, this physical juxtaposition results from the community of natures in those things that are juxtaposed. Consequently any change in one monad must imply either corresponding changes in the others, or else its removal to a different set of conditions and relations where differences will be less.

The qualitative nature of each monad is far from fixed, as the following quotations demonstrate: "the natural changes of the monads come from an *internal principle,* since an external cause can have no influence upon their inner being"[31]; "The activity of the internal principle which produces change or passage from one perception to another may be called *Appetition*"[32]; "they have a certain self-sufficiency (*autarcheia*) which makes them the sources of their internal activities and, so to speak, incorporeal automata."[33] Leibniz may be confusing metaphysics with physics here, since it is as clear that monads have wills of their own as that they have consciousness, in which case they cannot be automata. The will of a monad cannot fail to be free, moreover, since it cannot be causally subject to natural forces. The natural order is represented *in* the monad, which transcends it as a whole.

The reason why the individual nature (modified by the internal activity) necessarily determines also the form of external activity lies with the principle of Continuity, which implies a measure of equality among all closely related beings. By this means, all beings secretly condition one another without any question of direct action. Thus the way in which each monad acts in relation to its world determines for good or ill the nature of the counter-actions induced by it. No inner qualitative state is therefore purely private, but rather each selects the external relations that make up its environment without direct action thereupon; such would be a fuller account of the "ideal" interaction between monads which Leibniz speaks of.

Curiously, where he does speak of interaction of this kind, it is in connection with physical interaction:

For all is a *plenum* (and thus all matter is connected together) and in the *plenum* every motion has an effect upon distant bodies in proportion to their distance . . . this inter-communication extends to any distance, however great. And consequently every body feels the effect of all that takes place in the universe so that he who sees all might read in each what is happening everywhere.[34]

But no matter whether this principle be applied to monads or bodies, it can be seen that Leibniz is employing a Neoplatonic concept which we have already considered at some length in Chapter 2, the doctrine of Cosmic Sympathy, by which Plotinus reconciled interaction of entities with the unity of the world. Whether Leibniz was conscious of this connection or not, it serves well to show the continuity of his thought with that of the Neoplatonists.

Leibniz denies interaction between monads not only by reason of their simplicity, but also by reason of the way in which each of them is conceived to develop wholly from within, according to a law of its own. This still leaves open the question as to whether the working-out of this inner law is freely willed or predetermined. This condition is stated as follows: "Every present state of a simple substance is naturally a consequence of its preceding states in such a way that the present is big with its future."[35] Here, at least, causality is admitted within the monad, if not outside it, although the part played in it by the will is not specified. However, the extent of the will's activity must make up an important part of each "present state," and so some freedom of the will would not be inconsistent with this conception. The monad would, among other things, be capable of redirecting the tendency of its own inner law, which would have to have implications for other monads, however indirectly.

If there is no direct interaction, there is still some kind of interaction. The fact that all monads remain in relation, forming a coherent whole, implies that they are all acted on by a governing principle. The kind of interaction referred to above, to some extent involving the body, is closer to common sense, because body-soul interaction is a familiar idea, even if not sufficiently understood. Conversely, the direct action of soul on soul would be less problematical in principle, but here again we do not understand in detail what this would involve, only that, given the law of Continuity, it must be a reality.

Besides, Leibniz's denial of interaction must invite comparisons with Hume's criticism of causality. What for Hume are sequences of ideas developing according to numerous different laws or regularities with no physical basis are for Leibniz the coordination of many conscious beings which are kept in relation to one another according to the principles of Continuity and Plenitude. Yet Leibniz, like any published philosopher, believes that his philosophy must influence other minds (as is equally the case with those who deny or ignore free will).

But if this is to happen without direct interaction, the principle of Continuity must be enough to ensure that the prevalence of an idea in one's mind will be matched by a similar development in other persons to whom he is related. By adopting any consistent kind of life, then, one ensures that an equivalent of it will be realized in other minds which are closest to his own by their inner nature and tendency, with or without any specific action to influence them.

If free will is combined with this conception of the self, it would imply that the inner workings are complex enough for there to be a choice among real alternatives in its content. If this were not so, the effective isolation of each monad would still be enough to ensure that it was truly the cause of the action which emanated from it, only in this case it would be lacking in the further perfection of acting from a choice determined by rational judgment. There seems to be nothing in the conception of a "simple substance" which would be inconsistent with this power, so that it is all the more strange that Leibniz does not seem to refer directly to it, especially as he is attempting to formulate an implicitly Christian philosophy. One may argue that free will, in the sense of the monad's ability to be determined from within, is too essential to the construction of this kind of philosophy for Leibniz to have deliberately excluded it.

In this case, each monad, or each of the higher kind among them, would possess a form of causality which is the more powerful in that it does not need to act overtly. Another factor in this causality would be the extent to which the direction of its action is in accord with the inherent nature and purpose of these beings. This would significantly affect the power of the indirect causality involved, and would also throw some light on the social impact of numerous spiritual leaders in history, whose influence was far beyond anything they manifestly did, or even could have done. It also has some bearing on Taoist and Confucian idea of individuals rectifying their world by a rectification of themselves. The denial of direct interaction does not therefore exclude a more subtle and pervasive influence. If the "mediation of God"[36] is requisite for this, it will be so inasmuch as God orders the world according to Continuity: a significant change in one person must therefore induce corresponding changes in others, simply by action of presence, if continuity among beings is unalterable.

In view of Leibniz's disbelief in direct interaction, what he does say about activity deserves special attention. "Outward" action in fact functions as the measure of a being's (inner) perfection. Conversely, passivity is the result of imperfection. As in the earlier discussion, perfection itself is measured solely in terms of the distinctness of the perceptions. The manner in which A acts on B is said to be by A's containing something which can serve as an *a priori* explanation for B. No examples are given to illustrate this, and one cannot expect to find them in the natural sciences, since these do not deal in *a priori* causes.

The use of the word *act* is not appropriate here, as action necessarily implies something taking place in time, whereas logical relations are not temporal at all. Even if a relative distinctness of perception implied a greater inner activity, it still could not literally be an activity "on" anything.

It is not denied that there is interaction among bodies, however, and each monad is related specifically to one body, and thus it is not easy to deny that the monads are affected by these interactions. The real interaction of bodies follows from the idea that "all is a *plenum*." Because of this condition, interactions are inescapable, as there are no voids, and they can spread their effects ever more widely beyond themselves for the same reason. Because of all the linked interactions, only the indistinctness of the perceptions prevents the state of the whole universe from being discerned by any one of its conscious parts.

Strangely, Leibniz says that any increase in the expression of one substance is always conjoined to a diminution in the expression of another, this being presented as an implication of the idea of the *plenum*. These increases and decreases in expression are also movements to greater and lesser perfection, which is again to be understood in terms of distinctness of perception:

> The action of one finite substance on another consists only in the increase in the degree of its expression conjoined with the diminution of that of the other, in as much as God has so formed them that they accommodate themselves to one another.... For it can happen that a change which augments the expression of one diminishes that of the other.[37]

If no efficient causality obtains between different substances, the increase in perfection of one and the decrease in perfection of the other must directly contradict what has just been deduced in regard to Continuity. It implies a competitive relation between all beings on almost all levels, for which there is insufficient evidence, and there is no reason why the gain of one should be the loss of another where nothing material is involved. We have already considered the argument for the exact opposite claim, that an increase in the perfection of one being must result in corresponding increases for other beings.

This idea can only be valid on a very elementary level; for example, the more land on a farm is used for growing potatoes, the less land it will have for other crops, but this is not exactly philosophy. On the intellectual level, it has no relevance. Did Leibniz think that the publication of his ideas caused a reduction in the consciousness of everybody else? Or that the lives of saints made other people worse? At the same time it would render Continuity inoperative, by breaking continuity between beings upon the least exertion by any one of them. In this case, the effect of any change in one individual would always be nullified by an equal and opposite change in another.

According to Leibniz, the idea of the monad excludes direct interaction between minds, or between minds and bodies. As if in support of this, he gives no indication that monads have wills, and suggests no reason why this might be so. Instead, there is the idea that all active relations are owing to God's pre-established harmony, and not to their own causality. But in that case, no individual substance would actually do anything, and this result is no different from absolute determinism. This is a strange result for a philosopher who sought to vindicate religion and justify the ways of God to man. Because of these issues, I cannot follow Leibniz beyond a certain point.

In reality, the monad can easily constitute a microcosm or a world exempt from natural forces without any need for passivity. Having a will, it has power over its own body, and therefore over other bodies as well, indirectly. There is no need to doubt the common-sense assumption that transcendent minds communicate through the use of immanent bodies, since we have no truly adequate reason to think otherwise. There is one reason one might be inclined to think so, however, and that is a desire to minimize a failure to explain causality by claiming that there is really nothing there to be explained.

Neoplatonic Comparisons

Leibniz's idea of each monad reflecting from its own point of view both God and all the other monads can also be shown to be Plotinian, only with the reservation that for Plotinus the soul belongs primarily to the realm of Forms. In a particularly visionary passage he effectively expresses what Leibniz would make one of the main themes of the *Monadology*:

> And each of them contains all within itself, and at the same time sees all in every other, so that everywhere there is all, and all is all and each all, and infinite the glory. The sun, There, is all the stars; and every star, again, is all the stars and the sun. While one manner of being is predominant in each, all are mirrored in every other.[38]

Even the Leibnizian analogy of the mirror is here, besides the recapitulation of the presence of all in all which is so essential to the idea of the monad. Leibniz is therefore not expressing an idea which is purely original to him. If he did not read Plotinus, he could still have acquired the Neoplatonic concepts from his reading of the Scholastics, who knew a paraphrase of the *Enneads* as the "Theology of Aristotle," and Proclus's *Elements of Theology* as Aristotle's "Liber de Causis."

Among other distinctive ideas in this realm, it should be noted that the idea of the "best of all possible worlds" is also a Platonic concept, and Aristotelian besides, inasmuch as according to the *Timaeus* the world is created in order that all things should be as much like the most perfect model as possible. This idea also appears explicitly in the *Enneads*: "Since there is no Universe nobler than this, is it not clear what this must be? A representation carrying down the features of the Intellectual Realm is necessary; there is no other Cosmos than this; therefore there is such a representation."[39]

This again is a consequence of the Principle of Plenitude, which is equally essential to both Leibniz's philosophy and Neoplatonism. It is therefore strange that the idea of the "best of all possible worlds" should be so much identified with Leibniz, who did no more than clearly articulate what was really common to the tradition stemming from both Plato and Aristotle.

It is also interesting to compare what Leibniz says at *Monadology* 83 with what Proclus says in his *Elements*, prop. 195:

> Among other differences which exist between ordinary souls and minds [*esprits*], . . . there is also this: that souls in general are living mirrors or images of the universe of created things, but that minds are also images of the Deity or Author of nature Himself, capable of knowing the system of the universe, and to some extent of imitating it through architectonic ensamples [*echantillons*]. . . .[40]

and:

> Every soul is all things, the things of sense after the manner of an exemplar, and the intelligible things after the manner of an image. . . . Accordingly it pre-embraces all sensible things after the manner of a cause, possessing the rational notions of material things immaterially . . . of extended things without extension; on the other hand it possesses as images the intelligible principles, and has received their Forms. . . . Thus every soul is all that is, the primal orders by participation and those posterior to it in the exemplary mode.[41]

In the first passage, Leibniz draws a distinction among monads between "ordinary souls" and those which have the rank of mind. The former are simply reflectors of the universe to some degree or other, whereas minds are reflectors of both the universe and God.

Their ability to reflect God involves their possession of "architectonic ensamples" which make the mind as it were a small divinity in its own sphere.

These "architectonic ensamples" correspond to the "intelligible things" which the (rational) soul possesses in the manner of an "image" in the second passage—these being the archetypes or Forms, though it is true that Leibniz generally conceives of them in a more materialistic manner. He thought it enough if the primal patterns of all things simply preexisted as microscopically scaled-down versions of themselves, as though this were enough to account for the ways in which things appear to us. In both texts one can clearly see the idea of soul or monad as being in some sense a microcosm, whether solely in regard to cosmic realities or in regard to these and purely intellective ones as well, though Proclus considers only the latter case, because he is concerned only with rational souls.

There is a significant carelessness of terminology in *Mon.* 83, however: it is said that souls in general are "living mirrors or images of the universe of created things." Taken literally, they cannot be images *and* mirrors at the same time, because there is a fundamental difference between an image and the mirror which in some sense creates it. In fact it is the analogy of the mirror which is really intended, as can be seen from what Leibniz says elsewhere—besides which a soul which was no more than an image of other things, such as bodies, would absurdly be beneath the level of material things, and not above them, as souls must be if they are to be anything like the reality which Leibniz speaks of.

The soul "with mind" is nevertheless only an image in relation to the Deity, as in the Proclean passage, since "minds are also images of the Deity or Author of nature Himself," as Leibniz puts it. This is not contradictory, because being an image in regard to Deity is quite consistent with the kind of superiority ascribed to it in relation to nature in the above. This implies that for both Leibniz and Proclus the rational soul is a mediator between the divine and the natural, though Proclus makes this point with greater clarity.

It has already been pointed out that the Identity of Indiscernibles is essentially a Platonic conception. An explicit reference to it appears in Plotinus, in reference to the uniqueness of the First Principle: "There can only be one such being: if there were another, the two (as indiscernible) would resolve into one, for we are not dealing with two corporeal entities" (*Enn.* V, 4, 1). The reason for the application of this to corporeal things has already been given above. Because of these and other assimilations, Leibniz's ideas about identity offer the most natural completion to those of Plato, Plotinus, and Augustine. He is also of exceptional authority because, in the words of William Barrett,

> Leibniz was, to put it bluntly, the best-educated philosopher of his period—and by this I mean educated within philosophy itself.... Generally, indeed, he saw the continuity of Medieval with Greek philosophy and thus had a sense of the unity of Western thought that was lacking in most of his contemporaries.[42]

His assimilation of the Neoplatonic metaphysic is so thorough that he does not need to make conscious applications of it or appeals to it. At the same time, he modifies it with borrowings from mysticism, theology and natural science. Although this gives rise to some apparent confusions between physical and metaphysical speculation, few other philosophers have said so much that was relevant in a constructive manner to a spiritual conception of personal identity.

Notes

1 *Phaedrus*, 249d–250b.

2 *Meno*, 85e.

3 Robert Latta, *Leibniz: The Monadology*, 368 (New Essays).

4 Ibid., 369, *New Essays.*

5 *The Trinity*, Bk. XV, Ch. 12.

6 *Phaedo*, 79 d–e.

7 Latta, *Monadology*, 30.

8 Ibid., 44.

9 Ibid., No. 47, note 75.

10 Leibniz, *Discourse on Metaphysics*, XIV.

11 *Monadology* 1–6.

12 Ibid., 3.

13 Ibid., 7.

14 Introduction, Part II, R. Latta, 37.

15 *Phaedo*, 74e.

16 R. E. Cushman, *Therapeia*, Ch. 6.

17 Paul Henri Michel, *The Cosmology of Giordano Bruno*, 97–98.

18 A. O. Lovejoy, *The Great Chain of Being*, 331–332; also cf. ibid., 254.

19 Latta, *Monadology*, 63n102.

20 Ibid., 72 and 73.

21 *Elements of Theology*, Props. 207–210.

22 Latta, Introduction, 115–17.

23 Ibid., 383–84.

24 *Monadology*, 57.

25 Ibid., 60.

26 *The Idea of Principle in Leibniz*, Appendix I, 364.

27 *Monadology*, 48.

28 *Principles of Nature and Grace*, Sec. 3, p. 409 (Latta ed.).

29 *Individuals*, 121.

30 Ibid., 124.

31 *Monadology*, 11.

32 Ibid., 15.

33 Ibid., 18.

34 Ibid., 61.

35 Ibid., 22.

36 Ibid., 51.

37 Leibniz, *Discourse on Metaphysics*, XV.

38 *Enn.* V, 8, 4.

39 *Enn.* II, 9, 8.

40 *Monadology*, 83.

41 *Elements of Theology*, Prop. 195.

42 *Death of the Soul*, 21–22.

5

An Empirical
Account of Identity

The Subject from a Different Point of View

In the previous chapters identity has been approached in a theoretical manner, one which depends directly on the subsistent reality of the soul. The argument has also been articulated in terms of the Platonic conception of Form and instantiation. But now that the idea of a substantive identity has been accounted for on this basis, we can turn to a different kind of argument for the same conclusion, where the subject is approached from the opposite direction, as it were, so as to derive it from facts which are open to common observation.

Since it is on the empirical level, among the natural manifestations of the person, that problems can arise for the idea of a unitary identity, it is only appropriate that identity should also be deducible on the basis of these diverse appearances. To do this, we shall not need to alter anything which we have affirmed so far, since the one standpoint neither affirms nor denies the other. The difference involved is like that between solving a mathematical problem by means of a formula and doing so by means of a series of approximations.

For example, one could find the area of a circle by analyzing a quadrant of it into a grid of square areas, or else find it from the product of pi (π) and the square of its radius. The latter method is the more elegant, but it requires us to justify the use of this quantity pi, which is far from easy to do. In general, the solution of such problems by means of formulae is bound to involve more complicated assumptions than their solution by cumulative or graphical methods, so their relative strengths and weaknesses roughly balance one another.

The convergence of these two methods reflects the possible convergence between metaphysical and empirical ideas of identity. To demonstrate this it will be necessary to account for the fact that empirical descriptions of identity can often appear to be opposed to real identity, not supportive of it.

Identity in Locke's Essay Concerning Human Understanding

According to Locke, identity results from an act of comparison between something as it exists at one time and place and as it exists at another time and place. A direct correspondence in this regard would thus constitute identity. Bradley would use a similar line of reasoning to show that what constitutes a thing is really ideal by nature, because it is dependent on thought in some such way as this.

On Locke's model, just the continued occupation of a given place will establish identity, any number of other changes notwithstanding, because he takes it that only one thing can fill the same place at any given time. Occupancy of a unique region of space for a continuous period of time would therefore be crucial for identity of a certain kind. From this, Locke concludes that "one thing cannot have two beginnings of existence, nor two things one beginning."[1] Two things cannot exist in the same place at once, any more than can one thing in two different places. This is most clearly the case with regard to material substances or bodies.

However, Locke maintains that we know of three kinds of substance: namely, God, finite intelligences, and bodies. For God there is no problem with identity, because a being who is omnipresent, unchangeable, and without beginning, besides being unique, is not susceptible of any of the difficulties which beset the identities of finite beings. There are no comparable beings with whom He may be confused, and no limits in either time or space which could evoke comparison with other beings or other realities. Although Locke does not seem to notice it, there is a possible clue here to the way in which finite beings may achieve their own identity. If the most absolutely unlimited being is the one whose identity is the most assured, it might well follow that finite beings could realize their identities by pushing back the bounds of their finitude as far as possible, actualizing their potentialities to the fullest extent, and so realizing the degree of infinitude which pertains to their unique natures.

As there are different degrees of infinity, this development of the self could be seen reflected in the infinite extension of a line in relation to a plane, or of a plane to a volume. In general terms, the greater the extension of a consciousness, and the more it comprehends, the more truly individuated it will be, and so much easier to identify. Far from being opposed to individuation, universalization rather increases it by the enrichment of its content.[1a]

Locke observes that each finite being is conditioned by the time and place of its origin for as long as it exists. This goes some way towards accounting for the uniqueness of each being, as these exact combinations of time and place are by definition unrepeatable. The identical place of origin may be repeated at different times, and the identical time of origin may be multiplied at a number of different places, but never both together. Moreover, if the various parts of space and time have intrinsic qualities, these qualities must be shared by whoever or whatever originates in them, in addition to the qualities of the physical locality.

God, finite intelligences, and material bodies differ mutually to such an extent that all three can occupy one and the same part of space or act in it. This does not apply to the intelligences and bodies among themselves, however, as bodies exclude one another from the same space, and minds exclude one another by their own form of individuation. Failing the latter condition, there would be no guarantee that the thoughts one is thinking are one's own and not those of some other mind. In practice, we identify our thoughts as being our own by the elements they have in common with our past thoughts, and their relevance to our present needs.

Material and Spiritual Substances

Locke observes that if two bodies could occupy the same place, so could any number of others at the same time, and in fact all of them could do so, and the same thing applies to the individual "thought spaces" of different minds. The principle of individuation which disallows this is said to be existence itself. Existence binds each entity to a given time and place, with its unique origin as already observed, and its relation to differentiation appears in its derivation from *ex-stare*, "to stand out." One could say that Being means Being-different.

But the continuing identity of a body or material substance depends on the fixity of the number of atoms of which it is composed. This identity is lost with either a loss or gain of atoms which is large in proportion to the original quantity, though the component particles can often be rearranged without affecting the identity, as for example in fixed quantities of gases or liquids, whose molecules are in a constant state of random motion.

For spiritual substances, the criteria for identity are less simple, however. This kind of entity can be said to have parts only in the sense of having internal variety and complexity, but unlike with the material substance, these "parts" are not arranged externally to one another. Rather, to continue the spatial analogy, it is as though they were all joined in a single center with each one in contact with all the others. Unlike material substances, their conscious powers and activities cannot mutually exclude each other, but rather fuse without confusion. Consequently the addition or subtraction of such "parts" from this kind of substance cannot have the same effect as with material substances, besides which they are not continuously present like atoms, molecules or cells, but are often only there in potentiality.

Thus spiritual substances are said to be characterized by "motion" and "thought," these being both forms of succession. No matter how much is contained in these successions, the different elements involved in them are external to the substance *qua* experience, such that the substance sustaining them may have either few or many of them without *its* existence being affected. Like both material and spiritual substances themselves, these series of thoughts and motions are differentiated from one another by the different times at which they begin, as also are the separate parts of their contents. Locke maintains that the difference from material substances which this involves begins at a lower level than that of consciousness, namely that of the living organism.

We are given the example of the growth of a tree from a small plant, and how the tree may be lopped when fully grown; the great variations in its material bulk over time do not compromise the identity of the tree. It is shown that the idea of identity is not applied to the material parts of organisms as it is to inanimate things. In the present example, the identity is said to lie in the organization of the parts which directs their development into leaves and bark and so forth. This, together with animal and human life, consists essentially of a certain organizing activity, teleologically ordered to a single goal, in conjunction with which a continual stream of material constituents is assimilated and distributed. This points to an essential difference between the identities of the bodies of living organisms and those of material bodies, as discussed above.[1b]

Any attempt to equate a living being with its material constituents in the various stages of life from embryo to maturity would raise the problem as to how one could find a single identity running through such very different things: foetus, child, man. The different bodily forms which obtain in the course of one life differ from one another as widely as do the bodily forms of so many different persons at any one time. Therefore, by using the body as a basis of identity, we could in principle confuse one person with another. This shows that these physical states are insufficient for the purpose by themselves. In addition, we need an observed continuity between them, whether they be our own states or those of someone else.

Man and Person

At the other extreme, if identity derives from the soul alone, persisting through all the physical changes of the body, it might as well persist through the change from one person to another, as reincarnationists believe, as the differences between individuals need not be any greater than those between the different states of one individual. Attention must therefore focus on the single process of organic development, the continuity of which manifests a given individual. Such a process is unique and absolutely untransferable for the reason given above, and is therefore of major importance for determining a unique identity. The idea of the soul with which this assorts best is the Aristotelian, as it comes very close to being just this organizing principle, which is peculiar to one individual form alone, and which is inseparable from the body which it sustains.

Locke goes on to argue that the commonly accepted way in which the word "man" is understood shows that it is in fact just this idea of living organism with a specific form organizing its matter, which is everywhere accepted. He offers the example of a parrot which could hold an intelligent conversation, without that causing anyone to think of calling it a man. Conversely, though some human person should have no more intelligence than an animal, he is still called "man," whereas one is no nearer to giving this name to a parrot which displayed a human intelligence, if such a thing were possible.

But there are other ways of explaining our reactions to these things. Many persons may in fact be unthinking enough to suppose that the human physical form is our essential reality if they were asked to say what this reality was, but our real conviction lies deeper. It may rather be that the belief that man is defined by his intelligence is so deep-seated that a human being with no intelligence is felt instinctively to be an impossibility, and that it is this which makes us unable to deny that such a person is human. This could also be explained in terms of the human state as being an intelligence incarnate, an *enhylos logos*, as discussed earlier.

The human form signals the presence of this intelligence in so many cases that we cannot break the association, even where it may appear inappropriate. This same emotional conviction about ourselves accounts equally for our inability to apply the name "man" to a parrot, even if it should manifest a human intelligence. Even if all parrots spoke rationally all the time, they would be taken for a race of "rational animals," as Locke puts it, but not as human beings, for "it is not the idea of a thinking rational being alone that makes the idea of man in most people's sense, but of a body so and so shaped, joined to it. . . ."[2]

If this reaction is explained in the way indicated above, we shall not be bound to accept Locke's conclusion as to how the physical human form should constitute human identity. In the *Philebus,* Plato explains why there is no sort of good that anyone would accept at the price of losing mind and with it the ability to know what good we in fact had.[3] This placing of mind in a unique category clearly does not cohere with our giving the human physical form an equivalent status in identity. The solution to this conflict may be to say that being human does not result from either our rational or animal natures, but from some third function which unites them. In this connection, one should recall what we said earlier about the symbolism of head and heart,[4] where the lower of the two forms the center.

When the discussion proceeds to the meaning of *person,*[5] the state of self-awareness is considered essential. This is expressed as "the sameness of a rational being," and is also a reference to what has elsewhere been called the "second-order" consciousness which observes the acts of perception and emotion in the primary consciousness. The continuity of this higher or more inward consciousness is the connecting thread which unites all the diverse elements of life's experiences. This is also what is expressed through the "I think" in Kant's synthetic unity of apperception as it embraces the manifold of self-intuition.[5a]

The Problem of Self-Continuity

The identity of the person extends as far back in time as this self-awareness, because memory is conceived as essential to it. The temporal continuity of this identity is interrupted by both sleep and forgetfulness, but it has another kind of continuity which is maintained by recollection. This self-awareness is used to define the person, "it being impossible for anyone to perceive, without perceiving that he does perceive." Exceptions to this occur in dreams and in some states of inattention while one is awake, but these in fact underline the importance of the two levels of consciousness in the make-up of true personality. In the last quotation, perception cannot be understood in quite the same way each time, because the perception that one is perceiving is of a more subtle kind than the perception of sensory objects and the content of feelings; but with this reservation it constitutes an important observation about the conscious person.

But the constant interruptions of consciousness on both subtle and sensory levels mean that we never have anything like the whole series of our past actions in mind at any given time. Sound sleep and close attention to present matters equally make us oblivious of our past selves, and it is in this connection that Locke draws a distinction between the question of whether to speak of an identical *person* is present or an identical *substance.* The question whether we are now the same thinking being who experienced something we remember is the question whether we are still the same substance. For the purpose of personal identity this is said not to matter, on the grounds that different substances can be united into one person by a single consciousness shared by them, as are the different physical parts of one animal by the same life. Similarly, the continual change in composition of a living body remains subject to bodily unity because of its continuing life.

Personal identity, Locke contends, is comprised of a single continuous consciousness which may reside in a succession of immaterial substances as easily as in a single one. This is to assume that the substance is no more than a container, rather as the regions of space appear to be for the objects in them, and to exclude the idea that it gives a quality of its own to the consciousness. It also involves the assumption that consciousness is not inherent in the substance, so that this consciousness could be transferred from one substance to another without being changed. Passage of time and change of substance thus would be equally unable to disrupt the unity of a continuous consciousness.

As Locke expresses it,

> And therefore those who place thinking in an immaterial substance only . . . must show why personal identity cannot be preserved in the change of immaterial substances, or variety of particular immaterial substances, as well as animal identity is preserved in the change of *material* substances. . . .[6]

This view of substance and identity overlooks a major problem raised by the transition of consciousness from one substance to another; if it can effect this transition by itself, does it really need a substance to inhere in before and after, if it does not need a substance during the transition? But if in fact it cannot exist without a substance, we should have to interpose a third substance C to sustain it while it was no longer in A and not yet in B. Likewise, we may have to posit further substances D and E to mediate between A and C, between C and B, and so on.

On this basis, one might well doubt whether consciousness can really enter or vacate an immaterial substance at all. Kant held that it was only by virtue of substance that change or transition of any kind could be experienced. This would imply that the vacation of substance by consciousness means losing the condition under which transition could take place at all: "Origin and extinction are not changes of that which originates or becomes extinct, ... only the permanent is subject to change"; the rest of this passage has been quoted more fully earlier.[7]

When Kant speaks of substances here, he does not explicitly distinguish between material and immaterial substances, but from what is said in the above, it is clear that this is a question of a substance in which perception of change can take place, which identifies it as immaterial. The principle enunciated here, to the effect that only the unchanging can register change, tells against Locke's idea of the movement of consciousness from one substance to another. This could not happen without a transition through no-substance, while the absence of such an interval would mean that the two substances were in fact one. This might be avoided by having a third substance to contain the two substances between which the consciousness was migrating, which would ensure that the change could be experienced. But in this case, the third substance would be the only effective one, and the two others would be without meaning.

For this reason, we do not have to accept Locke's hypothesis that "if the same consciousness ... can be transferred from one thinking substance to another, it will be possible that two thinking substances may make but one person."[8]

After this, Locke proceeds to the converse of the above question, namely, whether two persons could exist consecutively in one and the same substance. The principle of change and substance taught by Kant does not apply here, as the hypothesis is that all the consciousness that one being has of its past may be irretrievably lost, and replaced by another sequence of recollections. The transition from the former to the latter state could presumably take place in one and the same substance. This, it is said, is something which is believed in by "all those who hold pre-existence," that is, reincarnation. Locke emphasizes the fact that no one is able to remember any of the past actions of those whom they might be reincarnations of. This memory, being essential to identity, must be present, and without it, the case for reincarnation apparently fails.

But we may also be able to exclude reincarnation by falsifying the hypothesis of successive consciousnesses in the same substance. If none of these consciousnesses has any direct access to any of the others, as is the case with reincarnations, the situation within this substance would be indiscernible from that of two separate consciousnesses, each in a different substance. Since this idea gives us no basis on which to distinguish two consciousnesses in two substances from two consciousnesses supposedly in one substance, nothing results from putting the two into one substance. We may therefore conclude that the disjunction of the two consciousnesses does after all mean two different substances as well, and that the notion of mutually exclusive consciousnesses in one substance is unintelligible.

The fact that reincarnation obviously implies a change of body, even though the soul were not to change at all, is also used by Locke as an argument against it, and as a means of distinguishing between person and man. An example used is that of the soul of a prince reincarnating (still conscious of himself) in the body of a cobbler when the soul of the latter departs. To everyone but himself, this would make him just the same cobbler as before, and so the body must have an important part to play in our identity, even though it is not as essential as an unbroken span of consciousness. This change would mean that the prince was the same person without remaining the same man. What constitutes the man clearly cannot reincarnate, and accordingly nothing like a complete personal identity can be transmitted by it.

What constitutes the person, however, is conceived here as the possession of the consciousness of past and present actions together, regardless of the relation to substance. No intrinsic time-limit can be placed on this span of consciousness, which would serve to establish one's existence over a thousand-year period if only memory were to reach that far, just as surely as our memory of what we did a minute ago assures us of our existence then.[9] Besides, the body's part in our identity is still included here, as the full person is "that with which the consciousness of this present thinking thing can join itself makes the same person and is one self with it, and nothing else. . . ."[10] Such is the compound being which can attribute all its recollected actions to itself.

But that this "train of perceptions" can really be united by one identity is attacked by Hume on the grounds that this identity is never experienced as the perceptions are. (This need mean no more than the commonplace that we do not experience a bright patch of color in the same way as we perceive the fact that we do thus experience it.) As Locke has said that personal identity does not lie in an "identity of substance"[11] but rather in an "identity of consciousness," his definition is open to empiricist criticism on the grounds that conscious unity or identity does not make sense without substance, and so should not be retained when the role of substance has been made equivocal at best. Thus Locke's conception of the self, if taken a stage further, would end by dissolving it.

Hume admits that a kind of unity can arise from a mere "customary association,"[12] such that if a number of facts are always recalled together, imagination will create intrinsic relations between them. Subsequently, this subjective unification will be projected into the recollections themselves, creating a false sense of objective identity. Certainly, if personal identity thus resulted from nothing more than "a union in the imagination" applied to things having no real bond between them, it would be only a case of an *ens rationis* which would have no personal meaning or value. It is probable that Locke is at fault here in downgrading the role of substance while tacitly retaining it, intentionally or not, and that the only consistent conclusion would be the dispersion into multiplicity which Hume introduces, if substance were untenable.

However, the faculty of imagination is not, as such, a "perception" any more than is substance, besides which it must have some kind of central coordinating role in order to form the subjective impression of unity. This would mean that it could not be one more reality on a level with sense-impressions, as Hume would require, but must rather belong to some unitary power of the self which Hume's argument was meant to rule out. There is a dependence of multiplicity on unity which makes the latter almost impossible to exclude, and this will be relevant in our more detailed treatment of Hume on identity later on.

From Locke's definitions, personal identity would depend largely on the second-order consciousness which cognizes each successive act of empirical consciousness, this being the awareness that it is we who walk when we walk, we who see the sky when we see the sky, and so on. Because of this, it could follow that it is part of the essence of each moment of consciousness that it should comprise a perception of equality between something essential to itself at that moment and at the previous moment. (This could not be the same thing as the second-order consciousness alone.) There would then result a knowledge of self-identity from this on-going linkage of perceived equalities, as the idea appears in the treatment of personal identity by Joseph Butler in *The Analogy of Religion*.

A Condition for Veridical Memory

As to what exactly it is that should be essential to the self, we may begin simply with its content at any given moment. While analytical treatments of this, such as Bradley's, show that this cannot define the self,[13] it can still serve self-unity provided short enough time intervals are taken for the perception of equality to be applied. Content cannot change very much at short intervals, and one only needs a perception of a general equivalence between successive short intervals for there to be grounds for identity on this basis.

This relation of successive moments falls short of actual identity, but its closeness to it is important because of the proportion of the content which in fact is identical. Although there is no complete equality of the content as a whole from moment to moment, it approaches completeness when the intervals become very small, besides which there is the self-perception of the perceiver himself.

The latter can be seen to be identical with himself *qua* perceiver in any previous moment. Thus the second-order consciousness can perceive the percipient being over and above the contents of perception in the first-order consciousness, and the identity of each state of the empirical self with the next is seen just as one sees the congruence of one triangle with another. In this way the identity of the individual self is dependent on the identity, or at least the uniform operation, of the rational reflexive consciousness which is set over it.

We do not need to arrive at actual time instants for this purpose, as all we need are time intervals which can be defined as being as short as required. The perception of the equality of the self with itself at successive moments according to Joseph Butler's use of the idea can be illustrated by means of these successive temporal states A, B, C, D, E, in which our arrival at B is accompanied by the perception that $B = A$; and where our arrival at C is accompanied by the perception $C = B$; and at D, $D = C$, and so on. The self at, say, N would most probably also be able to perceive his identity with A, B, C, and so on, though this cannot be insisted upon. Full personal identity, however, comprises the sum total of all these serial acts of self-identification.

The use of the extremely short time interval in the above presents the easiest possible task for the memory, with the result that it can be taken as veridical when it spans such short intervals. In this way we escape the difficulty in theories of identity which are based on long-term memory, which cannot be assumed to be veridical because of the ways in which mistaken memories can occur.

In this connection, one should note the analogy between this conception of identity and that of a prolonged process of proof in symbolic logic. If the premises and all the various stages of the proof are self-evident, no matter how many of them there are, we can accept the final result, even if we do not remember the earlier steps of the proof. Possibilities of mistakes in logical processes may arise from the different and unfamiliar nature of stages in its content, but in this respect they differ from the moment-by-moment identity process, because in the latter all the component steps are the same—e.g., P, not not-P, not not-(not not-P), and so on—and this uniformity of operation gives us an additional reason for taking the memory to be free from error in this process.

This conception of identity is also an answer to claims that some individual has become "a different person," for example where a former criminal becomes a good citizen. During the transition from the former state to the latter, the process of self-identification from moment to moment goes on just as uniformly as at times when no change in the personality takes place. This conception of identity is not tied to content. It shows that it is only possible to become a "different person" from the perspective of external observation, particularly where that observation is frequently interrupted.

The essential idea here agrees with that of Locke to the extent of being based on memory, but differs in being based upon the shortest span of short-term memory rather than the long-term memory. It also removes the difficulty as to how one can believe oneself to be the same being as one was when in infancy, most of which one no longer remembers. Even if one could now remember nothing of the earliest part of one's life, it is enough that it was remembered in times subsequent to it, and that those subsequent states are now remembered. In this way the present state is joined to the earliest one as surely as the last link of a chain is joined to the first, no direct contact between the extremes being needed for them to form a continuum.

Moreover, Locke's idea of identity's dependence on conscious recollection is criticized by Butler on the grounds that this consciousness *presupposes* identity:

> But though consciousness of what is past does thus ascertain our personal identity to ourselves, yet to say, that it *makes* personal identity,... is to say that a person has not existed a single moment, nor done one action, but what he can remember; indeed, none but what he reflects upon. And one should really think it self-evident, that consciousness of personal identity presupposes, and therefore cannot constitute, personal identity: any more than knowledge, in any other case, can constitute truth, which it presupposes.[14]

To try to derive identity from consciousness is therefore to reverse the true order of things, and is even question-begging.

An Empirical Account of Identity

Implications for Moral Responsibility

That identity should thus be independent of the longer-term forms of memory has an effect on questions of legal guilt. If Locke's conception prevailed, it would not be possible to try anyone for a crime they did not remember committing, even though proof was to hand, as one would not be able to say that the same person was involved, even if the same man or woman was. But if identity does not depend on long-term memory, this objection will not arise, and it would seem to be the more realistic position to take.

Besides criminal cases, there are those like the soldier who is a victim of shell-shock, such that he is unable to remember having fought for his country. According to the Lockean conception, this should make his identity too doubtful for him to be able to qualify for a pension. In a more general case, no one expects that the payment of their salaries should depend on how fully they remember what they did to earn them. Both for good and bad we cannot ignore the principle that actions continue to produce their effects, both for the agent and the world, no matter whether they are remembered or not. In regard to legal procedure, the disallowance of the accused's memory is in one way a normal assumption, for if the accused pleads not guilty he has *ipso facto* no memory of committing the crime, granted the innocence he is presumed to have at the outset.

This contrasts with what Locke says in Ch. XXVII, 18–20, where the identity of the person does not extend to that of the man, but only that of the person having the legal responsibility, since personhood and culpability are equally linked by Locke to conscious continuity and memory. But actions which took place when one was irresponsible through drugs or drink are not in the same category as those which are forgotten after having been done with deliberation. Contrary to Locke in this regard, the real issue is not the fact that the accused does not remember his past actions, but rather the reasons why he cannot remember them.

Where Locke justifies the punishment of those who do not remember what they have done, for instance because of drunkenness, it is because the action committed can be proved to have taken place, whereas the absence of any memory of it can not. This is consistent with an identity based on consciousness, but it ignores the fact that memories are not as important as the actual experiences at specific times and places they derive from. Otherwise it would be possible to replicate persons merely by replicating their mental contents, as in the supposed case of reincarnation discussed in the next section.

Identity and Mental Data: a Paradox

Another weakness in Locke's idea of personal identity is mentioned by A. J. Lyon in his quotation of an argument of Bernard Williams.[15] The context relates to reincarnation, but it is also highly relevant to the question of how far consciousness constitutes a person:

> If A.L. might logically become Socrates reborn by taking on (by whatever means) Socrates' mental characteristics and memory data, then somebody else, B.M., might logically do the same thing, at the same time. Then if this would make A.L. the same person as Socrates, B.M. would also be the same person as Socrates, and so A.L. would be the same person as B.M., which is impossible, since *ex hypothesi* they are different people.

Such considerations point towards a demonstration that Locke's idea is contradictory. Suppose an elderly general can remember capturing an enemy standard when he was a young officer, but cannot remember being beaten when a schoolboy. On Locke's reasoning, the general is the same person as the young officer, but not the same person as the schoolboy. However, if the young officer remembers being beaten as a schoolboy, he must be the same person as that schoolboy, and as he has already been admitted to be the same person as the general, it follows that the general too is the same person as the schoolboy, as two beings identical with a third are identical with one another. But this contradicts the original deduction from Locke's definition of identity.

This argument fits very well with our observations concerning the moment-by-moment formation of identity derived from Joseph Butler, for which recollection across longer periods of time is not necessary. Locke himself says that "nothing but consciousness can unite remote existences into the same person...,"[16] but he ignores the possibility of different ways in which this may occur. He also ignores the association of the person with all the unique combinations of time and place from which his memories derive and which can therefore never be duplicated, unlike the memories themselves.

This idea of personal identity based on the perception by the perceiver of his own successive states does not amount to a full knowledge of the self, because it results in knowledge *that* the self exists, not knowledge of *what* the self is, apart from its purely general attributes of being a perceiver and a knower. An individual nature is demonstrated, but not a unique individuality. This limitation is also indicated in a treatment of self-knowledge by John Scotus Eriugena: "if that interior idea which is in the human mind constitutes the substance of the things of which it is the idea, it follows that the very idea by which man knows himself may be considered his substance."[17] In the same place, Augustine is quoted as saying something similar about the substance of the self and its self-knowledge: "For the knowledge by which an intellectual and rational creature understands himself in himself is, as it were, a kind of second substance of him, by which he knows only that he knows, and is, and wills, but not what he is."[18]

The self-knowledge referred to here is of the kind which I have assigned to the "second-order" consciousness which knows the empirical consciousness. It extends itself through successive moments like a connective thread, and in this respect it differs from Locke's idea of identity, which requires memory extending over longer periods of time. As with Locke, it is a function of consciousness, but in a quite different way. The self, knowing that he is, and knowing that he knows himself, has therein two simple forms of knowledge whose self-verifying action is extended in time almost automatically. The unity of the person is hereby shown to have a transcendental cause under which even his most widely differing states are integrated.

The Effects of Quasi-Memory

Butler's criticism of Locke's idea of identity is examined by D. Parfit in *Reasons and Persons*,[19] with reference to the idea that memories, or consciousness of identity, must presuppose that identity, just as much as consciousness of being alive presupposes being alive. Parfit states that Butler's objection is still not answered by the modification to Locke's position which he himself has suggested. Even if one substitutes continuity of memory for single memories, and generalizes this to a "Relation R" which includes other kinds of psychological continuity, it is clear that there must still be something which possesses the continuity of existence which one is conscious of.

But Parfit claims that the effectiveness of Butler's answer depends on a concept of memory whereby one can remember only one's own experiences. Such a position is perfectly acceptable to common sense, but it can be criticized in regard to cases which may be impossible technically, but not physically or logically. For this purpose, Parfit introduces the concept of "quasi-memory." It is in some sense possible that the memories of one person could be transferred to another, perhaps by the treatment of a certain part of the brain with recorded brain-waves from the corresponding part of someone else's brain.

The question of quasi-memories is in any case relevant in the realm of the paranormal, where clairvoyance and apparent evidence for reincarnation are involved. There are well-known cases of individuals (such as Peter Hurkos) with psychic powers by which, it is claimed, they can participate in the memories of other persons simply by associating with them. Such possibilities are significant in this context because the relevance of alleged memories of past lives is closely dependent on the assumption that one cannot have memories except of one's own experiences. On the other hand, a transfer of memories by psychical means would create a kind of evidence for things which had not happened to oneself at all.

The conditions given for quasi-memory are as follows: (1) I seem to remember having an experience; (2) Someone did have this experience; and (3) my apparent memory is causally dependent, in the right kind of way, on that past experience. Condition (3) can be met whether the causal connection is physical, as by a brain operation, or owing to hypnosis or to extra-sensory perception.

There could be a problem of definition here, because the word *remember* implies essentially the presentation of something *again*. If there is such a repetition of anything which happens to someone other than oneself, this supposed repetition will be appearing for the first time if it arises in someone who never had the original. Such a thing would merge with the vivid imaginary experiences which are normally acquired from imaginative literature. Though we prefix it with "quasi," such things should not really be called memories at all, if we kept to the strict definition of the word. In this case, it would not be correct to include memories of things which have actually befallen one as a special class among quasi-memories, as Parfit does.[20] One person's memory may become an original experience for someone else, but "pseudo-memory" would be a better name for this.

Nevertheless, quasi-memories are in principle verifiable because they could be checked against the memories of the person from whom they were transferred. They could, as Parfit says, give us knowledge of other lives "from the inside." But if they were mistaken for normal memories, they would of course give rise to the belief that they were of one's own actions. However, the point of view of the original observer in the quasi-memory can easily be substituted for that of the third party who is contemplating it now. Provided one knows about quasi-memories, and can apply this idea to some of the things which purport to be one's own memories, one need not be deceived by them.

Where Butler's argument is concerned, it can now be maintained that continuity of memory is no grounds for taking all its contents to be the experience of only one person. Provided the memories show continuity, the unity of memory might even supersede that of personal identity. But this is just where the main difficulty lies. How can we hope to find any continuity between our memories of what we ourselves have done and our quasi-memories of what other persons have done? No examples are given to show how any such continuity could be achieved; Parfit speaks only of "overlapping strands of strong connectedness"[21] to provide the continuity, but this is an abstract idea with no practical applications, and it is hard to see how the contents of the memories in question can be more than merely juxtaposed.

If our quasi-memories were continuous among themselves, this would reveal to the fullest degree their lack of continuity as a whole with our own memory-series. Personal identity could not credibly be built up from such diverse materials. For this reason, this answer to Butler's argument is not so effective after all. Only if the quasi-memories could blend imperceptibly with the rest would it be so, and that seems not to be practicable. For example, how would someone who was convinced of the truth of, say, Heidegger's philosophy cope with the thoughts of someone who thought it to be untrue? Similarly, someone who was fond of cats might have to cope with "memories" of kicking cats. Possibilities of conflict naturally outnumber those of harmony, and if there were a "strong connectedness" among these things, it could only intensify the conflict.

The Unity of the Self

Parfit also suggests another interpretation of Butler's objection. It could equally well be taken to mean that the identity our memory makes us aware of is a fact separate from our remembering, which is something more than the continuity of our physical and psychological condition: "We are aware that each of us is a persisting subject of experiences, a separately existing entity that is not our brain or body. And we are aware that our own continued existence is, simply, the continued existence of this subject of experiences."[22]

One fact in support of this is that our self-experience is always a unity, whereas body and brain constitute a constantly changing composite, and so could never be equated with the former. Something which is only a relative unity of parts cannot be the same as something which is *per se* unitary. However, Parfit questions whether our memory really confirms this, and whether we have any direct awareness of our separate selfhood.

It should be noted that direct awareness is an awkward thing to challenge, because its presence or absence should be self-evident. There is certainly no point in denying it on the grounds that we do not have means of proving it, because if it were the subject of a proof, it could not then be direct. Besides the "subject of experiences," there is also the characteristic disposition of our will. This forms our teleological identity, and is open to direct awareness if anything is, although Parfit makes no mention of it. The typical direction of our will defines our individuality as much for other persons as for ourselves, in some respects even more than our physical appearance.

What Parfit is questioning is the idea that the subject of all our experiences is "a separately existing entity" apart from the brain and the body. Introducing the passage which he quotes from Reid, Parfit illustrates the unitary nature of personhood from the fact that no physical member can ever be found to constitute it:

> The amputated member is no part of his person, otherwise it would have a right to a part of his estate . . . it would be entitled to a share in his merit and demerit, which is manifestly absurd. A person is something indivisible, and is what Leibniz calls a *monad*.[23]

It is true that the absence of a physical basis for self-unity does not automatically prove the existence of a non-physical unifier, which I shall argue for further on. Reid's view is disputed by Parfit on the grounds that body and brain enter into everything we think:

> My personal identity therefore implies the continued existence of that indivisible thing that I call myself. Whatever this self may be, it is something which thinks, and deliberates, and resolves, and acts, and suffers. I am not thought, I am not action, I am not feeling; I am something that thinks and acts and suffers.[24]

Now if we deny that this subject is a separately existing entity, the effect of our denial is to efface the distinction between the subject and any one of its determinations, such as feelings or volitions, or things suffered. What typifies all these transitory modifications of the self is precisely that none of them is an independently existing entity. A pain, thought or volition, though it is a separate entity, has no kind of independent existence, but is always in a dependent relation to the subject. Consequently, if we affirm that the subject itself has no independent existence, like its thoughts and feelings, we are, firstly, ignoring a distinction which is perfectly intelligible, as we never confound the subject with its conscious states in practice.

Secondly, it seems that our denial of the subject's independent existence is not justified by reference to any more truly substantive reality, in contrast to which its unreality could be seen, rather as the supposed reality of our subjective being shows up the ephemerality of its different states. There ought to be a substance S, of which the subject himself could be seen to be a transitory modification, analogously to a feeling in the subject. If there is any such S, Parfit says nothing of it, and it seems that no one knows of any such thing.

But in that case, our denial of the independent existence of the subject is essentially dogmatic. In the absence of substance S we have no occasion to try to put the subject on the same level as its own transitory states. If thoughts and feelings are known to be dependent realities only, and the subject itself is at least *prima facie* independent in being, we can only doubt the subject for the sake of an experiment in doubt. It is well enough to argue in the abstract that something P is not an X, but the argument can hardly be conclusive unless one can instance some other kind of thing Q which undoubtedly is X, and which excludes P. If, for example, the paradigm case of this entity were a material thing like a paving stone or an apple, it would be only too clear that the non-material subject could not be included. However, this option is not presented, possibly because there is no source of convincing examples.

Whether Self is Experienced

The next argument concerns the question as to whether each of us is directly aware of himself as a Cartesian Ego, a persisting subject of experience. The first objection to this is simply that Parfit himself does not think that he has any such direct awareness, and so presumably neither do most other people. A lack of this kind of self-awareness is a part of certain kinds of handicap which occur on all levels of intelligence, and provides no basis for conclusions about minds in general. In any case, to argue from a lack of personal experience is to make too much depend on a negative. Even if it could be shown that the great majority have no such experience, it is still a kind of experience which one might expect to be possible for someone with the training of a philosopher, just as the trained musician is aware of many things in classical music which escape the attention of the general public.

An Empirical Account of Identity

If a philosopher in fact is not aware of himself as a permanent subject, this may well result from the way in which his mind is habitually used. This is possible because of a peculiarity in the nature of knowledge and the different ways in which we are free to engage in it. According to E.F. Schumacher, there are four distinct realms among which knowledge can be divided without remainder: (1) "what is going on in my own inner world," (2) "What is going on in the inner world of other beings?," (3) "What do I look like in the eyes of other beings?," and (4) "What do I observe in the world around me?"[25]

There is nothing to compel us to keep up any parity between these four realms; in fact, we can concentrate almost entirely on realm (4) without causing ourselves any immediate problems, and this is what scientific thinkers generally do. Philosophers who treat philosophy as a refined form of natural science think in the same way, and accordingly find that the other three realms, especially realm (1), seem unreal through the lack of mental activity in them. But there is no intellectual justification for this, because it is part of the essence of philosophy that it is concerned with knowledge *per se,* and not just a subdivision of it, however important. Attempts to ignore this are in reality regressive in tendency, since they would take philosophy back to what it was in its Presocratic beginnings when it was still not separate from natural science.

In view of the above, it appears that doubts about our ability to know the self as an independent entity arise from a one-dimensional conception of knowledge and a consequent failure to assimilate what can be done to achieve such self-knowledge. In this connection, Schumacher quotes W.T. Stace[26] concerning a meditation practice which seems to be common to all cultures, based on fixing one's concentration on a simple object or thought, so as to finally exclude all others, and even come to have no object at all:

> One would suppose *a priori* that consciousness would then entirely lapse and one would fall asleep or become unconscious. But the introspective mystics—thousands of them all over the world—unanimously assert that they have attained to this complete vacuum of particular mental contents, but what then happens is quite different from a lapse into unconsciousness. On the

contrary, what emerges is a state of pure consciousness . . . it has no content except itself.

One need not be perfect in this technique to be able to experience how the non-empirical consciousness can be approached, as the effects of any state of deep concentration can show what is involved in this. Stace also relates this to experience of the self:

> One may also say that the mystic gets rid of the empirical ego whereupon the pure ego, normally hidden, emerges into the light. The empirical ego is a stream of consciousness. The pure ego is the unity which holds the manifold of the stream together.[27]

In the light of such experience, there is not much use in arguing as Parfit does, on the basis of our average, everyday consciousness that "Such awareness [of separately existing subjects of experience] cannot in fact be distinguished from our awareness of mere psychological continuity. Our experiences give us no reason to believe in these entities."[28] If we confine our experiences within certain limits, this will of course be a statement of the obvious.

As Stace indicates, the distinction between the self and "awareness of mere psychological continuity" is precisely what meditation techniques serve to reveal. At higher levels of concentration, we have power to control the quantity of our conscious contents, and so to approach the ground and medium of their connection. This is at the opposite extreme from the state of absorption in the observable world, referred to as realm (4) in the schema above. We are not naturally compelled to know only the "empirical ego," as Stace calls it, and so a direct knowledge of the independently existing self is always a possibility.

The Question of "Branch Line" Identity

In connection with what he calls "the branch line case," Parfit argues that even if it is admitted that we have direct awareness that we are separate entities, it would not be conclusive. This is because it is logically (though not practically) possible that there could be an exact replica of oneself somewhere else, doing the same things and thinking the same thoughts. If, then, someone says to himself, "I exist," it is possible that the same thing could be being thought by his replica. Now while this could also be the expression of a direct experience in the replica, it clearly would not be indicative of the existence of the man whose replica it was.

However, the idea of Replica or Identical Copy is far from being a simple idea, and it gives rise to at least three distinct possibilities. The first case is where it is in effect a perfect clone of oneself, living an independent life in this world. Being a real and separate person, the clone's thoughts and actions have no connection with one's own, so that no matter how often one may apply the *Cogito* argument to one's own existence, there is no reason why the clone should ever do so. Clearly, one can see that this form of the Replica is of no use for the above argument.

The second case is where oneself and one's replica live the same life, with all the same actions and thoughts. The conditions for this to be physically possible conflict with the natural conditions of life, for if we were simply in different parts of the same world, we should have to be occupied with different things. In order really to do and think the same things, we would need to have the same homes, family, possessions, and environment. That in turn would call for parallel universes, which again is not logically impossible. Suppose it is so, and two identical lives unfold in parallel; but the problem now is that, given this perfect equality, we can no longer know who is imitating whom. The "I exist" will now be thought by two equally real beings, in whom the duplication of it need not make it any less true. This conception of the replica is therefore also of no use.

The third case is where one's replica is causally determined to do and think the same as oneself by one's selfsame actions and thoughts. Here, at last, it is clear that if I should think, "I exist," the corresponding thought in my replica will be a falsehood. But a replica of this kind, necessary as it is for the objection against our direct experience of self-being, has one fundamental flaw. *I myself am not imitating anyone;* if my replica is of the kind which slavishly imitates me, therefore, it cannot be a true replica of *me.* Such a replica is therefore logically self-contradictory, and not just technically impossible.

There are other cases of conscious duplication of the knowledge of one's own existence which are owing to insanity, as where Napoleon's knowledge of his existence is copied in the mind of a madman thinking: "I am Napoleon." This shows that duplication of a mental act cannot, in itself, cast doubt on its unique reference to the self. There is, in fact, no reason why the thoughts of our automaton-replica should count for any more in this respect than those of the madman. One's own "I exist" would be guaranteed by one's being sane as much as by one's not being an automatic imitator. All this indicates that "branch line" identity is not one which should be taken seriously.

This is not the only way in which our identity could possibly be multiplied, however. Locke argues that what appears to be the single conscious self could in fact be a series of different ones, each transferring all its contents to the next.[29] Each such new entity, having the memories of the previous ones, could believe that these made up its own history:

> I grant, were the same consciousness the same individual action, it could not [be transferred]; but, it being but a present representation of a past action, why it may not be possible that that may be represented to the mind which really never was, will remain to be shown.

Parfit states that memories and all other psychological features could be passed on from one conscious entity to another without our being aware of the fact. Whatever was passed on would be accepted by each new entity as its own life-story. The peculiar thing about this argument is that it is almost exactly the same as an argument to prove that the world began just a moment ago, when God made it complete with mature living creatures, remains of dead ones, fossils, and nations with long histories and people with memories. Without judging either application of this argument, one can safely say that its credibility is just as great or just as small in either case. Besides, the main question here has already been fully answered in our treatment of the transference of consciousness from one substance to another, and the multiplication of consciousnesses within one substance.

When one advances a hypothesis, one must have a reason for doing so which reflects some practical need. Suppose the same line of reasoning were applied to physical things, and it were claimed that every ten seconds the Rock of Gibraltar was spirited away and replaced with another which was indistinguishable from it. All this would do would be to needlessly multiply the problems of a single material substance by as many times as these magical substitutions occurred. The natural idea of personality involves no difficulties comparable to those which arise from the above kinds of criticism, and the hypothesis of serial identities in one substance, put forward apparently without evidence, violates Ockham's Razor, which is a strange thing to find in modern philosophy.

Notes

[1] *An Essay Concerning Human Understanding*, Vol. 1, Bk. II, Ch. XXVII.

[1a] See Ch. 2, 71–73.

[1b] See Ch. 2, 64–66.

[2] *Essay*, Vol. 1, Bk. II, Ch. XXVII.

[3] *Philebus* 21b–c.

[4] Ch. 2, 105.

[5] Ch. XXVII, 9.

[5a] Kant's use of this idea did not involve a thinking substance, but it is implicit in a substantive conscious identity.

[6] Locke, ibid., Ch. XXVII, 12.

[7] See Ch. 3, 161.

[8] *Essay*, Ch. XXVII, 13. These views of substance are only suggested by Locke, but I respond to them in case they should be taken seriously.

[9] Ibid., XXVII, 16,

[10] Ibid., XXVII, 17.

[11] Ibid., 19.

[12] *Treatise* I, Part IV, Ch. VI.

[13] *Appearance and Reality*, Bk. I, Ch. IX.

[14] Joseph Butler, *The Analogy of Religion*, Dissertation 1.

[15] *Encyclopedia of Philosophy*, Ch. 20.

[16] Locke, ibid., XXVII, 23.

[17] *Periphyseon*, Bk. IV, 7.

[18] Ibid.

[19] D. Parfit, *Reasons and Persons*, Ch. 11, 219–23.

[20] Ibid.

[21] Ibid.

[22] Ibid.

[23] Ibid.

[24] D. Parfit, ibid.

[25] *A Guide for the Perplexed*, 75–76.

[26] Ibid.

[27] Ibid., 88–91.

[28] Parfit, ibid.

[29] Ibid.

6

Answers to
Analytical Problems

Philosophy and Science

This chapter will be mainly concerned with criticisms of the metaphysical idea of the unitary self which has been discussed in the previous chapters, and with counter-arguments to these criticisms. Before attempting this, however, I wish to present a general criticism of scientific explanation, because of a high probability that skeptical thought in regard to personal identity is indirectly an effect of the natural sciences.

The prestige of science, with its constant advances and flow of new theories, has put philosophy on the defensive, and has led it to try to treat its problems in ways patterned on those of science. This implies the denial or neglect of much valid philosophy for no other reason than that the retention of it might imply a static position which would compare unfavorably with the progressive appearance of science. Thanks to this attitude, the commonest, if unacknowledged, presupposition behind anti-metaphysical thought is that, if all else failed, there would always be scientific explanations available, and that these could possibly become complete enough for there to be no need for any others.

Materialistic and empiricistic theories do not contain grounds for serious differences with physical science, and could even complement it; as long as this point of view is felt to be reasonable, the kind of understanding sought by metaphysics will not be properly valued. However, one cannot reasonably object to this view of science unless one can show that the explanations belonging to the natural sciences fail in relation to philosophy by their essential nature, and not merely by reason of gaps in their knowledge which may be filled at some point in the future.

For this reason, we shall begin with an attempt to define scientific explanation in a way which distinguishes it from the kind of explanation sought by metaphysical thought. If it can be shown that science necessarily falls short of the range of realities treated by philosophy, those philosophies which tend to leave the problem of identity in the hands of scientific study will be found correspondingly ineffectual to the extent that they do this, with the effect of adding relevance to the critical arguments that will be discussed later.

Scientific Explanation

The subject matter of science is a world of physically individuated things, each of which can be shown to have effects on a relatively small number of other such entities directly related to it. This may be a matter of electrons interacting with other electrons and sub-atomic particles, or of molecules with molecules, living cells with living cells, and of fields of force between them; the pattern of interactions is generally familiar.

The relationships between things of this kind are, in the minimal case, always of a one-to-one, binary sort, no matter how great the complexity of the combinations they form. They are not only binary, they are extrinsic, as where two elements combine and are then separated again; both are separate subsistent entities both before and after their interaction. The supposed universality of scientific explanation would imply that everything can be reduced to combinations of these binary-extrinsic relationships. The so-called "n-body problem" illustrates the way in which scientific knowledge is confined to this particular relational level. An exact mathematical account is possible only for a system of two bodies, as with a moon orbiting a planet. For a system of three, four, or more, one has to make a sum of the binary combinations involved, so as to find an estimate of their total effect.

In the general case, if three things A, B and C are related in this binary and extrinsic manner, they give a set of three reciprocal relations $A \leftrightarrow B$, $B \leftrightarrow C$ and $C \leftrightarrow A$. If one of them, say, B, is removed, the relation C↔A would remain unchanged. Similarly, a system of A, B, C, D would give relations A↔B, A↔C, A↔D, B↔C, B↔D and C↔D; and here the removal of, say, C, would leave the relations A↔B, A↔D and B↔D unaltered.

There is in principle no upper limit to the number of elements which can be related as systems of binaries in this way, but the question remains as to whether this kind of relationship can explain everything. If there should be a reality which requires a fundamentally different kind of relationship, scientific method could not be capable of universality. To find such a reality, we need look no further than knowledge itself, including that by means of which the scientific scheme itself is deduced. For knowledge, the irreducible relationship is not binary, but ternary; it can also be shown to be intrinsic by nature as well, which makes it differ categorically from the realm of the binary-extrinsic relations. This relationship involves the knower, the thing known, and the act of knowing. If any one of these is removed, the whole ternary relation ceases without remainder, because the two remaining elements can form nothing but a binary relation. If one supposes that knowledge of, say, a rosebush requires only the duo of oneself and the rosebush, one only has to remember that the withdrawal of one's attention by other concerns, or the intervention of darkness, will eliminate the Act of Knowing. In this case, both the Knower and the Known (defined by this relation) cease to exist *qua* Knower and Known, and for this reason I call the relation "intrinsic."

The ternary relation is essential to the Platonic theory of knowledge, which is expressed by R. E. Cushman as follows:

> empirical knowledge presupposes a threefold union or concurrence ... there is, first, the implicit identity of the self-identical Form with the Form as apprehended *a priori*, i.e., *ante rem*, by the knowing subject. Secondly, there is an identity of the self-identical Form with the Form *in re*. Otherwise stated, the Form, by participation or ingression, contributes the intelligible structure of the particular thing. In the third place, there is the concurrence of the Form *in re* with the Form as apprehended by the knowing subject (*ante rem*) independently of all sensible experience; and it is this

latter concurrence which constitutes the moment of empirical knowledge.[1]

This conception of knowledge as a three-fold relation is of course not original, especially as the doctrine of the Trinity clearly implies it. According to R.G. Collingwood, this doctrine is a paradigm of knowledge on which the intellectual soundness of a civilization depends.[2] Even without the metaphysical ideas of oneness in trinity and trinity in unity, the essential relation can also be expressed more simply as the relation between Subject, Signifier, and Referent where the Signifier is a symbol of the Referent used by the Subject. Even in these terms, what has been said of the ternary relation remains the same. If the Signifier were removed, Subject and Referent would retain nothing of this relation. Without its presence, in however elementary a form, the Subject or knower has no way of manifesting to himself the fact that he knows the Referent.

The distinction between binary and ternary relations is also expressed in even less metaphysical terms by John Searle in his distinction between the syntactical operations in digital computers and the semantic operations that accompany them in conscious beings.[3] Relationships of syntax are necessarily of the binary-extrinsic kind, whereas semantic ones are ternary-intrinsic because they link the subject to both the syntactical symbol and its meaning. Searle concludes that the development of the power of computers by the rules of syntax could progress forever without giving rise to the consciousness of meaning inherent in the semantic relation.

This conclusion can be generalized in terms of what was said before, to the effect that scientific explanations could likewise progress forever without reproducing the ternary relationships upon which scientific knowledge itself depends. Therefore the end-product of scientific thought consists in effect in a lie about its own origin, when taken to be all-comprehensive, one which becomes all the greater as scientific knowledge increases. The basic limitation of natural science is therefore that it is produced by intellectual processes which are not representable in the kind of world which science is designed to describe. Consequently it relates by definition to only a part of reality (even though that part may be unlimited at its own level), and so cannot be taken as a model for philosophy.

This position allows two possible meanings to empirical treatments of identity. On the one hand, they cannot be relied on when they are presented as a complete account of the person, but on the other hand they are quite acceptable when their aim is to increase knowledge of aspects of personality in realms which are open to science. Consequently, the following criticisms will apply only in regard to the former of these two alternatives.

Criteria for Personhood

An example of the treatment of the person from an empirical point of view appears in a paper by Ardon Lyon which serves to show what is involved in this approach to identity.[4] The main idea here is that properties which are neither necessary nor sufficient for personhood if taken singly may yet be adequate for this purpose if taken together.

This point is made by comparison with the question as to what it is that makes one an uncle. There are four ways in which one may be so: (1) by having a brother who has a child; (2) by having a sister who has a child; (3) by having a wife who has a brother with a child; and (4) by having a wife with a sister with a child. None of these four conditions can be either necessary or sufficient, because the full nature implied by the word "uncle" is distributed among a group of formally distinct relationships. Uncle-hood can thus be quite well understood without there being any one unitary concept involved, and similarly personal identity might be fully accounted for without any unitary principle.

The three criteria for personhood offered here are (1) keeping the same body; (2) keeping the same memory; and (3) keeping the same personality. To remain the same person, one should fulfill all three of these conditions, but in practice it is found that we do not always satisfy all of them. In any case, no one of them is either logically necessary or sufficient.

Memory is neither necessary nor sufficient because it is always logically possible for someone else's brain to be programmed with all of one's own memories. The question as to their veracity is not raised here, although if they were true for oneself they could not be so for someone who has not had one's experiences. What is at issue is identity based on the mere retention of a set of memories, regardless of their origin, and such as could be manifested to an outsider. It is maintained that one can remain the same person despite losing one's memory, but that this does not mean that memory is not a part of identity. The same applies to a radical change of personality. One can remain the same person just having the same memory and the same body. With losing or completely changing the body, the case may be more hypothetical, but logically the result is the same as before.

On this basis, Lyon opposes R. G. Swinburne's position that body, memory and personality are evidence for personal identity but do not directly constitute it, and that what is neither necessary nor sufficient for X cannot be part of the meaning of X. Some conditions, on the other hand, are necessary and sufficient in this connection, such as having the same teeth, fingerprints, or blood type, but it is clear that their logical sufficiency does not bring us any nearer to the real nature of personal identity. Similarly, artistically quite unimportant details in a picture can be decisive for identifying the artist, like the material it is painted on, or the composition of the paint. Something empirically *de facto* sufficient may easily have properties which are far less sufficient to account for the real person than some other property which is nevertheless logically not sufficient to define him.

Should we try to judge by essential criteria or not? One could do so if the subject of the inquiry were better understood, but as things stand, one does not know how to recognize the essential definition. This difficulty is an example of Plato's paradox[5] that one cannot ask for a definition of anything unless one somehow knows it already. However, this is as much a problem for skeptical theories of identity as for affirmative ones.

Self as Extensive Quantity

Instead of considering whether we know any essential reality in identity, Lyon proceeds to a view of the person which would make it a quantitative thing like the temperature of a room, on the grounds that, whereas a child of ten is a person, a fertilized egg is not, and that there is no actual point at which the non-personal egg can be said to become a person. He argues that for this reason the immorality of taking life increases gradually with the passage of time, being practically nil at the time of the fertilized egg. Lyon does not consider whether there could be more than one meaning for this indeterminacy about the person, although these facts are also consistent with the idea that there is really no variability in degree of personhood, but only varying degrees of manifestation of it; after all, if we remain persons even when we are asleep and thus are not manifesting our personalities, why may not our personhood be merely concealed in our earliest stages of development?

If applied to the Moon, Lyon's line of argument would suggest that it was only truly a Moon somewhere between first and last quarters, and that as a thin crescent in its first and last phases it could not really be called a moon at all. Few would see any sense in this, because if we cannot find a clear dividing line between the "real" Moon from its earliest and latest appearances, this could just as well be because it was just as much itself in its smallest manifestations as in its fullest. The same alternative applies to the case of the fertilized egg and the ten-year old child discussed above.

Lyon further argues in a similar fashion that someone can be half-way between being a brother and a sister if their parents have another child: "since someone can be part way between being a male and a female, having characteristics of both."[6] Here again, thought is confined to appearances, despite the fact that the difference between the sexes is a matter of X and Y chromosomes, and does not depend on appearances. One might as well suppose that a high-pitched note comes closer to being a deep note by being made fainter in volume; in reality, what it actually is is not affected by the force, or lack of it, with which it strikes our ears.

The argument for near-persons evidently conflicts with legal practice, as we are told that "It seems, incidentally, to be part of a judge's professional training to ensure that he should *illogically* rule that borderline cases shall not be deemed borderline. . . ."[7] What is really being criticized here is not merely legal practice but something common to both science and philosophy, since the main function of each is precisely that of seeing through appearances to the essential. Rational thought has to reach the inherent disconti-nuities of things, without which one could not even identify bor-derline cases, which must differ absolutely from paradigm ones or else there would be no point in making an issue of them.

Lyon argues that "the logic of the situation" requires that cases of near- or part-personality should be possible as distinct from per-sonality in varying degrees of development. This could only be the case if personhood consisted wholly in externally verifiable proper-ties like those of memory, body and character, while these did not imply the existence of any soul or substance expressing itself in them. Given these three properties, the argument that their varia-tions prove that the sum-total to which they belong is itself a vari-able quantity is too reliant on the one-sided interpretation of the absence of clear dividing-lines in personal development.

Part of this line of argument is that the exact idea of personal identity can be set aside in favor of the more general idea of staying effectively the same person. The assumption behind this is that it will be easier to think of oneself as the same person one was many years ago than to think oneself identical with him. But the difficulty involved here is wholly due to the attempt to equate the self with its perceptible properties. If the latter are the essence of the self, iden-tity will of course be a puzzle, but there is no such problem with the self *qua* perceiver and knower, which logically can and must have a mathematically strict self-identity, according to our account in Chapter 5.

Besides, there is probably not much point in arguing for some less-than-identical "sameness," because, its more modest objective notwithstanding, the idea of a relative identity seems to remain dependent on the idea of an absolute identity, for the same reason as it would be pointless to say, "You look like the Prime Minister," if one did not know what the Prime Minister looked like. More to the point, if there were such a relative identity, it would not matter much to anyone, because what one wants to know is whether this being is still *me*, not something approximating to me.

Where an analogy is presented between a person and a road, and parallels shown between them, one should note at the outset that the comparison with an unconscious artifact presupposes the conclusion about personality which is being argued for. This analogy is used in further support for the idea of the person as corresponding to a variable quantity. The way in which a narrow lane may widen out into a main road is implied to parallel the development of the fertilized egg into a person, suggesting again that there may be degrees of being the same person. The truth of this is defended on the grounds that there is nothing to personality except what can be observed by outsiders. However, this idea would commit us to something which nobody believes: namely, that we should cease to be persons when we go to sleep, and become persons again when we wake up.

Such an account of personality depends too much on analogies. One first must be able to prove that analogies between non-living things and unconscious organisms are valid in principle, or one will assume too much. The failure of Behaviorism to reduce consciousness to behavior would tend to prove the opposite of what these analogies imply.

Moral Implications of the Materialist Theory

One should note that the same kinds of argument could have been used if the subject of this discussion had been illness rather than personhood. Illness could be discussed as though it were nothing more than the symptoms which were observable by other persons. Pain, for example, in all but its extreme forms, could easily be shown to be a number of quite insignificant things on this basis. It is curious that the general conviction that our influenzas, bilious attacks and headaches are in their own way unitary identities manifesting themselves in outward signs is so strong that no one bothers to challenge it, while the conviction about our own selves seems less sure in some minds. The explanation of this is probably that the reality of things that make us suffer is necessarily an emotionally charged issue in a way that the nature of selfhood is not, for some persons; but for all that, the principle involved in the two cases is all too similar.

The reductionistic arguments considered here are a useful example of the way in which the reality of personality is criticized today.

Lyon even defends it from a moral point of view, on the grounds that the possible reduction of the person to nothing should not form an argument for euthanasia because one could believe this "and still be unwilling to hurt a fly." That is always possible for a split personality; the Nazis were opposed to cruelty toward animals. In any case, to argue at length for a position and then claim that it really makes no difference can only cast doubt on the sincerity with which the argument is being presented. Reductionistic thought can hardly avoid subterfuges like this, as its implications are never entertained except for the sake of argument.

There is also an absurdity in such disclaimers, because the issue is that of taking life, which is treated as though our conception of what that involves is unaffected by beliefs about the nature of human life. If our reasoning is designed to alter our beliefs about the nature of human life (and there is no other purpose it could have), then it must correspondingly alter our beliefs about the *taking* of human life. To pretend otherwise is to show a rather low estimate of one's readers' intelligence.

If other lives were simply aggregates of phenomena, the idea of causing death would be changed completely, and this cannot be ignored by those who argue on those lines. That they believe that their ideas actually will make a difference to the way life is treated is vouched for by the fact that they argue for them, and they cannot be altogether unaware that a negation of the person is really inseparable from a negation of morality. If there were no real persons, what meaning could moral values have?

The Body's Role in Identity

In the same paper quoted above, Lyon observes that whereas identity is primarily dependent on mind and personality from a theoretical point of view, in actuality damage to the body can have a quite disproportionate effect on the brain, and therefore on memory and personality. Thus the role of the body in identity is more important than it theoretically should be. There is a reference to other philosophers who have argued that bodily continuity is a condition for remaining the same person, and Lyon disputes this with the example of Gregor Samsa (in Kafka's *Metamorphosis*), who slowly turns into a giant insect. The reason for thinking of this creature as remaining Gregor, but with an insect's body, is presumably the continuous transition which was involved; but this is really a weak reason.

Having argued that the body is specially important for identity because of the effects of injuries to it, it does not seem very consistent to argue that one could thus exchange one's body for that of a different species without ceasing to be the same person. This would imply that our identity was bound not to the actual body we possess, but simply to a body, of whatever kind. It is in any case hard to see how the difference to one's identity resulting from injury to the body could be any greater than the difference made by its transformation into that of an insect.

This argument is based on the assumption that to speak of Gregor having the body of an insect does not involve any self-contradictions—but this still contains the assumption that the identity "Gregor" is not logically tied to any one kind of body, and in this way one may be assuming what one is trying to prove. In fact, we cannot so totally sever identity from the actual form of the body without also severing it from most of the things which make it significant for us; the body is a necessary though not sufficient source of identity on Lyon's assumptions, and it cannot have too great a scope for change without canceling this function. (Body and person cannot be inseparable either, on the other hand, because in that case the body *would* be a sufficient condition for identity.)

Where Lyon argues that "two people can have an equal claim to being G.F. for physical reasons," on the grounds that "G.F.'s body logically might become replicated," he assumes certain things about the nature of bodies: firstly, that uniqueness is not essential to the body's nature, whereas we showed in the previous chapter that a living body is formed in the course of a unique history of unique place-time combinations. In this case, we cannot simply say that it is logical to assume that a given body can be replicated.

For this reason, we do not need to suppose that unique personal identity could be undermined by the possibility of two persons having an equal claim to being the same person because of having indistinguishable bodies. The difference between a body which has been fabricated so as to look the same as another and one which has grown continuously in harmony with one's own development from the beginning of one's life is a reminder of the paradoxes that "branch-line" identity was shown to give rise to in the previous chapter.

However, Lyon tries to reinforce his idea of the replicability of bodies by arguing that to be the same body one need not have "a spatio-temporally continuous life history," on the grounds that in physics, electrons "jumping orbits" do not have any such continuity. This argument, however, rests on the assumption that sub-atomic particles like the electron are *bodies*, even if very small ones like the atoms of classical physics. This is not how modern science sees them, for it treats them as waves just as much as particles. A body for science is a combination of atoms, and one which is large enough in number for all their indeterminacies to average out in a determinate mass. Given this condition, one cannot abstract bodies from the property of continuity.

Finally, there is the question of the meaning of the claim that injuries to the body can evidently alter identity. If one understands the body as a medium through which one's identity manifests and expresses itself, the effects of physical injury need only imply an external suppression of something which continues to exist regardless. This point was made in Chapter 1, in regard to the Aristotelian argument as to how sight may be lost through a defect in the eye and then recovered by the physical correction of the eye. It would be very different if the body were what actually constitutes our individual natures and our identities, as common sense is wont to suppose. To see why this need not be believed will be the objective of the next section.

Individuation and the Body

The occasion for this analysis is provided by certain statements in a book by A. Kenny[8] which has personal identity as its main theme. Kenny speaks of mind rather than soul, which he takes to mean "immortal mind," similarly to the way the word is used here. More precisely, he defines it as "a capacity to acquire intellectual abilities"[9] and offers no further definition, though this appears incomplete and inconclusive. If it is a capacity, we need to know what it is a capacity of. If we say that it is of a mind, the definition may be true, but only as a tautology. If we say that it is a capacity of the body, we make a category mistake, and the definition is without meaning.

We may go on to say that it is a capacity of a person or of a human being, but that would call for another definition. If "person" is defined as "union of body and soul," then "person" would differ from "body" by the addition of another reality, namely the mind or soul, which leaves us with the same problem as before. Nevertheless, this definition is used repeatedly, as where intellect is again defined as "an ability to acquire abilities,"[10] which seems to serve the same purpose of avoiding the idea of a distinct spiritual substance in our being.

Supposing it were a matter of defining "dog," and we were to proceed in the same way, we should have to call it "a capacity for manifesting canine qualities." But here again, we have only the two alternatives of completing it with the words "by dogs" or "by something other than dogs," with the same results as before. Kenny is trying here to avoid making mind a distinct reality, and the reason why he thinks he can do so is made clear where he expresses doubt whether certain psychic activities can take place "in the absence of bodies to individuate the souls."[11]

No analysis of "body" is ever offered, so we are left to think of it in the manner of unscientific common sense, in which case it can easily be accepted as our source of individuation. If we can make that assumption there need be little resistance to the way in which he treats mind and soul, because one can believe that our individuality is surely founded on the body at all events. If the concept of body is analyzed, however, it can easily be shown that only inorganic bodies realize Kenny's meaning, as these only involve a combination of a fixed number of atoms which are in principle permanent, all of them having a fixed set of relations to one another.

Bodies of living organisms, on the other hand, have no such stable composition, their entire content being replaced every few years. Bizarre as it must seem to common sense, these are not, strictly speaking, bodies at all, but rather slowly flowing liquids. As such, they have no means of individuating themselves, let alone minds. The living body's permanence of form imitates that of the true body, the inorganic, up to a certain point, but even then it is only in appearance, since its permanence is essentially like that of the curve of a waterfall or the arc of a fountain. Its physical form persists *despite*, not *because of* its material content, every particle of which, even in the bones, is either arriving or departing. Its relative permanence is thus not based on a material structure, despite appearances.

If in fact the only corporeal basis for individuality were really confined to inorganic bodies, it would appear that either the idea of individuality must be given up where living beings are concerned, or else it must have a basis which is not corporeal. It is here that we encounter a substantive reason for positing the soul-substance to which Kenny is so opposed. The Substantial Body is thus refutable by simple scientific considerations, which puts it in worse case than the Substantial Soul, so that we cannot claim that there are no adequate grounds for supposing the latter. If we ignore this, it may turn out that Kenny's opposition to the "Cartesian myth" of soul and body is itself based only on a Scholastic myth of bodily individuation.

This conclusion is amenable to the Platonic principle that bodies *qua* bodies have no causal power, because the causal power in them is owing to the Forms instanced in them, if they are inorganic, or Soul and Forms if living. Belief in the body's power to individuate minds or souls is also opposed to the simple common-sense objection that, after death, the bodies of living creatures begin at once to de-individualize, that is, to decay and disperse. If bodies were really the source of individuation, one would expect them to maintain this property without any help from life or soul, on the grounds that their possession of this power would mean that they should be able to provide individuation for themselves both before and after sharing it with other kinds of being such as souls. The natural effects of death thus show how the individual nature depends on the non-corporeal part which has departed, and that far from being the source of individuation, the body's individuation is only what it receives from the presence of the soul.

There is no doubt a biochemical account of the way in which

organic bodies maintain their individual forms, but this should not alter our argument, because all science can do in this regard is to fill in detail as to what is involved in the ingestion, incorporation, and elimination of the body's molecules and cells. Such technical accounts are simply analytical expansions of the claim that "it is alive," enriching the idea somewhat but not changing it. To resume the former comparison between living bodies and liquids, if the actual comparison were with a mountain stream, its permanence of form would be due essentially to the form of the mountain, and obviously not to its "matter," the water running in it. In this case, the relation of the soul to the body would be like that of the mountain to the stream, and just as the stream is constantly made up of new water, so the body is made up of ever-new matter. This is also why I suggested that the word "body" is more precisely descriptive of inorganic solids.

Cartesian Questions

Kenny argues further[12] that if the emotions get their names from purely private experiences, no one else should know what we mean by the words we use for them. But this argument seems to ignore the question of our unity of nature, the way in which all human beings are formed in a similar manner. Since all are broadly similar on the corporeal level, why may there not be a corresponding similarity among human subjectivities? This point applies equally whether one maintains that there is a separable soul or that it is only a "capacity" of somewhat.

Given a correspondence of subjective natures, the same general patterns of emotion would be bound to arise. No matter how completely private they were in themselves, they would obtain a public character from their mutual correspondences. Once again, "one would never know that the experience one called by the name of a particular emotion was the same as that which others called by the same name."[13]

But we do not just hear names given to emotional states. We also perceive the conditions under which these states are said to arise, which enables us to make comparisons with the emotions we ourselves are liable to have under such conditions. Communication is just as much an effect of correspondence between the communicators as it is a cause of it.

In the same vein, Kenny objects that "Even the words used to give private expression to Cartesian doubt would not have any sense in a world which contained nothing but a Cartesian ego."[14]

But must there really be "nothing but" this ego in existence for the Cartesian argument to apply? It is true that it requires us to assume that nothing else in the world is certainly known, but that is not the same as saying that everything else is non-existent. Possibly Kenny is trying to refute Descartes by making him seem to demand more than his theory requires.

If there were in fact nothing else in existence but the ego, the ego would certainly be meaningless, for like any other finite entity it can only be understood as part of a world. But that need not prevent its being the most fully ascertainable part of that world, as was explained in Chapter 3. Kenny also says that Descartes is identifying with his imagination, because he can only consciously identify with an imaginary representation of his intellectual mind, and not with that mind itself. The distinction here is illustrated by the fact that "an imaginary ability to speak French is not the same as the intellectual ability in which the knowledge of French consists."[15]

The question here is whether one is identifying with something purely and simply imaginary or with an imaginary representation of a reality. It is not enough to point out that an inadequate image is often used to focus the mind on a more subtle reality, such as the mind itself. Everything depends on whether such images point to something beyond themselves. No one fails to sense the difference between an imaginary representation of a place or person we regularly see and of a person in a novel, of whom we have no direct experience.

This distinction among the uses of imagination depends on memory, of course, but the fact that we can make it at all shows how mind works outside imagination. The same point is also illustrated by the fact that something may be discoverable by reason, while having a size which is not imaginable at all, like the Solar System, though we are aided in thinking about it by a mental image of an out-of-scale diagram of it. The inadequacy of this imaginary image detracts nothing from our rational knowledge of the reality it stands for; and likewise we have a true knowledge of our minds, partly through the aid of and partly in spite of the mental images we use for this purpose. This issue was referred to in Chapter 3,[16] where I argued that only reason knows both itself and the other faculties, whereas the latter do not even know themselves.

Concerning the use of language, Kenny cannot be sure that its public use came before the private, because these two things are really inextricable from one another. The facts will equally allow the idea that the communal organization of speech is an activity which is only made necessary by its having received its subject matter from private experience. The difficulty in agreeing about private experience would be limited by our common subjective nature. There may well be serious problems in finding a meaning for exclusively private realities, but for some reason not much attention is given to the difficulties in the idea of an exclusively public reality. It will not suffice to argue, as Kenny does, implicitly, that because language is a public means of expression it must be essentially devoted to public things.

In a world where everything is necessarily public, communication ought not to be necessary at all, since all the facts should speak for themselves. All statements would be of the same kind as "Nice day," or "Isn't it cold!" Public reality is of course unconcealed reality, and one does not easily see why we should require communication to link one unconcealed thing with another when this linkage is *ex hypothesi* common to us all. Given that the private is essentially the concealed, one could easily see the purpose of language if it were to create communication between the realms of the concealed and the unconcealed. In this case, each of these realities would owe much of its nature to being the polar opposite of the other, after the manner of Inside and Outside. If this is in fact the case, the public-reality philosophies will in effect be arguing for a world with an outside but no inside, or left without right.

The Cartesian position on these terms would imply a radical doubt about the polar extreme opposite that of the self, yet without this requiring one to doubt *that* it exists, but only to doubt whether one knows *what* it is. In this way, the knower does not have to leave himself meaninglessly unrelated.

The denial of private language has also become less acceptable in view of a criticism of Wittgenstein's thought, where it is a question of knowing whether one's use of language follows its rules or not.[17] It seems that the isolated person, using language alone, cannot be certain that his thought is obeying the language rules (although this problem seems to assume that these rules are imposed on us from without, like the rules of cricket, and do not arise from the inherent nature of the individual mind itself), whereas in public use this can be checked. However, it seems that it may be just as hard to show how the language community as a whole can know that its usage is following the rules. The language community has no one to judge its collective behavior, and so it is in the same position as the isolated thinker. Either, then, we say that neither the individual nor the community can use language (in which case, who can?), or else they both can use it, as was always taken to be the case until recently.

This problem only arises because the dichotomy between public and private language is a false one, since it exists only for thought, like that between the heat and light of a candle flame. The true difference between the two reveals that the private use of language is the primary reality. It is easy to see that all acts of public language are generated by acts of private language, while many or most acts of private language are only occasioned by acts of public language. There is therefore no reason for asserting that they are physically separate things unless it is to make an argument against the private use of language.

Body-Soul Interaction

The way in which the above questions have been treated implies an acceptance of some kind of dualism of soul and body, in general agreement with what was said in the earlier chapters; but this does not mean an acceptance of that dualism in the form in which Descartes articulated it. According to what we have said, the body is to the soul as instantiation is to Form, and so is an integral expression of the soul, and not something totally separate from it as Descartes would have it. This qualification eases the problem of interaction, besides allowing that soul and body can have certain things in common without compromising their separate natures.

If the soul were taken to be the primary reality of the two, we would then have to explain its ability to interact with the body and cause its motion. Conversely, if body and brain were taken as primary, we would not be able to account for our ability to know the truth. Truth involves a non-physical form of necessity, and evidently there is nothing necessary about the conglomerate of molecules and cells which constitutes body and brain. It may be argued that such a combination of contingencies could give rise to true statements by lucky coincidences, and given enough time it might even be expected. But this only pushes the problem a stage further off. If contingent being can give utterance to truth, this will be in vain unless there is a non-contingent reality to judge that it has done so adequately. This condition can only be fulfilled by a kind of being which is free from determination by the indefiniteness of matter.

Where soul-body interaction is concerned, it may be questioned whether such interaction is really any stranger than the control of a machine by means of radio signals. (Radio signals are accepted as physical things, and being physical they are able to act on the physical machine, though the difference between them and solid objects in degree of concreteness is so extreme as to stretch the idea of the "physical" to its limit.)

Provided we do not posit an absolute difference between soul and body, as modern philosophy usually does, this comparison could well be relevant. It should be noted that if we continue to define the soul as exempt from absolutely all physical properties, the interaction problem must be rendered insoluble in advance. To ask how two absolutely different things can interact is contradictory, and thus can only be a rhetorical question.

In reality, we know that the soul is fully conversant with space and time, and if Kant is right they are part of its nature as well; and these are also the two basic conditions for its experience of material entities. They are not *per se* material, but if in fact the soul can be informed by them in its own mode, corresponding to the way in which material things exist, there must be some community of nature between soul and body, however limited. On this basis, the difference between them for interactive purposes need not in principle be any greater than that between radio waves and machines. A closely related idea is expressed by Gregory Vlastos, according to whom Plato's idea of the soul is that it "contains no physical matter (no fire, air, water, earth) and has none of the properties of physical matter (such as temperature, density, weight) *except one:* it can move."[18]

Although it is pointed out in the same passage that, even in this shared property, there is a basic difference in that the soul's motion is self-motion while the motion of matter is imposed on it, motion of whatever kind necessarily combines the dimensions of space and time, which as I have argued are shared by body and soul in their several ways. Since they unite in the shared property of motion, active on the one side and passive on the other, we have here the Platonic solution to the interaction problem, the action of the "psychokinesis"[19] which mediates between the unchanging Forms and their mutable instances. That the interaction between soul and body must be an insoluble problem is too often taken to be an argument against the separate soul, and those who reason in this way manage not to notice that the whole problem has really been fabricated through nothing more than a misleading definition of soul.

Conscious Being and Duality

Something more remains to be said about the composite and unitary aspects of the person. The duality of soul and body is not the only one, since there is also the duality between the rational and irrational functions of the soul, and that of the two levels of consciousness, which I have called first-order and second-order consciousness, where these are the activities of the empirical ego and the pure ego respectively, as defined in the passages quoted from Stace.[20] These complexities in the soul are noted by Proclus, who says that it is at once "geometric" and "arithmetic," that is, continuous and discontinuous.[21] He makes the same point even more directly as follows: "the essence of the soul is one and not one; the root of its parts (is) in a state which is indivisible and truly one."[22]

From what he says further in this last passage, it appears that a distinction is being made which corresponds to the one I have referred to above between empirical and pure egos. From what Plotinus says of the distinction between the *aisthetikon* and the *logikon* operations of the soul,[23] he too is thinking along these lines, these two operations being the first-order or empirical consciousness and the second-order consciousness, respectively. This duality is widely enough recognized up to the present time to be uncontroversial. In a chapter entitled "The Nature of Mind," D.M. Armstrong says:

> Consciousness . . . is nothing but perception or awareness of the state of our own mind. The driver in a state of automatism perceives, or is aware of, the road. If he did not, the car would be in a ditch. But he is not currently aware of his awareness of the road. He perceives the road, but *he does not perceive his perceiving,* or anything else that is going on in his mind. He is not, as we normally are, conscious of what is going on in his mind.[24]

This passage clearly expresses what we mean here by the internal duality in the conscious self. It is also important because it instances a way in which the two sides of the duality can be experientially separated, one where the unitary side or pure ego is practically suppressed. This case is symmetrical with the opposite kind of example cited by Schumacher and Stace,[25] where mystics withdraw entirely from the empirical ego or first-order consciousness and concentrate fully within the inner consciousness which transcends all particular contents.

There is no question of there being two different substances in the soul or conscious being, but rather two essentially different modes of activity in a state of balance with one another. Some further light thus needs to be shed on the relation between them, but before this is attempted, it should be observed how this analysis of the self affects the controversies of modern philosophy where they tend to a denial that there is any conscious entity or Cartesian ego to be the possessor of the successive mental states.

Modern treatments of this subject assume, with very few exceptions, that they do not need to take account of any conscious principle except what I call the first-order consciousness, or the empirical ego. If the inner self or pure ego is thus excluded, the task of materialistic thought is made too easy, and the conclusion that our mental states need have no possessor can hardly amount to more than a truism, within such an artificially reduced field of discourse. The first-order consciousness has in any case no concern with self-awareness, since it is in essence the same as the consciousness which we share with the animals. The endless accumulation of particulars and concretes it produces is so clearly unadapted to the idea of a unitary self that one may wonder why so much argument has been expended on proving that there is no conscious self on this basis.

This point of view is partly the result of the tendency toward greater specialization; in this case it has had the effect of splitting something which philosophy requires to be a unity. Before modern times, the philosopher was something of a mystic as well as a naturalist, while the mystic was something of a philosopher, and so on. The fact that there are distinctions which they did not make does not prove that they might have reasoned falsely about things which they considered as undivided. Descartes, for example, no doubt thought of the conscious self as the combination of pure and empirical egos, which in practice it is. He had no reason to try to rework his arguments so as to make them apply to either of these halves of the conscious being in isolation, as only the union of the two could be considered as a person. When analyses are applied to aspects of consciousness which go below what can constitute a person, one may forget that the results of such thinking cannot have the right to dictate our idea of personality as such.

Experience of the Self

Apart from theoretical considerations, some objections raised against a substantive self rest simply on the contention that no such thing is experienced. One answer to this has been made in the previous chapter, in regard to mystical concentration and to the way in which attention can shift between the two extremes of consciousness. Under modern conditions, most people have a mental development which is dominated by the empirical extreme, so that it is not surprising that modern philosophy should have taken it as a norm.

This attitude appears in the treatment of identity given in P. F. Strawson's work on this subject:

> One can ascribe states of consciousness to oneself only if one can ascribe them to others. One can ascribe them to others only if one can identify other subjects of experience. And one cannot identify others if one can identify them only as subjects of experience, possessors of states of consciousness.[26]

This text shows that the subject of experiences is thought to be a nullity, and that there cannot be any mode of conscious experience other than that which presents its particular contents.

This does not take account of the meaning of the fact that the field of consciousness can be cleared of contents by an effort of concentration, so as to bring one closer to an awareness of the pure subject and not to mere unconsciousness. It was through ignoring this possibility that Hume said he could never discover himself without a perception and could not discover anything but perception, and the philosophers who have followed him have taken this condition as though it were fated.

Strawson questions why (1) states of consciousness are ascribed to anything at all, and (2) why they are ascribed to "the very same thing as certain corporeal characteristics, a certain physical situation...."[27] He seeks to show a connection between the answers to these questions. The very fact that we tend to think of a person as a compound of two subjects, one a subject of corporeal qualities and the other of experiences, is taken to mean that the idea of a subject cannot be "logically primitive" after all, in regard to our idea of a person. Rather it must seem that "person" is the primary idea which is then qualified through two different kinds of subject.

For this reason, the subject of experiences would have to be something other than oneself, and since one must ascribe experiences to oneself, one cannot ascribe them to a subject. Strawson concludes his argument by saying: "So the concept of the pure individual consciousness—the pure ego—is a *concept that cannot exist*; or at least cannot exist as a primary concept in terms of which the concept of a person can be explained or analyzed."[28]

Treating the idea of the person in this manner, he puts the self on a level with its contents. There is a parallel between this reasoning and the objection of a scientist that he does not believe in the soul because he has not found one in a test-tube, without realizing that if he could do so it would be no such thing.

This does not mean that the existence of the subject or pure ego must simply rest solely on the results of deep meditation, however, for there are more indirect approaches to it. The distinction between subject-of-physical-properties and subject-of-experiences is surely admissible, from one point of view at least. It exists for an external observer who sees that another person has physical properties and so infers that he also has mental experiences. But what are for the observer physical properties are for their possessor just a sub-category of experiences.

The question then is why preference is given to the point of view of an observer. That the nature of a being can only be known from external observation is certainly scientific orthodoxy, but it is philosophy, not science, that this question belongs to. The arguments quoted above are highly representative in that they make it clear what is the fundamental objection of modern thinking to the pure ego. It is simply this: that in relation to its conscious contents, it is *epistemically null*. As this involves a fallacy, it could well be named the Epistemic Fallacy. Reality is more than epistemology, and there is no difficulty in finding examples of other such nullities which are nevertheless so well known to be real that no one bothers to question them.

A mountaineer who had climbed Everest may well be able to convey a minutely detailed account of the ascent, supplemented with film and recordings, until other individuals knew as much about it as he did. But the one difference between them that remains is the mountaineer's experience of actually having climbed Everest. This is obviously not *per se* transferable, and it is also epistemically null in relation to all the lecture-material on the ascent, since its nature transcends all the information pertaining to it while adding nothing to that information. But besides this, we can easily see that, far from being nothing, it is the central reality in this example, to which all the communicable knowledge is accidental or adjectival.

The argument from this example can be generalized to cover the case of the pure ego and its experiences, because essentially the same thing is involved. The ascent of the mountain is a special case of the experience in general possessed by the central faculty of self-awareness. The relation of the pure ego to its mental experiences corresponds to the relation of having-climbed-Everest to the description of it. Thus the fact that a logical proof for the existence of this entity is not strictly possible, as one cannot place oneself outside it, need not mean that we cannot form an account of our experiences which will make its reality apparent.

Let us return to Strawson's scientifically oriented assumption that the person is truly known by outside observation. If we get to know the mountaineer through external accounts we shall of course share all the information concerning him, but the all-important thing that constitutes him *qua* mountaineer is not shared at all, for the reason already given. Objections to so-called "privileged access" in this connection seem inseparable from a denial of the difference between first-hand and second-hand experience, which no one would endorse except for the sake of argument. If "privileged access" were not a reality, certain other basic distinctions would become meaningless as well, such as the distinction between one's own writings and those of others; originality is irredeemably private.

If, however, first-hand experience can be generalized from the above case, one can see that this does not support the idea that persons can most truly be known *ab extra*, not just because something in experience is incommunicable but because experiences are parts of biographies which are necessarily unique. Furthermore, in their biographical setting experiences are always interwoven with acts of volition which do not *per se* enter into knowledge, and so are not communicable. For these reasons, epistemology (or its realm of publicly accessible knowledge) cannot be taken as all-inclusive, in which case conclusions based on it alone have little force.

This point should be linked with what was said in Chapter 4 about the way in which identity is based on a continual flow of volitions.[29] Epistemically, it adds nothing to what we can communicate about ourselves, but it is essential to the reasons why experiences are chosen and why their sequels are such as they are. Such things serve to explain why experience of the self is well founded without being within the reach of scientific demonstrations.

No-Self and Pathology

There is a radical criticism exemplified in the writings of D. Parfit according to which the concept of a self distinct from body and brain is illegitimate *per se.* It involves a direct attack on the idea "that we are separately existing entities, distinct from our brains and bodies, and entities whose existence must be all or nothing... a Reductionist's main claim is that we should reject these beliefs."[30]

In support of this idea he claims that both Wittgenstein and the Buddha would have agreed with it, and that it should therefore have a claim to universality. These are two rather ill-assorted witnesses to call upon, and where the Buddha is concerned, it is most likely that his negations of self or soul were owing to the fact that his declared purpose was to teach not metaphysics but rather a certain way of life. His denial of the self is in any case unique among the founders of religions, and its practical consequences do not seem to hinder its followers from retaining their individualities, whether consistently or not.

When such denials of the self are taken literally, problems arise in connection with the action of the will. For example, can the will operate in this case in such a way that there is no awareness of a self having a will directed to the end of proving that there is no self? Can the exponents of impersonality avoid behaving like someone shouting angrily that he is not losing his temper? There is something about them which recalls a cartoon from the 1960's of a hippy answering a telephone: "I'm not here, man." The Reductionists surely believe that they will go on being able to do all the same things just as well as before, and even take responsibility for them; and no one supposes that they would be willing to forfeit the recognition owing to their achievements, though this would seem to follow from their philosophical suppositions. But if the self is not real, one must suppose that the world is somehow changed by the belief that it is real, or else not take the trouble to argue against it. But if one is to argue against it, by whose activity is this done? Not that of a self, of course. Similarly, there does not seem much point in asking who is going to be enlightened by the conclusion that there is no self.

Such questions concern something too much involved in concrete experience to be confined to the abstract. The question we need to consider is whether the elimination of the self can be experienced in real life. The answer to this lies in the observation of William Barrett, quoted in the Introduction, concerning actual loss of self and insanity. Rather than being a characteristic of man's true condition, the symptomatology of morbid psychology shows that no-self is the daily experience of innumerable schizophrenics.

Short of schizophrenia, there are many instances of states of mind which are not interrelated, or not related adequately to the being who should own them, and which are associated with some form of mental failure. This applies even in the mildest cases, where it is only a question of mistakes made through absent-mindedness. Such failures do not result from a lack of consciousness as such, because one is certainly conscious of many things in such cases, yet there is no effective relation of each of them to the others, since they are not related to the central control of the pure ego. But to take such things as reasons for a denial of the reality of the self is to opt for the life of a cabbage, no matter what deep thoughts may be used to support it. This is clear enough to some psychologists, such as R. F. Baumeister: "Most actions make use of the self, and shedding the self can only bring inaction. The main exception is low-level, meaningless activity, done on impulse, without responsibility."[31] As with denials of free will, therefore, denials of the self militate against high-grade activity, and leave the low-grade kind unaffected. That may be coincidence—or it may reveal something about the motives of modernistic thought.

All acts of understanding take place between a mental grasp of a given object and a mental grasp of one's own self. Of the two, it is that of the self which must come first, both logically and chronologically. This grasp of the self is the grasp of the second-order consciousness upon the empirical or first-order consciousness. Where this kind of awareness is subject to long-term disruption, there is no self for all practical purposes, and this is inevitably manifest in insanity or mental deficiency. This is not to say that a powerful grasp of the self will guarantee anyone success in intellectual pursuits, but that the lack of it will guarantee failure at them. Without the primary relation between the two levels of self, the work of the mind cannot even begin.

There seems to be no likelihood that a literal absence of self could be redeemed by what is discovered about the self in religious experience, because those who practice a religious exclusion of self never cease to be manifestly real selves. Besides the fact that "self" in religious thought nearly always means "ego" or "egotism," all attempts to find other ways in which one can be "selfless" draw one away from the position of its literal truth toward some moral form of selflessness, which is of course compatible with the existence a real self. From a more personal point of view, a practical reason for not accepting the Reductionist view of the self is that the belief that a real absence of self is a token of some higher wisdom can only tend to make many people with personality problems desist from efforts to achieve a genuine self, of which they would otherwise have been capable.

Notes

[1] *Therapeia*, Ch. VI, i.

[2] *An Essay on Metaphysics*, Pt. III, Ch. XXI.

[3] *Minds, Brains and Science*, Ch. 2.

[4] Ardon Lyon, "On Remaining the Same Person," *Philosophy*, Vol. 55 (1980).

[5] *Meno*, 80c–81b.

[6] A. Lyon, ibid.

[7] Ibid.

[8] A. Kenny, *The Metaphysics of Mind*.

[9–15] Ibid., 20, 81, 31, 52, 60, 90, 90.

[16] Proclus, *In Rep.* Section 277, 20–30.

[17] A. C. Grayling, *Wittgenstein*, 110–11.

[18] Gregory Vlastos, *Plato's Universe*, Ch. 2, 31.

[19] Ibid.

[20] See Ch. 5, 182–84.

[21] *In Tim.* III, Taylor trans., 615.

[22] Ibid., 164; 15.

[23] G. J. P. O'Daly, op. cit., 22.

[24] In *The Mind/Brain Identity Theory*, ed. A. G. N. Flew.

[25] See Ch. 5, 182–84.

[26] *Individuals*, 100.

[27] Ibid., 102.

[28] Ibid.

[29] Ch. 4, 140–41.

[30] *Reasons and Persons*, Section 92.

[31] *Escaping the Self*, 68–69.

7

Some Metaphysical Issues

The Synthetic Unity

K ant's original synthetic unity of apperception will be seen to be relevant to much of what has been said about the two levels of awareness, although I have not made much reference to it so far. This is because Kant's text on the synthetic unity can too easily be read by the non-Kantian as a piece of high-level psychology which analyzes the way in which the rational agent masters his material. In reality, the intention is that this should be an account of a connective process which takes place whether there is any substantive self or not.

It is doubtful whether Kant's exposition of the synthetic unity contains an argument, or just an assertion. If one has a technical title for something, it creates a disposition to take it for real in any case. A similar if less probable example of this might be an "assimilative process of pedagogy" supposedly taking place in the minds of students, whether assisted by a teacher or not. The question as to whether a teacher is involved could thereby be passed over without the need for a direct denial, if that was what one wanted. If the synthetic unity is like this, it would therefore constitute a disguised assertion that there is no conscious agent organizing the mind's thoughts.

Kant was nevertheless aware of the two different orders of consciousness, observing that there is a "primitive apperception" based on the forms of the intuitions of space and time as well as another and higher apperception expressed by the "I think" which must accompany all representations.[1] In the latter, awareness of the outer world is blended with self-awareness. The unity of our experience does not come from the things we have experience of:

But the conjunction of representations into a conception is not to be found in objects themselves, nor can it be, as it were, borrowed from them and taken up into the understanding by perception, but is on the contrary an operation of the understanding itself. . . .[2]

Consciousness of an identical self is thus closely connected with this unifying principle of experience, through which all its different contents are mutually related. Their very existence as experiences consists in their relatedness to one another within the manifold of unification with which the mind embraces them. But the fact that this principle applies so clearly to objects would seem to create a presumption that it should not apply to the self. Intellectual disciplines involve an intensifying of the identification with the role of self-as-subject, and the fact that the latter can never directly be grasped as an object accounts for the difficulty here.

It is only with the higher of these two, the apperception, that one is fully a person: "I am, therefore, conscious of my identical self, in relation to all the variety of representations given to me in an intuition, because I call all of them *my* representations. . . . I am conscious of myself as a necessary *a priori* synthesis. . . ."[3] Thus any one person can "read" his own unity and identity into the unity and identity of the world as he perceives it, the perceptual world necessarily having to reflect these properties. But what he discerns in this way is only what pertains to any individual consciousness, not necessarily human either: a race of identical clones could be individuated on this basis. Therefore the foundation for personal identity given by the synthetic unity of apperception suffices only for the identity of personhood in general, and not for any unique person. The tendency of monistic theories is to leave the question there, and ascribe individual identity to some kind of deception, a point of view adopted by Schopenhauer from the influence of both Kant and Oriental teachings.

Up to this point, the account is similar enough to what we said previously about the empirical ego and the pure ego, but there is still a question of the agency and substantiality of the higher consciousness. There is no reason to doubt the relevance of causality in relation to the things grasped by the empirical ego. For example, this passage in the *Critique* is causally explicable in that each separate item in it can in principle be shown to have a cause.

These causes surely include things written by other philosophers, things said by Kant's colleagues, events in Kant's own life, and his own acts of reflection. But when all the separate contents have been accounted for in such ways, there is still one thing not accounted for: namely, the unity or coherence of the whole text. Must that alone be without any substantive cause? More must be required than a technical title which describes this cause without explaining it. If this cause is in Kant himself, it would most naturally be taken to be the substantive self of the philosopher. In view of this causal role, it would be best to treat the synthetic unity as an account of what we have treated as just one part of the real self, and not the whole manifest self, as it is in strictly Kantian usage. Such was the course adopted by the psychologist whose observations on identity will occupy what follows, even though his thought as a whole is not of any great philosophical importance.

Identity, Logic, and Morality

Otto Weininger's[4] approach to identity, which reflects the influence of Kant and some of his successors, maintains that while conscious content in general is of no use for defining identity, there is a special case of it which is essential for our ability to judge the identity of the self in successive states, and that is our conception of the principle of identity itself.[5] This idea is developed alongside a different version of the *Cogito* argument and applied to the reality of a noumenal, trans-empirical subject. Weininger shows that a consciously continuous mode of being is necessary both for logical and ethical experience. Even to connect things with the simplest logical relations, there must be this inner continuum, just as the development of a moral sense requires us to know that we are the same person who performed a given action at a given time.

It is through personal identity conceived according to the synthetic unity that "the structure, form, law and cosmos persist, even through the change of contents."[6] The perception of identity in the things we know is thus deeply involved with the identity of the self, and a development of the *Cogito* argument is used to establish the latter.

The principle of Identity or Non-Contradiction is axiomatic and self-evident; it is "the primitive measure of truth for all other propositions." Given this basic role, it does not need itself to be a particular truth, since it is the very principle of our grasp of truth. Neither does it necessitate the existence of an actual A where it states A = A, because it is still true though A be a griffin or a unicorn. This independence from any actually experienced A means that the real being involved here must come from elsewhere.

When the law of non-contradiction is stated, then, the real existence it evinces is that of the simultaneous existence of the first and the second A, such that the proposition A = A is none other than the proposition "I am," there being no other ground on which this truth can fall. The certainty of A's self-identity merges with that of the existence of the knowing subject.

This application of the principle of non-contradiction to the case where the knower understands himself at a given moment as identical with himself at a previous moment makes a connection between theoretical and experiential identities. This is relevant to what was said in Chapters 3 and 4 about our knowledge of eternal truths. That the eternal is intrinsic to the knower himself can thus be based on the inherence of the principle of non-contradiction in his mind.

Weininger further observes:

> Were I part of the stream of change I could not verify that the A had remained unchanged, had remained itself. Were I part of the change, I could not recognize the change. Fichte was right when he stated that the existence of the ego was to be found in pure logic in as much as the ego is the condition of intelligible experience.[7]

The law of identity or non-contradiction, then, is a key to our own identity, enabling us to obtain the "I am" from a modification of the "I think" which qualifies it by this special content. This self-being has the property of a relatedness-to-everything because of the universality of the Identity law, which recalls the Aristotelian idea of the soul as being, in a sense, all things, and the conception of man as Spirit based on his relatedness to the whole world as such.

While this is the same in principle in all minds, it is by no means consciously present to the same degree in each. Leibniz's idea of the monad serves precisely to include such cases where there is a universality without a consciousness corresponding to it, as all monads are representations of the whole world, but with varying degrees of adequacy. There are potential as well as actual microcosms. The reference to Leibniz at this point in the argument shows that the intention is to link it to the idea of the substantive self which is constituted by the monad, and distance it from a point of view which tries to dispense with a unitary self.

This therefore involves the idea of a spiritual substance, which Weininger also connects with ethical consequences, claiming that it is only through the belief that every person is "a monad, an individual center of the universe," that one can have grounds for not using other persons as means to ends. Such theoretical individualism is said to be the basis of the positive content of altruism, and that which makes the fewest difficulties for individual rights.

Duality in the Conscious Being

The idea that there is a higher self or pure ego to contain the lower, empirical self might be thought to lead to an infinite regress, requiring a third self to contain these two, and then a fourth to contain these three, and so on. This possibility resembles the progression from Knowing A to Knowing that I know A, to Knowing that I know that I know A, and so on. But in the latter example, there is a significant difference between the transition from the first to the second and that from the second to the third and all the subsequent stages.

"Knowing A" is a binary type of conscious relation which is equally characteristic of animals, whereas "knowing that one knows A" makes this relation self-reflective and ternary, so transforming it in a manner comparable to the way the addition of a third dimension transforms a two-dimensional representation. However, a further enhancement of the same kind is evidently ruled out by the fact that we do not have access to an order of relationship higher than the ternary, that is, one which is *intrinsically* quaternary or quinary. For this reason the change made by the first "knowing that" relation is not really multiplied with the addition of further reflectives after it, and for this reason their infinite regress does not affect the principle of identity involved here.[7a]

If the self in fact possessed a third-order consciousness, it would result in an advantage over those who have only first and second-order consciousness, of the same order as human beings have over the animals. Fourth and fifth orders would have corresponding effects, and so on, and the mere fact that humans are recognizable as a single species is enough to show the unreality of such suppositions.

The difference in degrees of reality between the first- and second-order consciousness is the inverse of the difference between objects and their optical images. The second-order function which reflects on the content of the first, and is the basis of ternary conscious relations, is the higher reality of the two:

> In a hierarchic structure, the higher does not merely possess powers that are additional to and exceed those possessed by the lower: it also has power *over* the lower, the power of organizing the lower and using it for its own purposes. Living beings organize and utilize inanimate matter; conscious beings can utilize life, and self-aware beings can utilize consciousness.[8]

This hierarchic order contains our two conscious levels under the names of consciousness and self-awareness, these being preceded by matter and life. Here, as in the previous discussion, nothing above self-awareness is found in man, although this does not rule out the possibility of still-higher orders of consciousness for other kinds of being.

This duality in human consciousness does not imply two substances, but rather a two-fold function peculiar to rational souls. This has already been indicated in Chapter 1, in connection with the motion proper to the soul, with its necessary division between the "axial" and "peripheral" components, and should also help to complete in the account given in Chapter 6 of the internal duality. The awareness of this duality has been recognized so long as to be reflected in the ancient languages: for instance, Greek, Latin, and Arabic all have two different words for "man," one implying strength and spirituality, the other weakness and mortality: in Greek *aner* and *anthropos* correspond to *vir* and *homo* in Latin, while in

Arabic *insān* and *bāshar* make the same distinction. This distinction is also implicit in the distinction drawn by Plotinus between the separable soul and the "couplement" or "conjoint principle" which is not truly separable from the body: "For every human being is of a twofold character: there is that compromise-total and there is the Authentic Man"[9]; and "the Couplement subsists by virtue of the Soul's presence. This, however, is not to say that the soul gives itself as it is in itself to form either the Couplement or the body."[10]

The conscious act of the lower soul, which we have called the first-order consciousness, is called by Plotinus *aisthesis*, while that of the higher is called *logizomenon*: "the *aisthetikon* of the soul deals with objects *external* to itself, and . . . its *logizomenon* deals with the representations coming from perception [*aisthesis*], and judges these."[11]

The presence of dualities obviously complicates the idea of identity, though it should not be forgotten that its unity has been assigned to the individual Form, which is instantiated in both the gross matter of the body and the subtle matter of the lower soul or Couplement. This leads to yet further complexities in the physical being, which can create difficulties for the idea of the person.

Fabre D'Olivet and Composite Identity

Fabre D'Olivet wrote a number of philosophical works in the late eighteenth century and the early nineteenth, including *Histoire Philosophique du Genre Humain*, the Introduction to which contains much that is relevant to the theory of identity. What he says of the human composite closely follows Plotinus, but with certain developments which are relevant to our present considerations, such as a fourfold division of man's composite nature, articulated in a manner conducive to personal development. Here he adds a fourth principle to the Platonic and Plotinian combination of body, soul, and intellect (although Plotinus argues also for a lower soul or subtle body), and to the New Testament combination of body, soul, and spirit.[12] There is a difficulty with the word *spirit*, because if it is simply reduced to meaning the intellect it does not account for the unity of the whole being. In other words, the combination of body, soul, and intellect does not, by itself, explain its own unity. This unity is a manifestation of the individual Form. Its overall unity is owing to the fourth principle, and it manifests the sum total of the tendencies of the three inner components, such that it can be referred to as the Will, in an enlarged sense as used by Fabre D'Olivet.

The will takes its direction from a combination of determining factors in the intellect, soul, and body, while not being simply reducible to them. What I am referring to in this connection is the full unity of the manifest person, of which the individual Form is the archetype. This manner of division and unification is graphically represented by D'Olivet in such a way that body, soul, and intellect are shown as three spheres, each with a rotation of its own, which it imparts to a fourth sphere which bounds all three, the latter representing the total will of the person. What the three inner spheres contribute to the motion of the will may be very unequal, and even conflicting among themselves, because they have a large measure of independent action and development.

The corporeal, psychical, and intellective spheres are arranged such that the middle one passes through the centers of the other two when all three are fully developed. This provides a basis for temporalizing the Plotinian concept of the psycho-corporeal complex, and has important consequences for the ways in which the intellectual faculty originates. These spheres are temporalized in regard not only to their growth, but also to the order in which they begin to grow.

The corporeal, centered on physical needs, is the first of them, fully present at the beginning of life. Only when it has expanded to its full extent does it impinge on the center of the next one, the central or animic, which was as yet unmanifest. This action from the lower sphere is enough to initiate the growth of the animic, which involves the development of the emotions. When this has reached its full extent, it activates the center of the third or intellective sphere, which then begins its own expansion.

Such, at least, might be called the normative pattern of this process, assuming that natural conditions will be adequate and not be counteracted by external factors. However, it is a consequence of the relative independence of these three bases of personality that the intellective does not have to wait for the action of the sphere below its own. Educational influences can act directly upon the center concerned, no matter how far the animic sphere is from being able to activate it. This applies in the great majority of cases in the modern world, of course, but personal differences resulting from those between natural and artificial forms of development can vary widely because of the extent to which the central or animic sphere may have developed at the same time.

However, if the average rate of development through the two lower spheres declines, while education and general cultural pressures remain constant, there will result a new kind of humanity in which there is an ever-deeper split between the intelligence and the personality as a whole. This deepens a corresponding split between those who have developed through the natural order (even if under deprived conditions) and those who have not. It causes them mutual incomprehension, not least where moral issues are involved. When, as in modern times, the acquisition of the intellective phase results more and more from its being as it were "kick-started" by external means, and less and less from natural growth and development, the possibilities for the future are apocalyptic, as the status, function, and even nature of the intelligence are changed as they never have been before. Whereas for Christianity, God (the Son) is the Incarnate Word, the god of modern man would have to be called the Disincarnate Word; traditional religion becomes unintelligible to people who may be highly intelligent in those domains in which intelligence is valued today.

Persons in whom the corporeal and intellectual spheres are not effectively connected by the animic sphere have only potential personal identities, since it is on the development of the animic sphere (symbolized by the heart) that the growth of personal identity depends. This fact about modern man was observed by C. S. Lewis, with no theoretical basis beyond Plato's tripartite division of soul-life into the Desiring, the Spirited, and the Rational, which he discusses in a book chapter entitled "Men Without Chests."[13] What most directly constitutes man as such is neither the higher nor the lower principle but the central or animic one, concentric with the fourth sphere. The failure of this central principle to develop would result in a humanity which was no longer in the divine image, if such a thing could be possible.

Further Remarks on the Composite

The fourth principle, relating to the will of the whole person, is not a product of the other three, even though it is affected by them without being a member of their group. (In this way, it expresses the typical form of the quaternary, which consists in a symmetrical group of three, to which a fourth is related in a rather different manner.) If there is a question of causality, it is rather this fourth which results from the three, as is illustrated in the same passage where the four principles are compared to luminous spheres: "[Man] may therefore be conceived under the form of a luminous sphere, in which three central foci give rise to three other spheres, all of which are enclosed within the first sphere."[14]

The foci of these inner spheres, and their location, are relevant to the question as to where the true self is manifested: "Among these three vital centers, the animic is to be regarded as the most fundamental. It is the prime mover upon which the whole human spiritual edifice rests and moves."[15]

In these terms, the animic sphere has the importance which Plotinus attributed to it as the "center point" of the soul, maintaining that "the We is the soul at its highest,"[16] and that it is the mediator between the sensitive and intellective principles. The discussion of the self is effectively a commentary on this part of the *Enneads*, as well as *Enn.* V, 3, 7, and one can see the same possibility of two different answers to the question as to what is empirically the real self. According to Plotinus,

> we ourselves think the thoughts that occupy the understanding—for this is actually the We—but the operation of the Intellectual-Principle enters from above us as that of the sensitive faculty from below; the We is the soul at its highest, the mid-point between two powers, between the sensitive principle, inferior to us, and the intellectual principle superior. (*Enn.* V, 3, 3)

In relation to the question of man as body, soul, and intellect, we can now show the agreement of Plotinus with Fabre D'Olivet, if this is not putting it the wrong way around, since the influence of Plotinus on D'Olivet is very extensive. The fact that he speaks of the "instinctive life" in addition to the body means that he considers the latter from an experiential point of view, besides which it does come under the heading of Body in his own diagrammatic representation of it. What he says of soul and intellect is practically the same as what has been adduced of them before, except that he sometimes uses the term "spirit" for the intellective life. Again, this is not the most suitable name for the third sphere.

The sphere corresponding to body or instinctive life relates to good and evil in a sensory manner, that is, between the extremes of pleasure and pain; while the animic relates to them as moral good and evil, with the related emotions of love and hate. The intellectual sphere is activated by inspiration and assent, and divides good and evil in the forms of truth and error. These principles alone could still result only in what D'Olivet calls a "determinate being," that is, one which is primarily object (i.e., consists only of a system of binary relations); but the function of the fourth sphere is like the addition of another dimension. It is represented as concentric with the animic sphere of the emotions:

> Upon the very center of the animic sphere, the primary motive force of the spiritual being, there rests another center to which the same place belongs.... This fourth sphere, inside of which the three spheres of Instinct (body), Soul, and Spirit (intellect) are moved, stands for effective power.[17]

This fourth principle is manifested as the final total power of the individual. But because of its comprehensiveness, it answers to the function of the pure ego, with its self-awareness.

The same could also be said in regard to the individual Form, of which D'Olivet's fourth sphere is the most direct instantiation. Implicit in this is the soul's agency, its "mid-point," which is in a special way a counterpoise to the multiple nature of the person, in that it can direct its energies to one level or another, creating what could be called a *de facto* identity by the creative power of this choice. This is where the nature of the whole individual is determined by what dominates in him, not unlike what D'Olivet says: "This sphere, the life of which continually radiates from the center to the circumference, is able to expand or contract itself in ethereal space to an extent which could be called infinite if this power is always where it wants to be."[18]

Identity is not a wholly static thing, therefore, but includes a capability for becoming various different kinds of things, the potential for which is present in man's microcosmic nature. The soul is the mediator between the instinctive and intellective levels in a dynamic and self-aware manner, whereas the spirit or fourth sphere unites all powers of the personality in a transcendent manner. Fabre D'Olivet traces this function from the human microcosm to the macrocosmic order, where man as a whole being is the active mediator between the realm of Fate or *natura naturata* and that of Providence or *natura naturans*. Although this cosmological role of the soul is not within the scope of the present discussion, the dynamic and creative function of identity will be considered in more detail later.

This conception of man as a composite being affects our understanding of what is implied by the separation of soul and body. It would imply that not two but at least four components of the being could potentially separate, though there do not seem to be any reasons for dissociating the intellect and the individual Form. Similarly, there are no reasons why the soul should separate from its vehicle or subtle body, and in fact the soul is always embodied, in at least a subtle matter, according to Proclus. However, body, the lower soul (the Plotinian *eidolon*), and the soul itself undoubtedly separate—the first two necessarily—and they undoubtedly disperse in corresponding ways. This implies that the soul (*animus*) and its subtle embodiment are faced with two possibilities. It may remain united to the intellect and the spirit, or it may remain united to the lower components. This is the most important instance of the creative aspect of identity.

In the former case, there would be nothing to prevent the soul's retention of its own nature, in conjunction with natures which are beyond change. Conversely, in the latter case the soul would remain connected to parts of the personality which necessarily cease to be related to their principle of unity, besides remaining wholly confined to the instantial or cosmic level. In either case, the soul is joined to something adapted to the soul's nature, but in radically different ways. In the former, it is joined to its nature in archetypal and causal mode, while in the latter it is joined to it in the mode of natural and unstable effects. Such is the metaphysical background to what religion speaks of as the salvation of the soul. The simple body-soul distinction does not serve this purpose, whereas the developed Plotinian version is well suited to it.

The Vehicle of the Soul

The reason for introducing this rather obscure Neoplatonic notion of a quasi-corporeal entity, intermediate between the incorporeal soul and the corporeal body, lies in the light it sheds on the question as to whether the soul can ever be truly disembodied. Neoplatonism has an *a priori* reason which it gives for denying such a possibility. Briefly, the soul is assimilated to the realm of Forms, or eternal realities, and as we actually know it, this eidetic nature is manifest in its embodiment. Now if, at some time, it could definitively cease to be embodied, this would almost certainly require a fundamental change in the causal powers of the soul. But the soul cannot undergo a change in its essential nature because it is one of the eternal realities, and so the fact that it is embodied now must mean that it will always be embodied in one way or another. This has clear implications for Christian theology, and could resolve one of the supposed conflicts between it and Platonism.

The idea of the soul's subtle embodiment is to be found in Plotinus, but the great majority of surviving references to it are in Iamblichus[19] and in Philoponus. Their writings refer to another, subtle counterpart to the material body which is separable from it, variously called the *ochema pneuma* ("radiant" or "luminous" spirit) and the *augoeides ochema* ("radiant" or "luminous" body). According to Philoponus, who taught at Alexandria in the seventh century, it resulted from the nature of the soul itself:

> For as the soul is a being of the cosmic order, it is absolutely necessary that it should have an estate or portion of the cosmos in which to keep house. And if the soul is in a state of perpetual motion, and it is necessary that it should be for ever in activity, it must needs be that it should ever have attached to it some body or other which it keeps eternally alive. For these reasons, therefore, they say it for ever keeps its radiant [*augoeides*] body, which is of an everlasting nature.[20]

Philoponus also says that the matter of this kind of body is not of the four elements, but of the fifth element or "quintessence," the "outflow" (*chyma*) of the transparent cosmic spheres. Similarly, Proclus speaks of a subtle embodiment of the soul which is not dependent on the material body: "Every participated soul makes use of a first body which is perpetual and has a constitution without temporal origin and exempt from decay."[21]

The reason he gives for this is that the soul has a fixed nature, in that it "proceeds from an immobile act of creation,"[22] whence it follows that if it animates a body at any time at all, it must always do so, as already argued. That this conception has a long history appears from the fact that the Pythagoreans believed that their discipline and virtue had the effect of purifying this soul-vehicle from the effects of gross matter, so that it might commune with higher entities.[23]

The thinking involved here centers on the idea of the soul having a series of "vestures" resulting from its descent to terrestrial conditions. Proclus also has the same idea:

> some are accustomed to say that [man's] gnostic principle (*to noêron*) corresponds with the nature of the fixed stars, his reason corresponds in its contemplative aspect with Saturn.... Moreover, the radiant vehicle (*augoeides ochema*) corresponds with heaven, and this mortal frame with the sublunary region.[24]

On this point, there is a disagreement between Proclus and Iamblichus, who treats the soul's vehicle as something which is necessary only in this world. In higher states, the soul can be disembodied even of the vehicle, but this is at the price of an inconsistency about the soul, which Proclus corrected later on. As already observed, the development from Iamblichus to Proclus continued its way into Christian doctrine: "The doctrine of the body of glory is the doctrine of Paul" (who did not teach the idea of the resurrection of the self-same material body). "Paul's doctrine as to the resurrection-body is summarized by Professor Charles as follows: 'This present body is *psychical* as an organ of the *psyche* or "soul," just as the risen or spiritual body is an organ of the "spirit." Thus as the psychical body is corruptible, and clothed with humiliation and weakness, the spiritual body will enjoy incorruptibility, honor and power. Hence between the bodies there is no exact continuity. The existence of the one depends on the death of the other. Nevertheless there is some essential likeness between them. The essential likeness proceeds from the fact that they are successive expressions of the same personality, though in different spheres. It is the same individual vital principle that organizes both.'"[25] "According to Paul the 'spiritual' body is not a body of pure spirit, which would be, philosophically speaking, an absolute contradiction in terms; but a body capable by its purity of manifesting the immediate power of the Spirit."[26]

The Question of Illusion

Some arguments against the reality of personality are based on criticism of the adequacy of our means of knowing it, but they rebound on those who use them. Philosophers like F. H. Bradley propose an Absolute as a more acceptable alternative to the self, but this kind of approach leads to some strange problems. With what do we cognize this Absolute? If it is with the supposedly illusory self that we do so, why should we have any confidence in what it claims to know of the Absolute? The Absolute, as we come to understand it, owes the quality it has for us to the peculiarities of our individual nature. If that nature were to be transcended qua individual, "we" should necessarily cease to see the Absolute in the same manner, and there would be no guarantee that it would still appear to have the same meaning or value as before. Our actual valuation of it is made possible only by a self-nature that the theory condemns as unreal, which is self-contradictory.

If, on the other hand, we know it by something transcending the self which we know as our own, the knowledge may be valid in this case, but how shall we know that it is *we* who possess it? Furthermore, if we cannot place any trust in the reality most obvious to us, how can we trust one which is necessarily more remote? Such considerations seem to be the doom of Illusionism. Something or other has to be real at the outset, if only as a stepping-stone from which to proceed logically elsewhere; and if there is no such reality, our speculation could only be a case of *ignotum per ignotius*.

An important line of argument used by monistic thinkers is to challenge the reality of things we know by showing how they contain contradictions. But the apparently contradictory nature of most of the cosmic realities when subjected to an analysis like that of Bradley is something which arises from the condition of our actual self. If they result only from the self's faculties, why attach any importance to them?

I have mentioned Bradley's criticism of the reality of the self because the nature of its attack is useful for bringing out the complexities of our problem with personal identity. At the same time, it makes us aware of the limitations of our common-sense idea of the self, which show the need for a more comprehensive conception of it. The point of departure of Bradley's criticism is the self of common sense, in which we believe as if by instinct. From what I have argued, the contradictions the self gives rise to do not imply its unreality, but rather the incompleteness of our knowledge of it. Finally, something more must be said about contradictory experiences, and how far they are a proof of unreality.

This critical method depends on our being able to show that the usual conceptions of most realities are self-contradictory when looked at closely. However, this method relies on an analogy between a human construct like a text and things in the natural order, such as substance and accident, selves, time, space, causes. Now it is clear that if a text contradicts itself it is rendered null, and that we can certainly know this to be the case. This is because a text can be known in its entirety, since it is simply a finite number of words and meanings put together for that very purpose. As logical consistency is essential to verbal communication, self-contradictions negate them, in a way that cannot be compensated for by anything else.

But when we apply this standard to things which do not arise from any purposive human activity, like substance, space, time, or self, we cannot have the same assurance about the role of logical consistency. That is, we cannot say that such realities are there just to be logically consistent for us, as one can with regard to a text. Also, unlike a text, they do not allow us a full and definitive knowledge of them, as they are not human constructs. Their full nature may well extend into regions quite unknown to us, and even beyond what we can know.

One consequence of this is that when such things are found to be self-contradictory, this can always be blamed on the present state of our knowledge or of our understanding. Some new discovery may make all these odds even at any time. But even if no such new knowledge were to be found, one could still not be said to have proved that self-contradiction in things must render them unreal in the same way as it nullifies a text. We can never know that a consistent account cannot be given of space, time, causality, etc., for all that such an account is beyond our present understanding. We merely know that we do not have one. Their contradictions, in other words, would then result from our limitations, not from any unreality in them.

In more recent times, a kind of critical argument similar to that of Bradley has been used again to infer the unreality of the individual "I." In this instance, the "I" is admitted to be unique by definition, but with the consequence that this brings it into contradiction with the multitude of other individuals who all call themselves "I" as well. Some hold that this plurality of unique selves is self-contradictory, and that this contradiction must imply the existence of the Divine or universal "I" which individuals unthinkingly suppose themselves to be.

But as I have just observed, self-consistency and self-contradiction are only *literally* applicable to verbal constructs, and the "I" is obviously not in that category. In itself it asserts nothing; it simply is, and so cannot be either consistent or contradictory. Besides that, the above reasoning should suffice to show that a contradiction here, even if real, would not ensure the unreality of the "I" in any case.

There is also another fact about the "I" which this kind of illusionist argument takes no account of. This lies in its being simply an indicator-word like *here*, *now*, *then*, *this*, or *that*; such words do not designate the natures of things in themselves, but rather the nature of their relatedness to us. In the case of *I*, the reference is directly to ourselves, but its exclusiveness has no deeper significance than that of *here* in regard to *there*. To suppose that the exclusiveness of the first person implies a parallel exclusiveness for the self it refers to is just a confusion of words with things. It would be as though one thought that the statements "this X is here" and "that Y is there" meant the attribution of qualities of "thisness" and "hereness" to X,

and "thatness" and "thereness" to Y. Here again, then, apparent contradictions are not a means of disproving the reality of the self. In
any case, when one refers to oneself as "me" or "myself" no such
issue as the above can arise, and that should suffice to confirm the
conclusion that such illusionistic critiques of the self are merely
semantic.

Notes

[1] *Critique of Pure Reason*, 94.
Transcendental Logic, Ch. 2, Sec.
ii, 12.

[2–3] Ibid.

[4] *Sex and Character*.

[5] See Ch. 5, 172–74.

[6] Ibid. (Weininger).

[7] Ibid.

[7a] This is maintained in regard to
natural phenomena—not logical
relations.

[8] E. F. Schumacher, *A Guide for the
Perplexed*.

[9] *Enn.* II, 3, 9.

[10] *Enn.* I, 1, 7.

[11] G. J. P. O'Daly, *Plotinus' Philosophy of the Self*, 41.

[12] See St. Paul's Epistles, 1 Thess.
5:23.

[13] *The Abolition of Man*, I.

[14] *Histoire Philosophique*, Introduction, III.

[15] Ibid.

[16] *Enn.* V, 3, 3.

[17] *Histoire Philosophique*, Introduction, III.

[18] Ibid.

[19] *On the Mysteries*.

[20] G. R. S. Mead, *The Doctrine of
the Subtle Body*, 66.

[21] *El. Theol.*, Props. 196 and 208–
10.

[22] Ibid., Prop. 208.

[23] Ibid. (Mead), 65.

[24] Ibid., 62.

[25] Ibid., 93–94.

[26] Ibid., 99.

Conclusion

Body and Individuation

To conclude this treatment of identity, we need first to recall the distinction between identity and the simpler idea of individuation. Individuation is the necessary foundation of personal identity, and much depends on what constitutes it. The common-sense belief that it is due to the body was denied because the enduring form of the body was shown not to be a specifically corporeal property. The corporeal substance itself is a flux, without any constant form, and so we cannot look to it as a cause of individuation either for personality or even for the body itself.

This is the reason for the emphasis which has been placed on the psychical and spiritual bases of identity. Much modern thought, by contrast, is strangely uncritical and unanalytical in regard to the body, as though it were something indestructible simply because of its connection to the higher faculties. Yet the spiritual significance of the body is not on its own level: where the body can be shown to have a positive role in our uniqueness as individuals, it is through a relative permanence and rigidity which owes nothing to its organic material, which is subject to constant replacement.

By virtue of these properties, which living organic bodies manifest without causing them, each body excludes all other bodies from the space it occupies, such that at any given moment a body's combination of spatial and temporal location is unique to itself. During a lifetime, it accumulates a large number of these unique space-time positions, the sum total of which is unique *a fortiori*. The body for which this is true is the combination of living matter (most of which is replaced every two-and-a-half years) and the structural form which instantiates eidetic realities. The latter are independent of the material of the body, and are the real and incorporeal basis of its individuation, that is, all that has to do with fixity, shape, resistance and causal efficacity.

Therefore, even where the body is instrumental in individuating the person, this condition is primarily owing to the soul and the non-material essences related to it, as death makes clear in its own way. The conception of the person as a union of body and soul in which the soul is separable and capable of existing apart from the material body has been argued for in the light of traditional conceptions. The theory supporting this idea is not altogether divorced from evidence, however, and although this evidence does not strictly constitute argument, it would be obscurantist to ignore it.

The advances of modern medicine have greatly multiplied the number of cases where patients have been resuscitated after having been close to death, and there are interesting similarities between the accounts of this experience given by those who remain conscious during it. Typically, they report that they find themselves with thought and perception outside of and above their body, looking down on it while it lies there with no sign of consciousness, as in the following account:

> I stopped, floating right below the ceiling, looking down. I felt almost as though I were a piece of paper that someone had blown up to the ceiling. I watched them reviving me from up there. My body was lying stretched out on the bed, in plain view, and they were all standing around it.[1]

Here, not only thought and self-awareness but also senses of sight and hearing were still operative from outside the body. C.G. Jung reports a similar experience, which he learned of from a patient of his in whose honesty he professes full confidence. There was the same experience of perceiving her own inert body and the activities of the medical staff, from a point near the ceiling. Besides this, on another side there was what she saw to be "the entrance to another world . . . [she] felt there was nothing to stop her entering in through the gate." In this case, the patient was also able to give some verifiable evidence for having been conscious apart from her body: "Only when she described in full detail what had happened during the coma was the nurse obliged to admit that the patient had perceived the events exactly as they happened in reality."[2]

There are other reports of this kind of experience which indicate that the disembodied self who undergoes this separation sees himself as a complete being, no matter what parts of the material body are damaged or missing. From these considerations it would appear that we experience the world through the mediation of the body's faculties, while these faculties do not need to be bound to the body, or be part of it, in order to function. If their bodily location is too badly damaged, perception will be prevented as long as soul and body are together, but it may resume when they are separated.

These reported phenomena imply that there are gross and subtle forms of the same experiences superimposed upon one another, which always pass unnoticed except when one is under exceptional stress. Such reports are very numerous, and no one has anything to gain from inventing them. If they can be taken at face value, they would reveal precisely the kind of experiential reality which the theory of the soul and body developed in the previous chapters would lead us to expect.

Empirical and Mystical

While we are considering the experiential background to our theory of identity, the objections raised in Chapter 6 to the reductionist conception should be recalled. The consciousness presupposed by this form of thought is always wholly empirical, which is to say it is made to consist only of what I have previously called "first-order consciousness." There is seldom any recognition of the contribution that can be made by the experience of mystics to this subject, where it can show how we have either actually or potentially the power to disengage consciousness from the world of sense-objects to a large extent. (If such a disengagement were complete, it would simply mean death, since it would leave no means of re-engagement.)

As with out-of-body experiences, this is dependent on testimony, which is abundant and consistent. However, it is not dependent on testimony to the same degree as in the former case, because those who are not mystics can still acquire some skill in meditation and gain at least a little first-hand experience of the inner side of consciousness. In this way one can see how the idea of consciousness is being artificially limited in much modern thought, not least where it excludes the role of introspection in the search for truth.

The conception of identity which would make it simply a result-ant of the body and the brain raises some curious difficulties, which, while not directly philosophical, nevertheless cast doubt on the ability of its exponents to seriously believe in it. The first con-clusion we should have to draw from this premise is that the kind of being one is must be decided by the kind of body one has. We may find something amusing in the consequences to which these philos-ophers should be committed by this. For example, the equality of the sexes allowed by enlightened opinion should not be merely wrong, but delusional. The same would have to be said for racial integration, and selection-procedures among those of the same race would have to rely on things like cranial measurements.

In contrast to this, the theory of spiritual individuality developed throughout the previous chapters allows some room for the views of those who believe in sexual and racial equality, though not as much as most of their advocates would want. Equality follows from the presence of the human soul in all persons, and inequality from the different uses made of its free will. That the soul is separable from the body implies that the basis of identity is only manifested by the body, not constituted by it. Soul relates to body as a formal cause, while the body in its natural life has an efficient causality of its own which does not have to follow automatically the norms of the for-mal cause. This relative independence cannot go too far without endangering the unity of the person, but within certain limits the individual can realize some possibilities which belong to the formal cause of mankind rather than those of the individual *per se*. This consequently allows for a number of things which are interchange-able in the lives of men and women.

With regard to belief in complete sexual equality and its conse-quences for identity, however, there is a particularly telling observa-tion by Stephen Clark to the effect that this idea presupposes that the true self is in fact a sexless, discarnate transcendental entity[3] which one might say is no more modified by the body it controls than a car driver shares the properties of his car. It implies an extremity of dualism which no sane dualist would accept, and it is most ironic that it should emerge from the social values of a culture which is utterly opposed to dualism in its theorizing.

Conclusion

The conception of body, soul, and intellect I have presented in this book can be seen to form a middle way between the implicit ultra-dualism of the egalitarians and the dogmatic stereotyping implied by the physicalist school.

Monism and Sources of Individuation

Although physical individuation arises from certain properties which the body has by virtue of its psychical principle, this is only the outer shell of identity. More importantly, there is the function of the will, with its continual flow of volition, which was considered in Chapter 4. It may appear that much of the time it is not in operation, but it is in reality wholly active in maintaining a state where no particular commands are needed.

The will, based as it is on the intellective, animic and instinctive powers and the various combinations they can form, always operates so as to realize what the whole being is orientated toward, as much when this does not coincide with one's conscious intentions as when it does so coincide. When it seems that one's will is unequal to a given task, it may still be working effectively for something which has not been directly chosen. This can arise from the fact that conflicting volitions can produce a resultant differing from all of them, as with mechanical forces.

For good or ill, therefore, the will continually works in a direction unique to the individual. The soul's inherent self-motion or "circular motion" expresses this dynamic aspect of it, which is an important representation of its function as mediator between changing and unchanging realities. We do not compare its self-motion with rectilinear motion because that would imply change purely and simply, whereas psychical change is always a union of the changing with the unchanging.

The intrinsic psychical motion is certainly motion in some sense, and the only physical motion which combines the changing with the unchanging is the circular kind. What is Platonically called the soul's circular motion therefore expresses by a close analogy the form taken by its individuating dynamism.

This inner individuation of the soul by its essential movement or volition is one of the two central elements of its metaphysical identity. The significance of this point appears especially in relation to a pantheistic and monistic conception of identity which has arisen in modern times in the wake of H.P. Blavatsky and Theosophy, and other popularized renderings of oriental thought. Such is the tendency which was anticipated in modern philosophy, starting with the way in which Kant separated the synthetic unity of apperception from the true self, which he placed in the noumenon. Once these two realities were no longer united on the conscious level, as they were for Descartes, successors of Kant such as Schopenhauer dispensed with the noumenal self as an individual entity, and so reduced all selfhood to its unity of apperception which is identical in all. His noumenal will is not recognizably personal.

The idea of personal identity implicit here has the charm of simplicity, and is undoubtedly a reality as far as it goes, since it is essentially what I have called the "second-order" consciousness or pure ego. If all this conscious being has to do is form a veridical image of everything else, including the empirical or manifest personality of its owner, it could well be said to be *a priori* the same in all beings. What then remains of the problem of identity is purportedly solved by declaring everything in our make-up besides this universal element to be more or less illusory. That this is a fair summary of what is asserted by the fashionable pantheism can be seen from a representative statement by Lord Northbourne:

> But your essential being must not be confused with the accidental accretions that are so closely associated with it, including, of course, your observable psycho-physical complex itself. If your accidentality alone is distinguishable while your essentiality is not, the same applies to your neighbor. That suggests that you and he are only accidentally two.[4]

This is the view of identity which makes the pure and empirical egos practically separate substances, and which theologically implies a radical denial of the Incarnation. It is also the idea of self which Plotinus criticizes for making individual differences depend only on so many different kinds of failure to manifest a given Form adequately, as opposed to the idea of all such differences among persons having their own formal causes, that is, individual Forms.

Conclusion

The content of the supposed true self according to the monistic or pantheistic conception is extremely small, if not infinitesimal, and many minds fail to see that the certainty with which its existence is arrived at is owing primarily to this lack of content. What could exclude it? However, a good deal of what I have said of the pure ego could be taken in support of the monist position. The two-fold nature of man as denoted previously by *logizmon* and *aisthesis* could be taken in this context to mean that only one half of it is truly real, as Northbourne in fact maintains. Such thinking denies any possibility of spiritualization for the natural self, and leaves only an abstract entity with no need for salvation.

In itself, this self-essence is simply a reflector of phenomena, and as such it cannot be thought to have any personal significance, since mirrors and recording equipment do as much in their own ways. The idea that the highest reality in us could be something so empty and passive would need a great deal of proof, instead of resting on mere assertion, as it typically does. It would above all require purposeful activity, which could not come from a mere reflector.

While the self's reflection of externals is essential to it, this is still no more essential to it than its volition, if only because we never see any grounds upon which the two could be separated. This integrality of the self with the will is what monist thinking always ignores, although it is the key to the issue. We are normally only aware of our volition when we give it a change of direction or intensity, but it is in reality continuous. It lies at the heart of what Plato called the soul's "motion" and what Leibniz called the monads' "appetition." Once its equality with the intellect is understood, the uniform perceptive function of consciousness is of no use for proving that all minds are one.

But what if, after all, it were the case that the pure ego and the will are substantially separate, and not just aspectually so? Such a real separation would require conscious transfers of information between ego and will, which in fact we never experience. We are able to will without having to inform the will by a separate operation, which should not be the case if there were a substantive separation between intellection and volition. Catholic theology makes a similar point in moral terms with its affirmation that intellectuality is not separable from moral values such as charity, an issue which has caused at least one leading figure related to the "New Age" movement to break with Catholicism in the interests of a supposedly pure intellectuality.

That the self should unite the universality of the pure ego with the individualizing action of the will agrees with a conclusion we have already reached in connection with the individual form. This is the basis of the mediating function of the soul and the grounds of its not being assimilable to other psychical entities. The tendency of monism to conflict with this has some interesting parallels with that of other schools of thought which are nominally poles apart from it, such as reductionism. Intentionally or not, they are joined in a fashionable attempt to explain the human by the less-than-human.

Dualities in Identity

Circular motion, even if understood in an analogical sense, involves a duality between its inner and outer aspects, and this gives us the means of combining two useful concepts. Center and circumference would naturally correspond to the duality we have discussed in terms of the pure and the empirical egos. We have also distinguished them as first- and second-order consciousness, which are sometimes capable of degrees of separation. This duality marks the difference between human and animal consciousness, as animals have only the first-order component, which does not include self-reflection.

Here we have a duality in consciousness in addition to that of the objective world and our representation of it. The latter involves a psycho-physical duality, and it is thanks to the power of self-reflection that we are aware of it. This dual nature of both consciousness and its subject-matter is common to both Western and Eastern thought. In Buddhist teachings, the two egos have been represented by two intersecting circles, each passing through the center of the other:

> This interpretation ascribes universal consciousness (the realm of archetypes) to the first circle, and empirical consciousness to the second circle (that which "sorts out and judges the results of the five kinds of sense consciousness"), and finally manas, the area of overlap. Manas is described as the balancing consciousness that "either binds us to the world of the senses or which liberates us

from it," and "the double character of manas which, though being without characteristics of its own, becomes a source of error if it is directed from the universal towards the individual, but directed in the opposite direction from the individual to the universal, it becomes a source of highest knowledge."[5]

Besides being also an expression of the "ascending" and "descending" activities of the Platonic Forms in a Buddhist source, the function of *manas* is one which we have assigned to the voluntary center of attention, or "mid-point" in Plotinian terms. But because Buddhism does not possess a doctrine of the soul, there is no telling in whom or in what these powers reside. The empirical consciousness is clearly the dynamic part of the combination, while the other is static, comprising the eternal archetypes. What is in question, then, is the union between the changing and the unchanging for which the analogy of circular motion was adopted, in connection with the soul's individuation.

The effect of this conception here is to make the two orders of consciousness aspectual properties of the soul, like the circumference and the axis of a rotating sphere. On this basis, they are present in each person as two basic functions of one soul, and their combination forms a unique individual. For this reason, we do not have to see the manifest personality or empirical ego as the irredeemable pseudo-entity it appears to be for some forms of doctrine, nor must we see the universal consciousness or pure ego as substantially identical in everyone like the synthetic unity of apperception. The analogical conception of circular motion is thus a bridge between two universal conceptions of identity which otherwise could appear mutually exclusive.

Christian and Platonic Ideas

The theory of the relation of the individual to the universal examined in Chapter 2 overcomes a conflict between religious and philosophical views of identity, particularly where Christian and Platonic positions are concerned. A philosophy which bases itself on finding the real in the universal would not appear to have much relevance for a religion which finds reality primarily in individual persons and particular actions and events. This has led many of the more tough-minded thinkers on either side of the issue to reject the other, while some have had a kind of instinctive conviction that both positions are valid, even though they did not see how this could be proved.

It is now possible see that the *eide* or universals imply a logical commitment to the formation of compound universals among them, which have progressively lesser degrees of universality. Such is the case according to the Principle of Plenitude, which is no less essential to Neoplatonism than the theory of Forms. This attenuation of universality has its limit in a Form which can have only one instantiation, and this is what we call the individual Form, of which the psycho-corporeal complex is the instantiation. The individual Form coincides with what we have also called the soul in an enlarged sense of the word, conceived as being separable from the body while being the Form of the body in a Platonic and not Aristotelian sense.

Although the two essential premises in this proof, the theory of Forms and the Principle of Plenitude, have been in use since ancient times, it appears that they have never before been used together in this way so as to establish the individual Form. Plotinus, who considered the possibility of such a Form, made no attempt to prove it, and neither did his successors.

This development therefore supplies something which always has been lacking in Neoplatonism, and which is necessary to show its compatibility with the Christian idea of the unique individual. It also supports the point of view of Leibniz, which is itself so largely a synthesis of Neoplatonic thought with a theology which comprehends individual destinies. It should be recalled that the nearest historical approach to the proof of the individual Form was found in the writings of Leibniz, in reference to the Scholastic *species infima*. Leibniz maintains that every substance is a "lowest species," but this conclusion is not proved, although the means of proving it, the Principle of Plenitude, holds a central place in Leibniz's philosophy.

The soul as an individual Form unites in itself properties peculiar to the Forms and those peculiar to their instantiations. For this reason we have a new basis for the traditional conception of the rational soul as the mediator between the realm of nature and that of the spirit; that it ranks highest in the natural order and lowest in the spiritual. This is what Aquinas expresses by the following: "the intellectual soul is said to be on the *horizon* and *confines* of things corporeal and incorporeal, in that it is an incorporeal substance and yet the Form of the body."[6]

The individual Form is the Form of the individual person, in the Platonic sense of the term, conceived such that the body is rather a material recapitulation of what the soul comprises implicitly. This dual nature is necessary for the function of the rational soul in the world, where it is a channel through which the Forms are drawn into nature in a creative and ordering manner. This is for Plotinus the *enhylos logos* or "enmattered Form," whose consciousness functions on two levels at once, as where the perception of sensory fire is mingled with an intellectual intuition of the *fire-eidos*.[7]

This bi-level consciousness is therefore the means whereby man can enhance the natural world through his relation to its archetypal originals, besides creating new things without natural precedent. This takes us beyond the simple body-soul combination deduced in Plato's *Alcibiades,* which by itself does not give us the true person. In the individual Form we also have the third basis upon which the person is individuated. The first is on the corporeal level, in the unique space-time combinations arising from the body's exclusion of other bodies. The second is the continual flow of volition, which expresses in action the essential nature of the person. This essential nature is a function of the individual Form, which both individuates the person and integrates him with the realm of Forms or universals.

Monistic and Dualistic Experience

The conclusions which have now been presented enable us to confront another question arising from monistic conceptions of identity. It may be asserted on the basis of mystical experience that there is ultimately only one identity, and that all other identities merge with it. W. T. Stace claims that all mystical experiences are essentially the same, and that the only valid explanation of them is the monistic one. They all involve "the experience of undifferentiated unity, which mystics believe to be in some sense ultimate and basic to the world."[8]

Let us accept for the sake of argument the contention that all such experiences are the same—though why there should be so little variety in the transcendent realm is far from clear—and consider what Stace says about their interpretation. The dualist explanation is not ruled out by an experience of "undifferentiated unity" *qua* unity, because this can be a unity in the experience of a subject, just as easily as a unity which supposedly absorbs the subject substantially, as monism maintains. Stace denies that these two types of interpretation correspond to separate realities: "But this suggestion, though superficially plausible, will not bear examination . . . there are common elements in them all which are much more fundamental and important. . . ."[9] In short, he concludes that only the monistic account answers to reality, and that all dualistic ones are only matters of "theological and cultural interests." Whether this makes sense or not depends on what we first think of God: is God a benign Creator who originates and sustains our existence? Or is He an aggressive competitor who creates nothing and resents the existence of anything but himself? Is the eternal Source of life the validation of all lives, or can it be the negation of them? There need be no doubt about the weight of "theological and cultural interests" on either of these sides, and to identify them all with those of Christianity is dishonest.

All such anti-personal doctrines are at bottom sado-masochistic, and far from being above human concerns, they appeal to passions which are as human as can be. Besides, arguments for such beliefs can nearly always indicate something else as well. For example, the monistic account of identity as articulated by Stace derives a specious support from a commonplace kind of experience which is by no means confined to mystical states. Any experience which is sufficiently absorbing leads one to forget that it is oneself who is experiencing it, yet without thereby altering the subject-object relation at all. Exciting films and football matches cause millions of minds to "lose" their individualities by just such a lapse of self-awareness. There is no reason to think things are essentially different in mystical experiences, in which case the dualistic account of them will apply whether the individual is aware of his perceptive act or not.

Conclusion

Immortal Soul, Transcendence, Free Will

The argument used for the immortality of the soul in Chapter 1 is based on the capacity for knowledge in general, and is not tied to any particular kind of knowledge. The faculties of knowledge and volition, distinct as they are, are not practically separable, residing in the psychical unity like the axis and circumference of a sphere. But with the action of the intelligence being distinguished from the flow of natural phenomena, and the action of the will being inseparable from that of the intelligence, the implication is that the action of the will is likewise not, in its essence, a part of the natural processes either, however much it affects and is affected by them.

This aspect of the will, which pertains to the empirical ego by reason of its action on the outside world, is central to both its freedom and its powers of creativity, referred to above as its "*logos-function*," bringing the Forms into the material world. All acts of free will are essentially creative, and all creative activities are exercises of free will. This conception of free will has been shown to be closely associated with psychical self-motion, where it was linked to the operation of knowledge. Like knowledge, it requires an agency outside the series of natural phenomena. This self-motion is effective as much in concentration and meditation as in bodily motion.

Knowledge, self-motion, and (by implication) moral judgment all require an identity transcending the phenomenal flux processed by the empirical ego, and so does philosophy itself. All attempts to deny access to an independent realm of Forms or ideas are really so many demands that critical thought be stifled by imprisonment in subjectivity such that science, religion and culture should be simply the playthings of political and historical forces, and so merge with social behavior. As opposed to this, what has been argued for regarding the soul involves the joining of mind and will to a permanent reality above the level of the merely human.

The capacity for knowledge includes a knowledge of necessary truths; and among these we encountered the *Cogito* argument in a form which preceded that of Descartes. The significance of this is second only to that of the argument from knowledge *per se*, and it is logically the first particular thing known in regard to the knower himself. The universal role of knowledge and the individual's existence are combined in the *Cogito* argument, which thus bridges the gap between the individual and the universal in its own way. Skeptical objections to it cannot truly free themselves from it, and that weakens them.

The Leibnizian role of eternal truths and our knowledge of them shows how they support a knowledge of self-identity, because such things can only be known through acts of self-reflection. This is the aspect of our subject where the function of transcendence is equally relevant for both identity and free will. It is our "immanent transcendence."

How the Soul May Be Manifest

The essential, non-empirical reality which we have assigned to soul is manifest in an indirect manner through the private representation of the world it forms in each person, as was stated in the Introduction. The gulf between this representation and the world as it really is is constantly experienced in the amount of work we have to do in order to understand parts of the latter by penetrating the appearances of the former. Thanks to this fact of individual world-representation, there is a real sense in which soul can be said to be publicly manifest.

Besides being the seat of individual identities, this representing power is also the basis of both science and philosophy, because the real world is invariably veiled in representation. The more subtle faculties must take the materials of representation as though they were texts in unknown languages and learn to interpret them under those aspects of the real which pertain to philosophy and the sciences. By this means, the transcendental, unitary self is yet further manifest by the results of theoretical knowledge, or their discovery. The modern attempt to deny the reality of the mind is itself nothing if not a manifestation of the power of that mind.

Science and technology are thus inseparable, because the scientist constructs models which are not found in experience and then experimentally imposes them on nature so as to find how far its functioning corresponds to them. For this reason, there is a deep contradiction involved in the idea that modern, scientifically-orientated thought should necessarily "deconstruct" the self. Modern scientific thought is itself a creative endeavor wholly sustained by the thought and the volition of human mental agents, something poles apart from the mere passive reflection of facts which mental life is sometimes made out to be. Real personhood, to assure us of its existence, requires something more essential to it than the mental artifacts of science and philosophy.

Let us note the significance of this in regard to dualism. The soul is at one level the source of dualism, with its world of appearance which it opposes to the reality, but it does not leave us there because this is primarily the work of *its* sensory powers. The balance is redressed by its intelligence, which pierces the veil of the representation and brings us to the reality which we contrast with the latter. The soul continually creates duality with its lower faculties and transcends it with its intelligence.

For this reason we can see that denials of the dualist position imply a denial of the need for intelligence and science, for if we had truth and reality *gratis* in the first place, there would be nothing for intelligence and science to do. The question of self-creation arises here as well, because the effort to cultivate the necessary intellectual awareness will not be psychologically meaningful unless we first have a belief in the reality and power of the self and its faculties. If the effects of this belief, or of its absence, are not always clear in every person, they are more evident in society as a whole. The denial of the soul as a unitary and substantive self has gone hand-in-hand with an increasing loss of the freedom of the individual, as well as a decline in intellectual standards. Circumstantial evidence, perhaps, but the connection of these things is natural and logical.

A New Kind of Humanity?

That such a radical change as this could be possible can be understood from the account of the tripartite conception of identity deriving from Plato and the Neoplatonists, together with the temporalization thereof outlined in Chapter 7. According to this conception there is a natural sequence in which man can acquire his intellectual faculty in a way that is integrated with his whole being as a microcosm of the natural and the spiritual worlds. Only in this form can it carry out its true function, and it is to a humanity organized inwardly in this manner, albeit in fallen state, that the message of traditional religion is addressed.

But increasingly in the modern world the intelligence is awakened and developed by means that have no connection with the organic development of the person, with the result that its functions are becoming as artificial as the causes of its inception. The fact that this makes spiritual doctrines either incomprehensible or just interesting flights of fancy with no special claim to truth and no claims on us is not widely seen as the disaster it is because a "rootless" intelligence can be experienced subjectively as a liberation from limitations, or a sense of infinity.

However, to have an intrinsic—that is, objectively real—function, the intelligence must have a *necessary* function, which implies certain limitations, failing which its activity is like that of an engine racing with its gears in neutral. This condition is accompanied by a sense of identity which could embrace everything and anything without realizing its own being in anything. The natural basis of this widening split between the intelligence and the whole being lies in a weakening and a slowing-down of the rate at which man's energies flow from his corporeal ground or substance through his emotional and subjective self to his intellect, together with an intensification of cultural pressures which activate the mind in isolation. Those who are carried along with the consequences of this change will ultimately find that they are in pursuit of an impossibility like that of effects without causes.

The purely biological basis of personal identity is, of course, as evident as ever, being too basic to be affected in itself by the changes under discussion here. It is an undoubted reality, and if the only other major component of identity to be brought into activity is the intellectual faculty, the central component which combines the biological with the intellectual levels may be reduced to insignificance. In such individuals, the "directionless" condition of the unintegrated intelligence communicates itself to the consciousness of the body, in ways which become manifest in neuroses and an inability to see the intelligence inherent in spirituality. The identities of those who are affected in this way are held together by nothing more than the activity of the ego, with an intelligence which can mean anything or nothing. Such things result from human development taking place under unstable and anarchic conditions, in which spiritually valid standards are either not known or not distinguished from substitutes which are ineffectual or positively harmful. The best solution to this lies in identifying false options for what they are, and accepting a certain self-limitation against them.

In contrast to all morbid negations of the real self, the true development of personality integrates the faculties in a way which befits a kind of being who is a microcosm on all levels of reality, intellectual, rational, psychical, and material, as they grow out of one another in order. Development is in any case an essential part of identity, but nonetheless it is ignored in most modern thought, which assumes that we must remain exactly the same forever, and on an exclusively naturalistic level at that.

The real self is the counterpart of the world of universals from its unique point of view; and whether or not we can perceive ideal realities in the physical world, it is always possible to cultivate the preconditions for doing so. Far from being automatic, like physical maturation, this development needs to be sought in accordance with the examples of the archetypal figures who impart grace, such as are manifest in the ancient religions and heroic traditions and bring about a sharing in the life of the Divine Word. The power of the will increases when it aims at making effective the spiritual dimension, because there it is combined with a purpose which joins it to the purpose concealed in all existence. The human will in harmony with Divine Providence is more powerful than fate, and the practical discovery of this truth awaits us all. The question as to what we are merges with the question as to what we can be or are destined to be.

Notes

1 R.A. Moody, *Life After Life*, 36.

2 C.G. Jung, *Synchronicity*, 128.

3 Stephen Clark, *Anarchy and the Divine Order*, Vol. 1.

4 *Looking Back on Progress* (quoted not so much for the authority of the statement as for its frankness and directness).

5 Keith Critchlow, *Time Stands Still*, 35–36; quoting from Lama Govinda.

6 SCG, Vol. II, Ch. 68, 6.

7 O'Daly, *Plotinus' Philosophy of the Self*, 35–36.

8 *Mysticism and Philosophy*.

9 Ibid., 230.

Index

Index

www.ingramcontent.com/pod-product-compliance
Lightning Source LLC
Chambersburg PA
CBHW031244090426
42742CB00007B/309